5G Mobile Core Network

Design, Deployment, Automation, and Testing Strategies

Rajaneesh Sudhakar Shetty

Apress®

5G Mobile Core Network

Rajaneesh Sudhakar Shetty
Bangalore, Karnataka, India

ISBN-13 (pbk): 978-1-4842-6472-0   ISBN-13 (electronic): 978-1-4842-6473-7
https://doi.org/10.1007/978-1-4842-6473-7

Managing Director, Apress Media LLC: Welmoed Spahr
Acquisitions Editor: Aditee Mirashi
Development Editor: Matthew Moodie
Coordinating Editor: Aditee Mirashi

Cover designed by eStudioCalamar

Cover image designed by Freepik (www.freepik.com)

Distributed to the book trade worldwide by Springer Science+Business Media New York, 1 New York Plaza, Suite 4600, New York, NY 10004-1562, USA. Phone 1-800-SPRINGER, fax (201) 348-4505, e-mail orders-ny@springer-sbm.com, or visit www.springeronline.com. Apress Media, LLC is a California LLC and the sole member (owner) is Springer Science + Business Media Finance Inc (SSBM Finance Inc). SSBM Finance Inc is a **Delaware** corporation.

For information on translations, please e-mail booktranslations@springernature.com; for reprint, paperback, or audio rights, please e-mail bookpermissions@springernature.com.

Apress titles may be purchased in bulk for academic, corporate, or promotional use. eBook versions and licenses are also available for most titles. For more information, reference our Print and eBook Bulk Sales web page at http://www.apress.com/bulk-sales.

Any source code or other supplementary material referenced by the author in this book is available to readers on GitHub via the book's product page, located at www.apress.com/978-1-4842-6472-0. For more detailed information, please visit http://www.apress.com/source-code.

Printed on acid-free paper

*To my wonderful parents, **T.B Sudhakar Shetty** and **Veena Shetty**, who always supported me when required and always corrected my mistakes and raised me to become the person I am now.*

*I cannot complete my dedications without thanking my two wonderful kids, **Aarav** and **Atharv**, as without their love and understanding this book would not have been possible.*

Table of Contents

About the Authors

Rajaneesh Sudhakar Shetty is an industry expert in the field of telecommunication with 20+ years of experience in delivery of turn-key next generation 5G end-to-end mobility solutions for large customer accounts. He has proven credentials as a trusted advisor for customer delivery, solution architecture, software management, system architecture, test architecture, product management, and pre-sales for telecom products using state-of-the-art technologies with an excellent track record of technical leadership and management. Rajaneesh is currently working as a Senior Solutions Architect for Cisco Systems and is based out of Bangalore, India.

Rajaneesh Shetty has also:

- co-authored and published the book *4G: Deployment Strategies and Operational Implications*,

- filed several patents, primarily on the 5G core network domain, and

- published several 5G-related white papers in various forums, including the IEEE.org forum.

Guest Authors

5G Mobile Core Network would not have been possible without the contributions from two key guest authors:

Ananya Simlai, who contributed significantly toward the **"5G Overview"** and **"5G NSA Design and Deployment Strategies"** chapters of the book.

Ananya Simlai is a Telecom Specialist with primary focus on wireless 4G-5G mobility networks, cloud native, and network function virtual infrastructure.

She is a "trusted advisor" for key service provider operators in the AMERICA region and APJC regions, helping them address the technological challenges in the mobility domain as well as the infrastructure/virtualization domain, thereby enabling them to smoothly transition across technologies like 4G and 5G. Her expertise and exposure across mobility domains with various customers gives her the ability to identify and address the various challenges for both large- and small-scale deployments in an innovative and effective manner. She has worked with service provider CTO teams to design their 5G story and has been instrumental in designing, implementing, and successfully rolling out for one of the largest 5G mobile networks around the globe.

Ananya has also:

– filed patents on 5G mobility core network,

– spoken at international forums on 5G, and

– published defensive publications on 5G.

Filipe Rodrigues, who contributed extensively toward the "Packet Core Testing Strategy" chapter of the book.

Filipe Rodrigues is a very experienced engineer in the telecommunication field who is driven by innovation and challenge. He takes pride in delivering state-of-the-art projects to high-demand customers across the world. Filipe has vast experience across several telco areas, including RF designing, radio planning, LTE/EPC, 5G, and VoLTE. In the last few years he has worked extensively as a subject matter expert for the software delivery and testing methodologies, especially for telecommunication, delivering software projects, and helping the transition to automated testing and continuous delivery.

Filipe holds a Masters degree in Electronic and Telecommunication, a post-Masters study in Telecommunication, and an executive MBA.

Currently Filipe is working with Cisco Systems based out of Düsseldorf, Germany.

About the Technical Reviewer

**Omied Ghaderi** graduated with a Bachelors degree in physics and a Masters of Science in Electrical Engineering. He is experienced with mobile cloud core networks from both the vendor and operator side. He started with IP multimedia subsystem and then entered the packet core field with different projects and contributed in many end-to-end core network integration, commissioning, configuration, and upgrading for different operators. Omied is also experienced with Openstack and switch configuration for launching virtual networks as infrastructure for the cloud core. Currently Omied is working in Tokyo, Japan as a cloud core specialist on the operator side, and his interest is in 5G core solutions.

Acknowledgments

I decided to write this book because I felt there are gaps in how 5G is specified vs how 5G is interpreted vs how 5G is implemented. When I began to familiarize myself with 5G, I went through various specifications and books that helped me gain understanding of the concepts of 5G. When I started working on 5G, I realized that the books and the specifications were not detailed enough for me to be able to apply my learnings to practice.

My aim with this book is not just to cover the various aspects of 5G or 5G mobile core network but also to be able to help the readers understand the concepts and provide them with practical tips that they should be able to apply as input toward 5G network design and deployment.

This book is a collection of my experience that I gained by working with some of the greatest **engineers, architects, business professionals, and customers**. I would like to thank all my colleagues at **Cisco Systems** and all the past companies I worked with. I sincerely thank all my teachers, professors, and mentors who enlightened me with their knowledge and wisdom.

Finally, I would like to thank the readers of this book. I would love to hear from you all. Please send your comments, suggestions, and questions to my email at rajaneesh.shetty@gmail.com.

As the technology evolves, some of the examples of this book may require updating. I will try my best to keep all the content up to date at the book's site. I look forward to hearing from you all.

Introduction

Almost all telecom operators are planning their transition toward 5G. 5G transition is a lot more than faster speed. 5G enables new IoT experiences, massive connectivity, smart cities, decade-long battery life, ultra-responsive networks, and increased speed, and it requires a significant change in the radio, transport, data center, and the core network architecture along with the UE change (mobile handset).

This book is intended for those who wish to understand 5G and also for those who work extensively in the service provider environment, either as operators or as vendors, performing activities such as network design, deployment, testing, and automation of the network as a profession. By the end of this book, the reader will be able to understand the benefits in terms of CAPEX, OPEX while considering one design over the other. Consulting engineers will be able to evaluate the design options in terms of 5G use-cases, the scale of deployment, performance, efficiency, latency, and other key considerations.

5G Mobile Core Network Design, Deployment, Automation, and Testing Strategies begins with the following:

I. Chapter 1 is an introductory chapter to 5G: In this chapter, the reader will be introduced to the basics of the 5G network and some of the key concepts in 5G with comparisons of equivalent 4G features/concepts. The chapter acts as a foundation for 5G, which will be required before moving on to the advanced concepts introduced in the later chapters of the book.

II. Chapter 2 is about multi-access edge computing (MEC), the readers are introduced to the distributed data center architecture and its advantages. Design and deployment considerations for various MEC use-cases are discussed in this chapter, along with design strategies for MEC toolkits and advanced 3GPP Release 16 features.

III. Chapter 3 is about the 5G non-standalone (5G NSA) architecture. In this chapter, the reader gets introduced to the basics of 5G NSA, the various migration paths, and options for transitioning from 4G ➤ 5G NSA ➤ 5G SA. CUPS is also introduced in this chapter, and various design and deployment strategies/considerations are discussed in detail for the remaining part of the chapter.

IV. Chapter 4 is about 5G standalone (5G SA) architecture, where the reader is introduced to the 5G SA architecture, various network functions, and network slicing. Further the chapter gets into the details of some of the practical design and deployment considerations, especially from the core network point of view used in various operator networks.

V. Chapter 5 is about testing strategies for both 5G NSA and 5G SA. Different types of testing are discussed in detail in this chapter, along with some call models and practical considerations such as CI/CD integration and test automation.

VI. Chapter 6 discusses the need for automation in 5G and various aspects of end-to-end automation in 5G. The reader will get insight into the details of various core network automation considerations and best practices.

VII. Chatper 7 is concentrating more on the advanced 5G features where the reader can understand some of the Release 16 features like e-SBA, LADN, etc. The chapter also provides insight into non-public 5G strategies and, in general, how operators can use these advanced features to optimize their network.

CHAPTER 1

5G Overview

Welcome to the extraordinary journey of transformations that 5G will take us through. 5G gives us the means to revolutionize the world as we see it now.

Many of us wonder about the various generations of technology, the more recent ones being the terms 3G, 4G, and 5G. If we look at these terms as mere acronyms, it would just mean another incremental "G"; however, if we look at them in terms of the impact them makes in our daily lives, we would be able to not just understand the change but also feel it.

Since each of these generations of technology last more than a decade with a large overlap in their years of service, the real use-cases each enables is somewhat abstracted from the common consumer; more often it's a little cloudy.

However, let's reflect back solely on the impact these terms have had in our lives and to the end-user that would directly map to the technology behind them.

A History of Mobile Communication

In the 1980's the world of communication was disrupted by 1G, the sheer ability to break away from wired landline phones and to be able to wirelessly communicate made it popular. This also brought with it the dawn of mobile communication—the freedom of being able to connect to anyone from anywhere. The handsets were called "mobile phones," due to the simple fact that the consumer could be mobile with the phones. The generations of technologies henceforth would be called mobile technologies.

© Rajaneesh Sudhakar Shetty 2021
R. S. Shetty, *5G Mobile Core Network*, https://doi.org/10.1007/978-1-4842-6473-7_1

Then came the 1990's, and with that decade came 2G, the second generation of mobile technology. The notable difference from the first generation was that this brought in digital communication, as opposed to analog-based communication used in the first generation. In addition to significantly being able to reduce the size of the handsets and supporting voice calls, with this generation short messaging service (SMS) was introduced and became very popular. I am sure some of you will remember the days of "SMS" jokes making the rounds.

With the new millennium came 3G. Also note around this time the worldwide web was fast becoming popular and the user base expanded at exponential rates. Emails were very popular among enterprise and general consumers. Higher data rates supported email communication, internet access, and various other popular messenger services, "Blackberry Messenger" being one very famous among them. Another noteworthy first for this generation was the capability of video calls.

Figure 1-1 illustrates the Evolution of Mobility from 1G to 5G.

1G	2G	3G	4G	5G
First Generation of wireless cellular technology	**Second** Generation of wireless cellular technology	**Third** Generation of wireless cellular technology	**Fourth** Generation of wireless cellular technology	**Fifth** generation of wireless cellular technology
Analog communication	Digital communication	Digital communication	**Data based network**	**Data Based network**
Voice Calls	**Voice and Data (SMS)**	Voice, calls, Video calls, SMS	**Voice, Video, SMS over IP.**	Voice, Video, SMS over IP
		Mobile Internet – Email access and messenger services became popular	**High speed internet access,** video streaming,online gaming, real time apps.	**10 times higher speeds and lower latency than 4G.**
			Realtime online navigation apps like cab booking services could be supported. This is the world as we know it today	Next Gen Applications like connected car.
				Massive machine type communications for IOT devices
				Remote Surgeries
				Augmented reality and virtual reality applications

Figure 1-1. *Evolution of Mobility*

In 2010 the use of 4G picked up rapidly across the world. This was a pure data-based network. Voice was implemented over this IP-based network for the first time, although it was possible to fall back to 3G for voice during its early adoption. **LTE was hugely successful; it provided higher speeds of internet than ever before**. This completely changed the way we live our lives. **Smartphones exploded the market**, businesses were taken online, and consumers could shop and sell online. Online gaming picked up. Real-time navigation apps could bring in new services like mobile cab apps, and entertainment could be viewed online. With this came content providers as we know them today.

With the close of the last decade and into the 2020's we will experience the rise of the 5th generation of mobile networks. Like we have read to this point, each generation initiated a transformation in the way data was consumed and also gave way to innovative applications. We should see 5G more as a technology enabler, which would help us realize a sci-fi movie-like world. We should also see how the 5G revolution in worldwide communication will be driven by multiple features:

1. eMBB: enhanced mobile broadband

2. URLLC: ultra-reliable low-latency communication

3. mMTC: massive machine-type communication

5G technology will provide faster speeds than any of the generations discussed thus far. This will provide an immediate scope for both consumers and industries to adopt it for various applications. 5G is expected to provide speeds up to 10GB/s and latency of 1 ms or less. 5G will enable service providers to provide more capacity, and hence data-intensive applications can be catered to. Per its standards, 5G inherently caters to be ultra-reliable and has provisions to have no connection loss, enabling it to be adapted by critical applications in healthcare for applications such as remote surgery.

Due to the provision of low-latency and machine-type communication, 5G is expected to be heavily used in industries on factory floors for robotic communication. This is going to drive a paradigm shift and enable huge enhancements in vehicle-to-vehicle, vehicle-to-infrastructure, person-to-person, and vehicle-to-person communication. 5G is expected to bring in a large amount of industrial automation by paving the way for reliable robotic communication. Smart Cities would need massive IOT communication built into 5G. Concepts like network slicing for IOT to reserve resources for such applications have been clearly defined and standardized.

Figure 1-2 showcases some of the use-cases that 5G can offer as defined by 3GPP specifications.

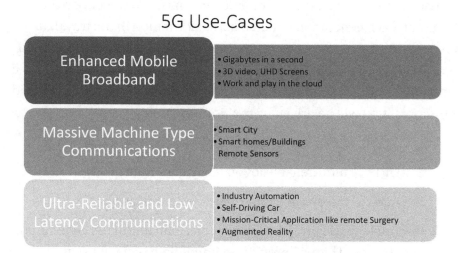

Figure 1-2. *5G Use-cases by 3GPP*

Autonomous vehicles will have large amounts of data to be transferred. To be processed more easily in the remote servers, the vehicles also need to have ultra-low latency for vehicular communication so that quick decisions can be made by the car following communication with other cars or reading signals.

5G also has provisions to be integrated with satellite communications to be used in remote locations and by various industries.

One of the major drivers for 5G is the rise of IOT devices and the adoption of edge computing. Content services are increasingly becoming popular, and 5G defines clear ways to bring mobile edge computing to cater to the rising market demand of high-quality video at high speeds by, for example, bringing content closer to the user and caching popular content.

Before we delve into the features 5G would provide that would enable a whole new world of applications, let's take a look at a market survey published by Allied Market research (*see* Figures 1-3 and 1-4).

According to a report published at their website, the 5G technology market is anticipated to be $5.53 billion in 2020 and is projected to reach $667.90 billion by 2026.

The following are some of the surveys published by connectivity, application and end-use.

- **Application graphs** would show the trend for adoption in various applications, such as the connected vehicle, monitoring and tracking, industrial automation, smart surveillance by use of drones, virtual reality (VR) and augmented reality (AR), and enhanced video services.

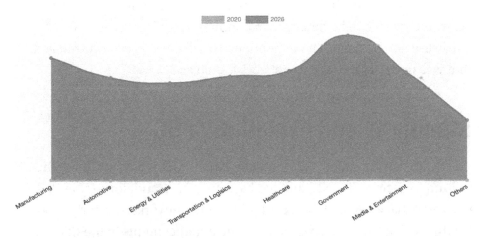

Figure 1-3. *Application graph(Source: Allied Market Research)*

- **End-use case graphs** will show the industrial adoption among manufacturing, automobiles, energy and utilities, transport and logistics, healthcare, government, media and entertainment, and others.

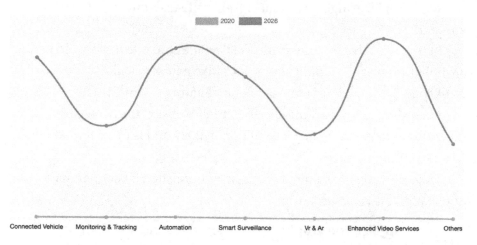

Figure 1-4. Technology Market by End use (Source: Allied Market Research)

One of the other key drivers for industrial adoption of a private 5G network is the ease of implementation and significant reduction in CAPEX. 5G would be able to be deployed in commercial off-the-shelf (COTS) hardware and hence has no dependency on expensive customized gear that was needed for previous networks, such as 3G.

Standards and Evolution of 5G

The 3GPP standards for 5G began with Release 15, which set down the ground for new radio (NR) and the basis for non-standalone (NSA) 5G networks that leveraged the existing LTE core networks; the early drop for this was in 2018. It also detailed some enhancements in the LTE core, such as control and user plane separation to be able to better cater to 5G adoption. Release 15 also had details for the 5G standalone (SA) core networks. Release 16, which was released in June 2020, had further features of 5G. Let us understand how we started with 5G, the contents of various releases, and in the details of Release 16, and what is planned for Release 17 that makes it so exciting.

Infrastructure-wise, a major difference between 4G and 5G is that 4G started the movement to a virtualized network, and 5G pushed it further to a containerized infrastructure.

Release 16 introduced more features, mainly focusing on industrial usage, among others. Figure 1-5 illustrates the details of Release 16. Further versions of Release 16 will continue over the next few quarters.

Release 15	Release 16
• NR- New Radio	Radio
• NR NSA ,5G Radio to work with LTE core	NR in unlicensed band
• NR SA, 5G Radio to work with 5G core	Industrial IOT
• Massive MTC and Internet of things	Accurate NR positioning
• Vehicle to everything communication (V2x)	NR for integrated Access and Backhaul (IAB)
• Mission Critical (MC) internetworking with legacy systems	5G Core
• WLAN unlicensed spectrum use	Enhanced SBA (eSBA)
• Slicing- logical and end to end networks	Private networks
• API Exposure – 3rd Party access to 5G services	Wireless/Wireline (Cable/BNG) Convergence + Access Steering
• Service Based Architecture (SBA)	Time Sensitive Network (TSN)
• Further LTE improvements	Cellular IoT (NB-IOT, CatM)
• Mobile communication system for Railways	Slice Management
• MEC	Network Analytics
	V2x Phase 3: Platooning extended sensors, automated driving, remote driving
	URLLC enhancements

Figure 1-5. *Releases 15 and 16 contents*

Release 17 is expected to be released in 2022. It introduces an exhaustive feature list that would truly mark the arrival of 5G (*see* Figure 1-6).

Release 17	
• NR MIMO	• NR Sidelink relay
• NR Sidelink enhancement	• RAN Slicing Enh. for small data
• 52.6 - 71 GHz with existing waveform	• SON / Minimization of drive tests (MDT) enh. NR Quality of
• Dynamic Spectrum Sharing (DSS) enh. Industrial IoT / URLLC enh.	Experience
• Study - IoT over Non-Terrestrial Networks (NTN) NR over Non- Terrestrial Networks (NTN)	• eNB architecture evolution, LTE C-plane / U-plane split
• NR Positioning enh.	• Satellite components in the 5G architecture
• Low complexity NR devices Power saving	• Non-Public Networks enh.
• NR Coverage enh.	• Network Automation for 5G - phase 2 Edge Computing in 5GC
• Study - NR eXtended Reality (XR) NB-IoT and LTE-MTC enh.	• Proximity based Services in 5GS
• 5G Multicast broadcast Multi-Radio DCCA enh.	• Network Slicing Phase 2
• Multi SIM Integrated Access and Backhaul (IAB) enh.	• Enh. V2x Services
• Unmanned Aerial Systems	• Advanced Interactive Services
• 5GC Location Services	• Access Traffic Steering, Switch and Splitting support in the 5G system architecture
• Multimedia Priority Service (MPS)	• 5G LAN-type services
• 5G LAN-type services	• User Plane Function (UPF) enh. for control and 5G Service
• 5G Wireless and Wireline Convergence	Based Architecture (SBA)

Figure 1-6. *Release 17 features*

Evolution to 5G and Overview of 5G Standalone Network

The 3GPP standards provided the service providers a path for gradual transition to a full-fledged 5G network. NSA is the steppingstone to a 5G network. NSA enables the NR (5G radio) to be deployed and to connect to a 4G core. In this arrangement the 5G radio depends on 4G eNB for all control plane messaging. 5G NR in this case cannot connect to the LTE control plane core network on its own—hence the name NSA, as it cannot stand alone without the help of a master LTE eNB and is dependent on it for all control plane signaling.

Another stepping stone was to separate the control and user plane completely. In legacy first-generation LTE networks the serving gateway (SGW) and the packet data network gateway (PGW) would handle both data and signaling to be more aligned to the 5G paradigm of separation of control and data. Control and data plane separation (CUPS) was introduced in 4G core as well. In that case the legacy SGW and PGW were split into control and user plane nodes. Hence both SGW and PGW after

CUPS have their own control and user planes that communicate with each other over a well-defined **Sx** interface over packet forwarding control protocol (PFCP). We will read about this in detail in Chapter 3.

The transition from 4G to 5G network is shown in Figure 1-7.

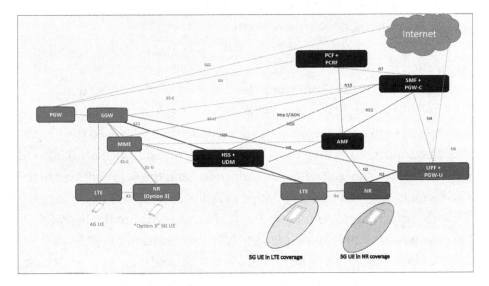

Figure 1-7. *4G to 5G Transition*

When the operator transitions to a network that uses the NSA option, as seen in Figure 1-7, the 5G NR connects to the LTE eNodeB for all signaling—in other words, the LTE controls the NR gNB. The data path, however, is separate, and the NR directly establishes a S1-U tunnel with the SGW for all data traffic and is encapsulated in general packet radio service tunneling protocol (GTPU).

As you can already guess, in the NSA option the UE IP address is allocated by the 4G core that is the PGW. Additionally the DPI, charging, policy, and so forth are managed by the LTE core. Only the access network in this case would be 5G—that is, the device would communicate to the 5G NR, and NR would send the data traffic to the SGW. Session mobility management is also managed by the 4G network. In a 5G coverage area, a UE with 5G UE capability would be served by the 5G-NR, and a 4G UE would continue to be served by a 4G eNodeB (eNB) even if it is in a 5G coverage area.

As seen in Figure 1-7, there are certain parallels that can be drawn with the LTE core gateway functions and the 5G Core NFs.

Let us go through each one of them.

The eNB can be compared to the gNB in 5G. It is basically the radio base station in 5G.

The next phase of rollout would be to launch 5G SA. When that is launched it is expected to coexist with NSA and legacy 4G. As seen on the right side of Figure 1-7, the 5G UE in the NR area in a SA-based deployment would be connected to the nr-gNB and thereby to the AMF/SMF/UPF and so forth; this is a simple use-case. Next, consider if the 5G UE moves to a 4G coverage area with no 5G coverage available, it would connect to the LTE eNB, which would connect to the MME and SGW, but the PGW in that case would be the interworking PGW located within the SMF. In this case seamless mobility can be obtained via N26, and context from 5G can be retrieved by the MME from access and mobility management function (AMF). Additionally the allocated IP address can remain the same between 4G and 5G, since the SMF and PGW is co-located and the UPF has not changed. The 4G UE in this type of deployment continues to connect to the legacy 4G gateway. And UEs with DCNR would keep connecting to NSA as explained earlier. This is how all the three types of deployments can co-exist.

Key Concepts in 5G

Data Network Name

The data network name (DNN) performs the same function and follows the same format as the access point name (APN) in 2G/3G/4G systems.

Packet Data Unit Session

The **packet data unit** (PDU) session is comparable to what is known as the PDN connection in 4G. The PDU session is set up to carry data between the UE and the UPF. All the control plane nodes in 5G are used to set up, manage, and tear up this connection. In the 5G network, only the UE, the GNB and the UPF are the network functions that are in the data plane; every other network function is in the control plane and contributes heavily to manage, control, and capitalize on the data plane.

There are three types of PDU sessions in 5G. The first is the **IP** type, which is used for the normal IPV4 and IPV6 traffic to and from the UE to the network. The second type is **ethernet;** in this mode ethernet frames are sent to and from the UPFs. This is to enable the UE to have a layer 2 connectivity. So one use-case of this type would be that the 5G UE is a part of a LAN, and this is connected to the UPF. The UE IP address would most likely be allocated by a DHCP server within the LAN; this is a classic enterprise use-case. In 5G one of the key principles is that it is access agnostic; hence, UPF would be able to terminate traffic from non-3GPP-wired or wireless access. The third type of PDU session is **unstructured;** in this type the PDU formats are completely unknown to the 5G system. The 5G system would not even know the payload boundaries, header boundaries, and so forth. The UPF in this case would only serve as the "pipe" for packet transfer. This type of use-case would mostly emanate from IOT devices.

Let's dive further details of how the PDU session is established. The easy-to-guess option is that it is initiated by the UE when it is powered on or wants to add another session to a different DNN. It could also be triggered by the network in case of emergency call with mobility registration.

There is a defined procedure for the establishment of the PDU session, after which the user would be able to make calls, browse data, and so forth. But how is it really set up? Let's go through the process at a high level.

11

When the UE starts the process of PDU establishment—say, when you toggle back from airplane mode—it will initiate a radio resource control (RRC) connection request to GNB with a PDU establishment request. The UE includes its preferred network slice, the DNN or the data network it wants a connection to, a PDU session ID (which is self-generated), a 5GSM capability that details the session management capabilities of the UE, and PCO options (which is similar to 4G). In case the NAS message doesn't contain the slice or DNN information, default values are picked up. The request is processed by AMF and sent to SMF, and then SMF further interacts with UDM for subscription details for the user, PCF for policy details, UPF for the n4 TEID, and CHF for charging, after which the SMF responds to AMF with success, which is forwarded to the UE by the GNB.

Subscription Permanent Identifier

All subscribers within the 5G Core are allocated a globally unique 5G subscription permanent identifier (SUPI). The SUPI is in the form of the traditional international mobile subscriber identity (IMSI) or network access identifier (NAI).

The service provider allocates this to each SIM card that is inserted into the UE. SUPI is never sent in clear text across the RAN, because if it is intercepted by rogue elements, the UE can be spoofed and can also result in DoS attacks.

Rather the UE is assigned a globally unique temporary identifier (GUTI), which is used to identify the UE over the radio link.

Utilizing the IMSI ensures various roaming and interworking scenarios are supported. This SUPI value in 5G can be the IMSI value, as used in previous generations, or it can be the NAI for non-SIM devices.

The SUPI normally consists of 15 or 16 decimal digits, which comprises of the mcc-mnc-msin.

Figure 1-8 shows the SUPI components.

MCC	MNC	MSIN
3 digits	3 digits	9 or 10 digits

Supi imsi-111222123456789

Figure 1-8. *Subscription Unique Permanent Identifier (SUPI)*

- MNC and MCC are the mobile network and country code used to identify the country and the specific service provider. A combination of the two can identify a mobile network uniquely across the globe.

- MSIN is the abbreviation for mobile subscription identification number. It consists of 10 digits and is used to identify a mobile phone subscriber by the service provider.

5G Globally Unique Temporary Identifier

5G-GUTI is used in 5G to keep the subscriber's SUPI (IMSI) information confidential. During the network registration, the AMF will allocate the 5G-GUTI, which is comprised of the globally unique AMF ID (GUAMI) and 5G temporary mobile subscriber identity. This information will be used to identify the UE over the radio access network to prevent snooping of SUPI. This information is changed frequently—hence, the name temporary.

Figure 1-9 shows the components for 5G-GUTI.

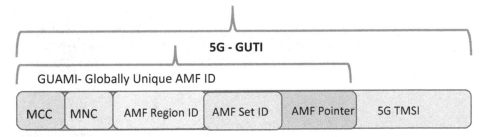

Figure 1-9. *5G-GUTI*

- GUAMI: stands for globally unique AMF ID. It is used to uniquely identify an AMF.

- AMF-Region ID: identifies the AMF region

- AMF-Set-ID: identifies a specific AMF set within the region

- AMF Pointer: uniquely identifies the AMF within the AMF-Set

QoS Model in 5G Core

The QoS model in 5G is flow-based as compared to 4G, which was EPS bearer level. As seen in FIgure 1-9, a PDU session is comprised of various QoS flows, and each of these flows are identified by a QoS flow identifier (QFI) value. When a UE establishes a PDU session to the data network, a non-guaranteed bit rate (GBR) QoS flow is set up, the UE or the application function can thereon create any additional guaranteed or non-guaranteed flows based on the need via the PDU modification process. The point to note here is that in 4G additional bearers were created to support different types of QoS flows, which is not the case in 5G. In 5G, the same PDU session can be modified to add or remove flows. For video or voice, the UE can initiate a PDU modification procedure to create a GBR flow needed for video or voice. A dedicated bearer, which was needed in 4G, is not necessary in this case.

Figure 1-10 illustrates how different QoS flows are bundled within a PDU session in 5G.

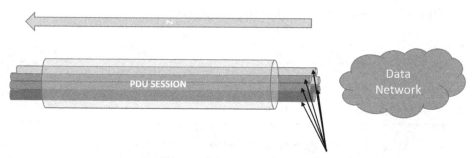

Different QoS Flows within the same PDU session based on latency, priority, or guaranteed or non- guaranteed bitrates

Figure 1-10. *QoS in 5G*

As you have probably guessed by now, the QFI value is comparable to the bearer ID of 4G. 5QI is the QoS identifier, similarly to QCI in 4G.

SMF allocates the QFI based on the QoS value.

Figure 1-11 shows the PDU session to QFI mapping in 5G.

Figure 1-11. *PDU session to QFI mapping*

As shown in Figure 1-10, the same UE can have two different PDU sessions—for example, one for IMS to connect to IMS slice with different AMF/SMF/UPF combinations and another for accessing data from the internet from another slice. The UE is responsible for assigning the PDU session IDs. For PDU session 1 for IMS, you can observe the same PDU session has a flow for IMS signaling and another GBR flow for voice. Similarly, consider the data PDU session of type V6, which has various QoS flows for different Qos types, but the PDU session remains the same until the PDU type changes. In the same example, if a IPv4 data flow is required, then a new IPv4 PDU session would have been set up. Another notable point is that within the PDU session, the QFI is unique, but for the same UE two different PDU sessions can have same QFI value.

Figure 1-12 shows the mapping of QoS between 4G and 5G.

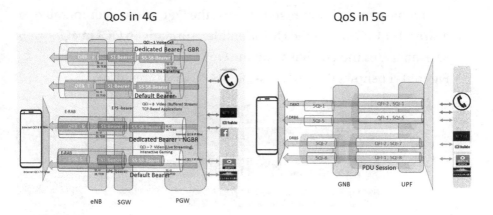

Figure 1-12. *QoS in 4G vs 5G*

Figure 1-11 shows the comparison of QoS in 4G vs 5G. In 4G a bearer was set up with different tunnel endpoint identifiers for each type of QoS class. However, in 5G the same PDU session is able to accommodate various QoS flows. In 5G the GTP tunnel for the data path is between the GNB and the N3 interface on UPF.

On the radio side the GNB is responsible for mapping these tunnels to data radio bearers (DRBs). The GNB may decide to map one or more QoS flows into the same bearer. Since only one GTP-U tunnel is formed for all these flows between the GNB and UPF, how is the GNB able to differentiate among the different flows? This is done by the new extension header of GTPU for QFI values in 5G UPF. To summarize, all QoS flows of one PDU session are sent in a single GTPU tunnel that is differentiated in the GTP header by the QFI field, as mentioned.

There are some more notable additions on the n4 interface between SMF and UPF regarding QoS management. The SMF provides instructions to the UPF via the PFCP messages. The information elements in the PFCP messages instruct the UPF about UE traffic classification, queuing, scheduling, and marking/remarking.

Packet Detection Rule: As the name suggests, this is used by the SMF to instruct the UPF on packet detection rules (PDRs), how to classify DL traffic using 5 tuple (source IP address/port number, destination IP address/port number, and the protocol in use), and to map it to a QoS flow. Similarly, UL PDR is used to verify UE SDF to QoS mapping before the UPF forwards uplink traffic to the DN. PDR also collects pointers to link the Forwarding Action Rule (FAR), QoS Enforcement Rule (QER), Usage Report Rule (URR), and Buffering Action Rule (BAR). We will discuss each of these here.

Forwarding Action Rule (FAR): This is to inform the UPF to forward the packet or duplicate the packet (for forwarding to lawful intercept [LI]). It also helps in QoS to DSCP mapping for the IP core elements. Differentiated services codepoint (DSCP) marking helps classify traffic that requires higher bandwidth or higher priority or is likely to drop packets. It works by using its header packet value that can be used to request high priority or best effort delivery for traffic.

QoS Enforcement Rule (QER): This is used to enforce bandwidth and latency for GBR or non-GBR flows. Throttling and rate limiting is applied with the help of this.

Usage Report Rule (URR): This is used to tell the UPF the usage reporting triggers (e.g., time, volume). This report contains the actual data usage by the UE and is sent to the SMF; the SMF then sends it to charging function (CHF) for charging.

Buffering Action Rule (BAR): This IE is used mainly for idle mode UEs and when data comes in for the idle UE it is buffered until UE goes back to connected mode. Hence this instruction helps the SMF inform UPF about the buffering action to execute.

Figure 1-13 illustrates the 5QI and QoS mapping in 5G. Note that 5QI 1 to QCI 9 is the same as QCI 1-9 in 4G.

5QI Value	Resource Type	Default Priority Level	Packet Delay Budget	Packet Error Rate	Default Maximum Data Burst Rate	Default Averaging Window	Example service	Applicable to
1		20	100 ms	10^{-2}	N/A	2000 ms	Conversational Voice	
2		40	150 ms	10^{-3}	N/A	2000 ms	Conversational Video (Live Streaming)	4G and 5G
3		30	50 ms	10^{-3}	N/A	2000 ms	Real Time Gaming, V2X messages, Electricity distribution - medium voltage, Process automation - monitoring	
4		50	300 ms	10^{-6}	N/A	2000 ms	Non-Conversational Video (Buffered Streaming)	
65		7	75 ms	10^{-2}	N/A	2000 ms	Mission Critical user plane Push To Talk voice (e.g. MCPTT)	
66		20	100 ms	10^{-2}	N/A	2000 ms	Non-Mission-Critical user plane Push To Talk voice	
67	GBR	15	100 ms	10^{-3}	N/A	2000 ms	Mission Critical Video user plane	
75								
71		56	150 ms	10^{-6}				5G
72		56	300 ms	10^{-4}				
73		56	300 ms	10^{-8}	N/A	2000 ms	"Live" Uplink Streaming	
74		56	500 ms	10^{-8}				
76		56	500 ms	10^{-4}				
5		10	100 ms	10^{-6}	N/A	N/A	IMS Signalling	
6		60	300 ms	10^{-6}	N/A	N/A	Video (Buffered Streaming) TCP-based (e.g., www, e-mail, chat, ftp, p2p file sharing, progressive video, etc.)	4G and 5G
7		70	100 ms	10^{-3}	N/A	N/A	Voice, Video (Live Streaming) Interactive Gaming	
8		80	300 ms	10^{-6}	N/A	N/A	Video (Buffered Streaming) TCP-based (e.g., www, e-mail, chat, ftp, p2p file sharing, progressive video, etc.)	
9	Non-GBR	90						
69		5	60 ms	10^{-6}	N/A	N/A	Mission Critical delay sensitive signalling (e.g., MC-PTT signalling)	
70		55	200 ms	10^{-6}	N/A	N/A	Mission Critical Data (e.g. example services are the same as 5QI 6/8/9)	
79		65	50 ms	10^{-2}	N/A	N/A	V2X messages	
80		68	10 ms	10^{-6}	N/A	N/A	Low Latency eMBB applications Augmented Reality	5G
82		19	10 ms	10^{-4}	255 bytes	2000 ms	Discrete Automation	
83	Delay Critical GBR	22	10 ms	10^{-4}	1354 bytes	2000 ms	Discrete Automation	
84		24	30 ms	10^{-5}	1354 bytes	2000 ms	Intelligent transport systems	
85		21	5 ms	10^{-5}	255 bytes	2000 ms	Electricity Distribution - high voltage	

Figure 1-13. *5QI Table*

Reflective QoS: Reflective QoS is a unique feature in 5G, but it needs additional support on the UE. If this feature is supported on the UE, the UE indicates it during the PDU session establishment or modification. When this is received by the SMF, it indicates the same to the UPF for a certain QoS flow, in which case the UPF will include it in the GTPU encapsulation header in a field called reflective QoS indicator (RQI) to gNB via N3 interface. GNB indicates the same to the UE, when UE detects the RQI set, it will apply the same QoS that is in downlink direction to all the uplink data packets—hence, any specific signaling for UL QoS is saved.

New Radio

New radio has some additional capabilities over LTE—it uses two frequency bands:

- Frequency Range 1 (FR1): This includes sub-6Ghz frequency bands; it is targeted for the enterprise segment.

- Frequency Range 2 (FR2): This is comprised of frequency bands in the mmWave range, which is 24-100GHz.

The NR has a key role in catering to the low-latency requirement of 1ms or less in 5G. It uses optimized orthogonal frequency division multiplexing (OFDM)-based waveforms and multiple access. Some of the key responsibilities of the NR are listed here and are very similar to the eNB functionality in 4G.

- One of the most integral functions of a base station is radio resource management. This involves radio bearer control, radio admission control, connection mobility control, and scheduling, which is nothing but the allocation of radio resources to UEs in both uplink and downlink. This is dynamic in nature and needs to be optimized to be able to meet the tight time constraints. The scheduler is a proprietary implementation and can be enhanced to improve efficiency.

- A new radio GNB performs IP and Ethernet header compression, encryption, and integrity protection of data. This is similar to the LTE eNB RoHC functionality.

- New Radio (NR) is responsible for selection of an AMF during attachment. The AMF list is configured on the GNB or can be obtained by query to the domain name system. It is important for the GNB to select the AMF in the pool in a round-robin fashion to ensure load is balanced across all the AMFs. Its also prudent to configure more than one AMF in a pool and size it to be able to take up all the traffic if the other AMF fails in the pool. Therefore, the GNB should be able to support the detection of AMF failures and choose the other AMF in case it fails.

- NR-GNB is responsible for the routing of user plane data toward UPF(s). In the 5G world, the N3 interface terminates on the UPF and starts from GNB. It is based on GTP. It carries the user data. The GTP tunnel endpoints are used to map traffic on N3 for a particular PDU session.

- NR-GNB is responsible for routing of control plane information toward AMF. It transfers the NAS containers from the UE transparently to AMF and SMF.

- NR-GNB is responsible for RRC connection setup and release between UE and itself.

- NR-GNB is responsible for scheduling and transmission of paging messages. Paging is critical to contact a UE that is in idle mode when there is data pending for it. For example, if a UE is in idle mode since the user is not actively browsing, then there is a VONR call toward the UE, and the UE needs to be contacted, but it may have moved from its original location to a new location when in idle mode. Therefore, to ensure that the call reaches the UE, it is necessary to ensure it comes back to connected mode. To execute this, the UE is paged, and paging is sent from the AMF to GNB and GNB to UE. When the SMF receives a downlink data notification for that UE, it sends the request to the AMF; the AMF in turn initiates the paging procedure and sends the request to the GNB. Finally, it is up to the GNB to identify and schedule paging messages for the UE in accurate paging occasions.

- NR-GNB is responsible for scheduling and transmission of system broadcast information. These broadcast messages can be originated from Operations Administration and Maintenance (OAM) or the AMF for various settings or tuning of radio settings for all the UEs in that GNB coverage.

- NR-GNB is responsible for measurement and measurement reporting configuration for mobility and scheduling. This is a critical task of the GNB; the measurement reports from the UE are the basis of all decisions for handover and mobility. The UE measures the signal strength and sends the reports to the GNB. The GNB will be responsible for scheduling these measurement reports so that the UE can send them. Thereafter the information in these measurement reports will be used for triggering handovers to a cell, which may show a better coverage in the report.

- NR-GNB is responsible for session management. It supports network slicing. The network slice information is sent in the radio SIB messages.

- NR-GNB is responsible for QoS flow management and mapping to data radio bearers. This is a very key concept in 5GNR. The PDU session from the UPF may contain various QoS flows with various 5QI values. It's up to the GNB to decide how it is mapped to various DRBs. It is possible to combine various 5QI values to the same DRB; it is also possible to have it on separate DRBs. It is up to the GNB to decide this.

- NR-GNB is responsible for UEs transitions from and to RRC_INACTIVE.

- NR-GNB is responsible for managing radio access network sharing. This would be crucial for onboarding roaming partner.

- NR-GNB supports dual connectivity and hence can be connected on both 4G and 5G.

- NR-GNB supports tight interworking between NR and E-UTRAN.

Access and Mobility Function

MME in 4G can be compared to the AMF in the 5G core network. However, in 4G the MME had both session and mobility management functions. In 5G the mobility management is done by AMF, but session management is delegated to the SMF. Let us go through the function of AMF in detail here.

- AMF is handles NAS signaling termination, which implies that the N1 NAS container is terminated at the AMF. It is also responsible for NAS signaling security and handles the encryption of NAS messages with the keys it obtains from AUSF. AMF further transparently sends the N2 NAS container to SMFA.

- AMF is responsible for handling AS Security control, this is very similar to the MME function in 4G. It is responsible for access authorization and also checking subscriptions for roaming rights.

- AMF handles 5G-to-4G handovers and does so with the help of an N26 interface with MME. Hence the context retrieval and transfer from 4G to 5G can be handled. For this to be implemented, it is necessary for AMF to support GTPv2 protocol with MME. Therefore AMF is responsible for inter- and intrasystem handovers, thus being responsible for mobility management control for subscription and policies.

- AMF is responsible for idle mode UE reachability. SMF is notified by UPF for any incoming data for the UE, the SMF then notifies the AMF, and the AMF is then responsible for control and execution of paging and retransmissions to the GNB.

- AMF has the support of network slicing and is used heavily to query the network slice selection function (NSSF) for proper slice selection.

- AMF is responsible for SMF selection. This can be based on TAC or region-based design and can also be based on DNN, slice, and so on. It is typically an operator discretion to configure the optimal method of SMF selection.

- AMF is responsible for selection of CIoT 5GS optimizations.

Services offered by AMF are shown in Figure 1-14.

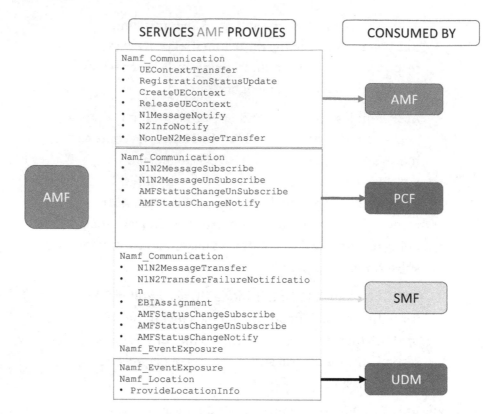

Figure 1-14. *Services offered by AMF*

The following should be considered while deploying an AMF:

- Network function repository function (NRF) discovery and NRF management can be configured as the same or different endpoints for its own discovery and for management of other NFs.

- Various procedure-based timers can be configured on the AMF, like T3550 (Registration Accept/complete), T3510 (Registration Request to Accept), T3522 (de-registration timer), and so on. Guard timers can be configured to kill slow procedures.

- Various security algorithms can be configured for ciphering and integrity protection.

- Static configuration for endpoints of peer NFs like SMF, UDM, AUSF, PCF, and so on, for fallback in case the NRF discovery procedure fails.

- The serving network ID, locality information that can be used for AMF selection, MCC, MNC, region ID, set ID, slice ID, and AMF pointer are configured.

- The diagram in Figure 1-15 illustrates the concept of AMF region, set, and pointer. As seen in Figure 1-15, the mobile network can be divided into various AMF regions according to the geographical area or the density of subscribers. Each region can have one or more AMF sets, and each AMF set can have one or more AMFs. The region ID addresses the issue if there are more AMF sets than what is supported by the AMF set ID. Hence, it is further categorized in regions, and each region can have set IDs that are repeated in other regions. The AMF pointer identifies one or more AMF within each AMF set within its own region.

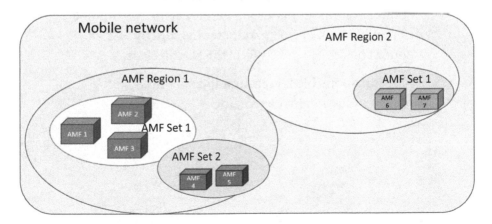

Figure 1-15. *AMF region*

- Tracking area identity (TAI) lists with various tracking area codes (TACs) are configured on the AMF. This is used for various purposes like paging and also SMF selection.

Session Management Function

The SMF can be comparable to PGW to a large extent in the 4G world. It is responsible for the IP address allocation and interacts with the charging and the policy systems just like PGW, but it also does session management. Let us go through the key roles and responsibilities of SMF:

- SMF is responsible for session management, which includes session establishment, modification, and termination. So when a PDU session establishment request comes to SMF from the AMF, the SMF allocates it an IP address and selects an appropriate UPF for it. The UPF selection can be based on DNN, location, and so on.

- The SMF then reaches out to the policy control function (PCF) and receives the various traffic steering rules, which it passes on to the UPF for enforcement. SMF thus serves as a manager of the UPF, serving as the controller for policy and QoS enforcement. Any update or modification of QoS parameters as sent by PCF is communicated to the UPF via the N4 interface.

- SMF is responsible for termination of NAS signaling related to session management.

- SMF is responsible for handling downlink data notification (DDN). The DDN is received by the UPF and sent to the SMF via N4. The downlink data notification is for any traffic coming in for a UE in idle mode. The SMF sends the DDN information to the AMF, which then starts the paging procedure.

- SMF supports LI. The LI tap is configured on the SMF, and the SMF then starts tap on UPF by asking the UPF to start duplicating the packets toward X3. So, the event details for a particular SUPI, when configured to be tapped on SMF, is sent via X2, and all the data is sent via UPF on X3. And SMF configures UPF to be tapped via sending duplication flag over PFCP on N4.

- SMF is responsible for charging data collection and support of charging interfaces. The data usage information is actually collected by the UPF and sent to the SMF over the session report PFCP messages. The SMF then uses the usage reported by UPF to send the information to CHF via N40.

- SMF is responsible for determination of session and service continuity (SSC) mode of a session. (SSC modes will be discussed in detail in Chapter 4; it is related to session continuity.)

Figure 1-16 shows the services provided by SMF.

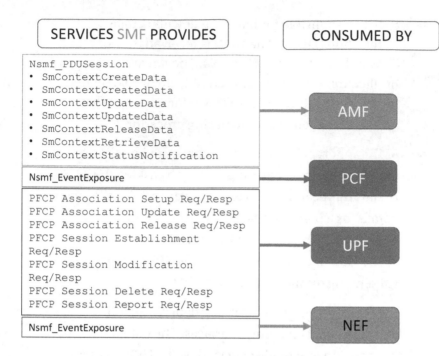

Figure 1-16. *Services provided by SMF*

The following are the configurable parameters on SMF:

- Of utmost importance is the UE IP pool configuration. It is from this pool the SMF will allocate the IP address to the UEs and also convey this to the UPF to be advertised out so that the user plane internet traffic can be routed for the UE on the appropriate UPF.

- NRF endpoint configuration for discovery of various NFs like AMF, PCF, CHF, UDM, etc. The NRF endpoint configuration can also be planned with endpoint failure in consideration; hence, two or more NRFs can be configured to serve as primary, secondary, and so on. It can also be configured to be round-robin across various NRFs so that failure of any one NRF won't cause overload on the failed NRF.

- Static entries for NF endpoints prove valuable when the discovery fails for any reason. Thus the same can also be configured.

- SBI endpoint configurations for the various services producers such as AMF, PCF, and so on that can be consumed by SMF.

```
Sbi endpoint
interface nrf
ip 1.1.1.1  port 8090. >>>> endpoint which is used by
smf to communicate with nrf
exit
interface n11
ip 1.2.2.2 port 8090  >>>> endpoint which is used by
smf to communicate with amf
exit
interface n7
ip 1.3.3.3port 8090    >>>> endpoint which is used by
smf to communicate with pcf
exit
interface n10
ip 1.1.1.4 port 8090    >>>> endpoint which is used by
smf to communicate with udm
exit
interface n40
ip 1.1.1.5 port 8090    >>>> endpoint which is used by
smf to communicate with chf
exit
```

- Various DNN configurations that are supported by the service provider would need to be present in the SMF.

- UPF details need to be configured as well as the the UPF selection criteria.

- Query parameters for various NFs are configured on the SMF—for example, query by DNN.

- Another important part of the configuration is the ability to handle failures. This can be configured on the SMF—for example, for a particular error code the SMF can handle by retrying to another endpoint. If there is still an unsuccessful response, the SMF can choose to continue or terminate according to configuration.

- The static traffic steering rules can be configured on the SMF.

- Converged charging, or online or offline charging, can be configured per design on the SMF.

- Lawful intercept is also configured on the SMF.

User Plane Function

As you have already observed, the SGW of the 4G node has been completely eliminated in the 5G world. One of the key functions provided by the SGW was to be an anchor for mobility. A similar function is provided by the user plane function (UPF). The UPF also has further responsibilities. **UPF as well as gNB are the only data plane nodes in the 5G architecture**. All nodes apart from these are only control plane nodes. The UPF is not a service-based interface, and it supports PFCP on the control plane and GTPU on the user plane.

- As discussed, UPF is the anchoring point for intra- and inter-RAT mobility as applicable.

- UPF is responsible for allocating UE IP addresses or prefixes (when supported) in response to a request by the SMF.

- UPF performs the role of the external PDU session point of connection to the external DN (internet or the application function).

- UPF is responsible for routing of packets and forwarding (e.g., support of uplink classifier [ULCL] to route traffic flows to an instance of a data network, support for branching point to support multi-homing PDU session, andsupport of traffic forwarding within a 5G VN group [UPF local switching, via N6, via N19]).

- UPF is responsible for deep packet inspection, including detection of applications based on a service-data flow (SDF) template and the optional PFDs received from the SMF in addition.

- UPF is responsible for the user plane part of policy rule enforcement (e.g., gating, redirection, traffic steering).

- UPF is responsible for LI (UP collection).

- UPF is responsible for traffic usage reporting.

- UPF is responsible for handling and enforcing QoS for the user plane (e.g., UL/DL rate enforcement, reflective QoS marking in DL).

- UPF is responsible for uplink traffic verification (SDF to QoS flow mapping).

- UPF is responsible for transport level packet marking in the uplink and downlink.

- UPF is responsible for downlink packet buffering and downlink data notification triggering.

- UPF sends and forwards one or more end-markers to the source NG-RAN node.

- UPF is responsible for functionality that responds to address-resolution-protocol (ARP) requests as well as the IPv6 neighbor solicitation requests based on informaton available in the local cache for the ethernet-type of PDUs. The UPF also responds to the ARP and the IPv6 neighbor solicitation request by providing the MAC address that corresponds to the IP address sent in the request.

- UPF is responsible for packet duplication in downlink direction, which is used in features like LI and elimination in the uplink direction in GTP-U layer.

Policy Control Function

PCF in the 5G world is very similar to the PCRF in the LTE world, save the fact that in PCF all interactions are based on HTTP communication (as opposed to being diameter-based in the 4G world). Let us go through the details of its responsibilities. Note that PCF plays a key role in implementing VoNR in 5G. It is not possible to support voiceover NR without PCF, as it communicates with the IMS core to receive rules to create voice PDU sessions.

- PCF supports an unified policy framework that governs network behavior.

- PCF supplies policy rules to the control plane function (CP) to be enforced by them.

- PCF accesses the subscription-related information for the user, which is relevant for policy decisions in a unified data repository (UDR).

- These dynamic rules sent to the SMF as a part of update notify messages, on the receipt of the same SMF, creates flows for traffic steering and sends it to the UPF for enforcement.

The PCF needs to be configured with all the policy rules and logic guiding the QoS for both voice and data. The PCF also has configuration for discovery via NRF Rx-related configuration to support voice and for EPS fallback. The PCF can also be configured with appropriate guard timers for specific transactions. This will help transactions taking too long to time out and retry.

Figure 1-17 represents some of the services provided by PCF.

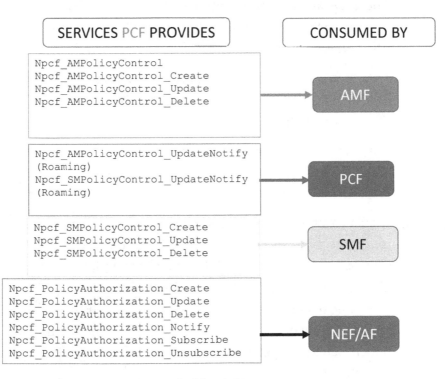

Figure 1-17. *Services provided by PCF*

Charging Function

The CHF in the 5G world has changed dramatically. In 4G there used to be separate nodes for online and offline charging services. In the 5G world, the implementation of charging has changed significantly. Let us go through the details here:

- In the 5G world, CHF does converged charging, which means that it covers online charging, offline charging, and the creation of charging data records (CDRs). CHF hence supports both online and offline charging.

- In the 4G world, PGW and SGW (roaming/MVNO) used to generate the charging records, which is no longer the case. SMF in 5G is only responsible for reporting the usage and requesting quota to the CHF. The CHF, in turn, uses the information sent to it by SMF to generate the CDRs.

- Therefore, SMF doesn't interact with the billing system, like PGW used to interact with CGF in 4G. All interactions with the billing system occur via the CHF.

- This is a service-based interface (explained in detail in the upcoming section) and is no longer diameter/GTP-based.

- CHF converges online and offline systems and hence fulfils the roles of rating function (RF), account balance management function (ABMF), and charging gateway function (CGF). CHF contains an RF that determines the value of the network resource usage, an AMBF that is the location of the subscriber's account balance, and a CGF acting as a gateway between the 3GPP network and the BD.

The CHF can thus include both the online charging function (OCF/OCS) and the charging data function (CDF/CGF)

- Slice information in the reporting by SMF to CHF can be leveraged to charge different slices differently as required by the service provider.

Figure 1-18 illustrates the services that are provided by CHF.

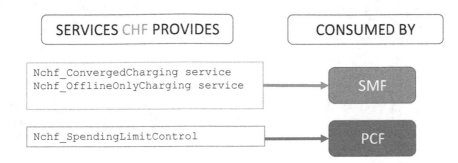

Figure 1-18. *Services provided by CHF*

The charging interfaces in 4G were diameter-based, and there were separate interfaces for online and offline charging—namely, gy and gz. In 5G, however, the charging interfaces are service-based. Both online and offline charging is now performed by a single entity called the CHF; this is called converged charging. As seen in Figure 1-18, it is responsible for online charging, offline charging, and creation of records.

Figure 1-19 shows the converged charging architecture in 5G.

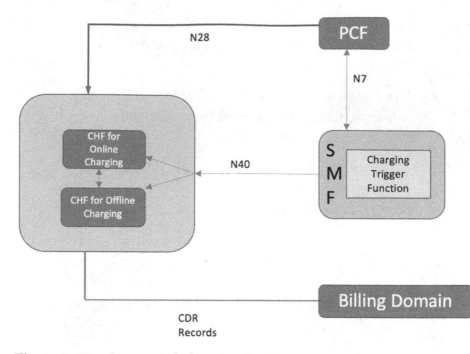

Figure 1-19. *Converged charging in 5G*

The CTF shown in Figure 1-19 is the charging trigger function that's located within the SMF. As seen in Figure 1-19, the SMF is configured in both online and offline charging, and the endpoint IPs of the online and offline sevices can be different, although it would be within the same CHF.

Another interesting thing is that we would be able to map the various charging-related parameters at this point. As we can see in Figure 1-20, the PCC rules between PCF and SMF map to the PDR in the UPF. The QoS Data from PCF maps to QosDesc in SMF and QER in the UPF. The charging data from PCF maps to chargingDesc on SMF and URR.

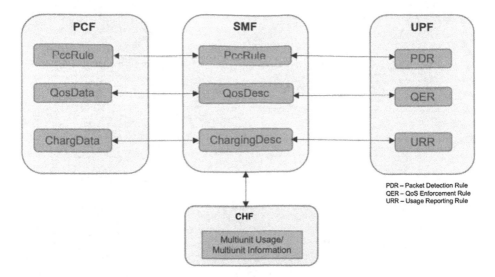

Figure 1-20. *Qos mapping*

Example of various snippets of the charging data block are shown in
Figures 1-21 and 1-22.

Figure 1-21. *Charging data block*

Figure 1-22. *Qos rules, PCC rules, ChargingDesc*

Authentication Server Function

The AUSF is similar to the home subscriber server (HSS) in the 4G world. It is connected to the UDM via the N13 interface and is connected to the AMF via the N12 interface. It is responsible for the following:

- implements the EAP authentication server for security procedures with AMF; and

- stores keys that are retrieved by AMF for security and integrity protection.

Figure 1-23 highlights the services provided by AUSF.

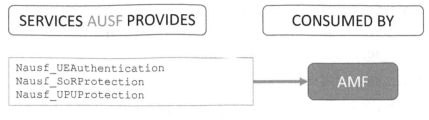

Figure 1-23. *Services provided by AUSF*

Unified Data Management

Unified data management is responsible for key management, user identification handling, access authorization, and so forth. The UDM uses subscription data, which includes authentication data that may be stored in UDR. Let us go through the responsibilities of UDM.

- The UDM is responsible for the generation of 3GPP AKA authentication credentials.

- The UDM is responsible for user identification-handling (e.g., storage and management of SUPI for each subscriber in the 5G core).

- The UDM is responsible for deconcealing the privacy protected subscription identifier SUCI.

- The UDM is responsible for access authorization based on subscription data (e.g., in roaming restrictions).

- The UDM is responsible for UE's serving NF-registration management, storing serving AMF for UE, and storing serving SMF for UE's PDU session.

- The UDM is responsible for support to service or session continuity by keeping SMF/DNN assignment of current sessions.

- The UDM is responsible for MT-SMS delivery support.

- The UDM is responsible for LI functionality—especially in outbound roaming cases where UDM is the only point of contact for LI.

- The UDM is responsible for subscription management.

- The UDM is responsible for SMS management.

- The UDM is responsible for support of external parameter provisioning, which includes the expected UE behavior parameters or network configuration parameters.

Figure 1-24 highlights the services provided by UDM.

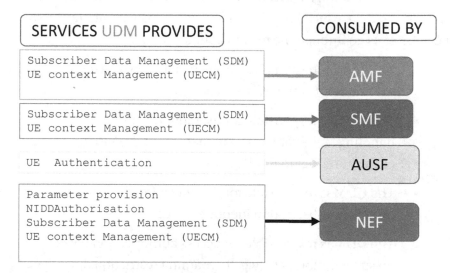

Figure 1-24. *Services provided by UDM*

Unified Data Repository

The UDR is contacted by the UDM for retrieval of subscription data. This is where the user details are actually stored. It also stores policy data and is connected to the PCF via the N36 interface. Let us go through the responsibilities of UDR:

- UDM is responsible for the storage and the retrieval of subscription data by the UDM.

- UDM is responsible for the storage and the retrieval of policy data by the PCF.

- UDM is responsible for the storage and retrieval of structured data for exposure.

- UDM is responsible for the storage of application data, which includes packet flow descriptions (PFDs) for application detection.

- UDM is responsible for the storage and the retrieval of NF group ID corresponding to subscriber identifier (e.g., the SUPI).

Figure 1-25 highlights the services provided by the UDR.

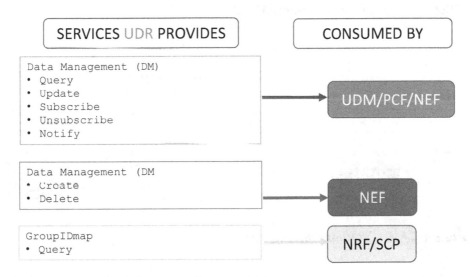

Figure 1-25. *Services provided by the UDR*

Network Slice Selection Function

Network slicing is one of the key aspects newly introduced in 5G. This will allow the service providers to provide specific portions of their network for specific use-cases; for example, IoT can have its own slice and enhanced broadband can have a separate slice. This ensures that the required resources are always available to cater to a specific type of traffic. The network topology in the IP core for these slices can also be tweaked to provide, for example, low latency for uRLLC and high bandwidth for enhanced broadband. This ensures the upkeep of SLAs for varying demands that suit the need of the application.

In a nutshell, slicing is the partitioning of the network architecture into virtual elements; in other words, it allows creation of multiple virtual networks over the physical infrastructure.

Figure 1-26 shows a very high level view of network slicing based on different types of services offered by the network.

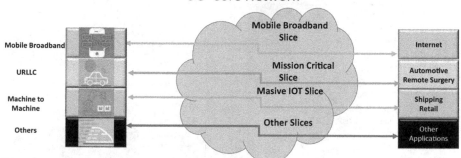

Figure 1-26. Network slicing 101

Slicing would result in savings for the operator, as they would need to be quickly able to deploy network functions that would cater to a specific use-case rather than deploying the full 5G core.

NSSF is the function that is used by the AMF to select a particular "slice" for a particular use-case. We will delve into details of network slicing in the upcoming chapter on network slicing.

NSSF is the node that is responsible for the slice selection. Its key responsibilities include:

- selection of the set of network slice instances serving a UE;

- determination of the allowed NSSAI and, when needed, mapping to the subscribed S-NSSAIs;

- determination of the configured NSSAI and, when needed, the mapping to the subscribed S-NSSAIs;

- determining the AMF set that is to be used to serve the UE based on its subscription and location.

Figure 1-27 shows the services offered by NSSF.

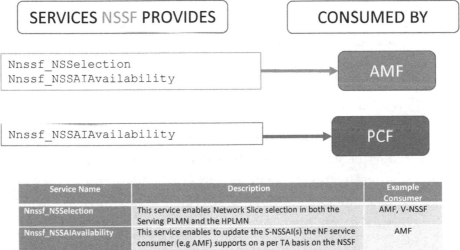

Service Name	Description	Example Consumer
Nnssf_NSSelection	This service enables Network Slice selection in both the Serving PLMN and the HPLMN	AMF, V-NSSF
Nnssf_NSSAIAvailability	This service enables to update the S-NSSAI(s) the NF service consumer (e.g AMF) supports on a per TA basis on the NSSF and to subscribe and notify any change in status, on a per TA basis, of the SNSSAIs available per TA (unrestricted) and the restricted S-NSSAI(s) per PLMN in that TA in the serving PLMN of the UE.	AMF

Figure 1-27. *Services provided by NSSF*

Network Repository Function

Before we can truly understand the functionality of the NRF, we need
to be introduced to yet another 5G concept known as the service-based
architecture.

Service-Based Architecture

While SBA is not a net new technology and has been used widely in the web
world, it is newly introduced in the telecom world. This is a proven method
to implement modularity in software applications. How is it relevant in the
5G world? The SBA is an approach followed to develop the 5G NFs; with
this a software is broken down into various communicating services.

SBA is a system architecture in which the system functionality is
achieved by a set of NFs by providing of services to other authorized NFs to
access their services.

- NF service: An NF service is one type of capability
  that is exposed by an NF (NF service producer) to
  other authorized NF (NF service consumer) through
  a service-based interface. An NF service may support
  one or more NF service operation(s).

- SBI: A service-based interface (SBI) represents
  how the set of services is provided or exposed by a
  given NF. This is the interface where the NF service
  operations are invoked (Namf, Nsmf, Nudm, Nnrf,
  Nnssf, Nausf, Nnef, Nsmsf, etc.).

To put this all together, service-based architecture is a system
architecture in which system functionality is achieved by network
functions providing services to authorized NFs that consume their
services.

For example, SMF and AF **consume** the services **provided** by
PCF in the example given in Figure 1-28 for policy creation and policy
authorization.

In 4G, there was a Gx interface between the PCRF and PGW and an Rx
interface between the AF and the PCRF to represent the same. However,
in 5G both these interfaces are replaced by N5 and N7, interfaces that,
respectively, are service-based interfaces.

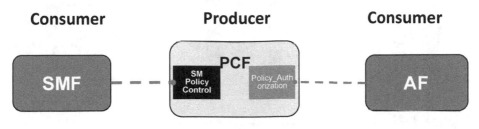

Figure 1-28. *SBA communication sample*

3GPP has chosen to use the widely adopted REpresentational State
Transfer (REST) architectural design model to support the design and
subsequent communication between the distributed applications and
functions that comprise the 5G core. In 4G the interfaces are based on
protocols like GTP, diameter, and so on, which are traditional telecom
protocols and not derived from a client server-based architecture.

Figure 1-28 shows a simple case when the consumer was aware of the
contact details of the producer and was able to contact the producer that
provided the service. However, if the consumer is not aware of the contact
details of the producer, it needs to undergo a process of service discovery.
This is similar to our real lives wherein when we want to look for a shop
that sells a brand of watches, we look up the web or a directory to get
the contact details of the seller. Similarly, the consumer service needs to
discover the producer. This process is aided by **NRF**.

Figure 1-29 shows the different communication models in 5G.

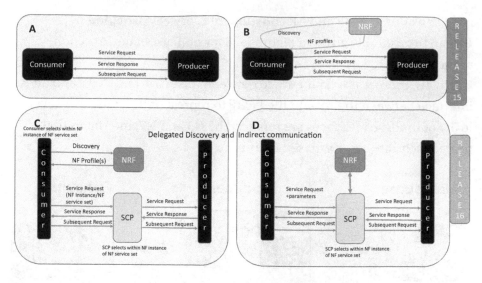

Figure 1-29. *Communication models in 5G*

Case A: The consumer has information to contact the producer to get its services.

Case B: The consumer is not aware of the producer details; hence, it undergoes a discovery process via NRF to obtain the information of the producer.

Case C: The consumer via discovery process receives an NF producer set instead of one producer. The consumer contacts the **service communication proxy (SCP)** and provides the NF set that is obtained via NRF. Now SCP has the logic to select the appropriate producer from the set. SCP has load balancing logic and is aware of which is the most appropriate producer to serve the consumer

Case D: This case is of delegated discovery. The consumer just contacts the SCP directly with the service request. The SCP then contacts the NRF to discover the appropriate producer. Once it gets the information from the NRF, it selects the appropriate producer based on its logic to cater to the consumer. The difference between Cases C and D is that in Case D the discovery is also delegated to SCP.

NRF: The Network Repository Function

NRF helps to provide the service discovery function. It receives NF discovery request from NF instances or SCP and provides information about the discovered NF instances to the NF instance or SCP.

- Supports P-CSCF discovery by the SMF

- Maintenance of the NF-profile of all available NF instances and their services they support

- Maintains SCP profile of available SCP instances

- Supports SCP discovery by SCP instances

- Sends notification about newly "registered/updated/ deregistered" network functions and SCP instances along with its potential NF services to the network function that has subscribed as service consumer or to the SCP

- Maintains the health status of NFs and SCP

- In the context of network slicing, based on the specific network implementation, one, two, or more NRFs can be deployed at different levels

- PLMN level: the NRF is configured with information for the whole network (all NFs)

- At shared slice level, the NRF is configured with information about sets of network slices available

- Slice-specific level: the NRF is configured with information about a specific slice "Nssai" level

Figure 1-30 highlights the services provided by NRF.

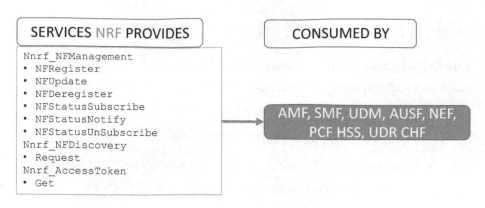

Figure 1-30. Services provided by NRF

Service Communication Proxy

The SCP has the following functions:

- indirect communication (as described above)

- forwarding of messages and routing to destination network functions

- message forwarding and routing to a next hop SCP

- provide secure communication between the NF's

- provide load balancing

- delegated discovery

Network Exposure Function

The network exposure function (NEF) is another new NF in 5G. As the name suggests, it helps to secure the exposure of network services over APIs for data, voice, subscriber data, and so forth to third-party applications.

The NEF will receive information from other network functions based on capabilities exposed by other network functions. The NEF will then store the received information as "structured data" using standardized interface to a UDR. The stored information can then be accessed and re-exposed by the NEF to other network functions and application functions and used later.

Some of the responsibilities of NEF are:

- With NEF, the NF capabilities and events can be securely exposed (e.g., third-party, application functions, edge computing).

- NEF will also store or retrieve information as "structured data" using the standardized interface (Nudr) toward the UDR.

- NEF also securely provisions information from external applications to 3GPP network.

- NEF provides means for the application functions to provide any information securely to the 3GPP network—for example, expected UE behavior, 5GLAN-group information, and service-specific information. NEF can authenticate/authorize and assist in throttling the application functions in such cases.

- NEF translates "internal external" information.

- It translates between information exchanged with the AF and information exchanged with the internal network function. For example, it translates between an AF service identifier and internal 5G core information such as DNN, S-NSSAI, and so forth.

- NEF handles the masking of network and user-sensitive information to any external application function according to the configured network policy.

- NEF will receive information from other NFs based on exposed capabilities of other network functions. NEFs will store the information received as "structured data" using a standardized interface to a UDR. The stored information can be accessed and re-exposed by the NEF to other network functions and application functions and used for other purposes like for telemetry and analytics.

Security Edge Protection Proxy

In order to understand SEPP better, let us take a quick glance at 5G roaming architecture.

As shown in Figure 1-31, SEPP provides a secure interconnect between 5G networks—in this case between a home and visited network. SEPP is responsible to provide end-to-end confidentiality and/or integrity protection between two 5G networks.

Following the 3GPP 5G security specifications TS 33.501 and TS 29.573, the SEPP provides:

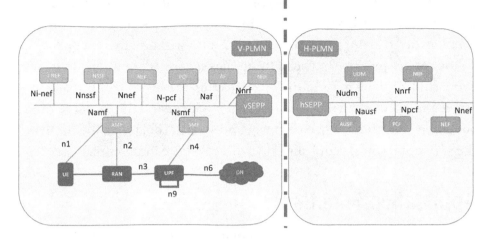

Figure 1-31. *Roaming with SEPP*

- A separate security negotiation interface (N32-c) and an end-to-end encrypted application interface (N32-f) between the two SEPPs

- Encapsulation of HTTP/2 core signaling messages using JOSE protection for N32-f transmission

- Operator control of security per roaming partner (via a key library)

- Trusted intermediary IPX nodes to read and possibly modify specific IEs in the HTTP message, while completely protecting all sensitive information end to end. Internetwork packet exchange (IPX) is a network layer protocol and provides connectionless datagram services for ethernet, token ring, and other common datalink layer protocols.

- Topology hiding is another important aspect of SEPP. The network topology, IP addressing scheme, and so forth, of the two networks are completely abstracted from each other.

Hence the SEPP protects the connection that lies between service consumers and service producers from a security aspect. Also the SEPP is not involved in duplication, the service authorization that is applied by the service producers. The SEPP applies security communication to every control plane message involved in inter-PLMN signaling; it acts as a service-relay between the actual service producer and the actual service consumer. For both service producer and service consumer, the result of the service relaying is equivalent to a direct service interaction.

Application Function

The application function is nothing but the application accessing the services of the 5G network. For example, IMS is an application function that provides the services to consumers of the 5GC to make voice/video calls. Hence AF has the following functions:

- application function's influence on traffic routing into the 5GS

- accesses the NEF

- interacts with the PCF for policy control

- IMS interactions with 5GC

Based on service provider solution, the application function is considered to be trusted by the operator and can be allowed to interact directly with applicable network functions.

Application functions not allowed by the service provider to directly access the network functions would use the external exposure framework via the **NEF** to interact with relevant network functions.

REST and HTTP2 Methods

To be able to understand the messaging between various 5GC NFs, it is important to understand the concepts of REST and the various HTTP2 methods. Unlike 4G, most of control plane signaling in 5GC is via HTTP2. The legacy protocols like GTPv2 and diameter are no longer carried forward in 5GC. All control plane communications are via RESTful APIs using HTTPv2 methods.

What is REST?

REST is popularly defined as:

> *"REST, or Representational State Transfer, is an architectural style for providing standards between computer systems on the web, making it easier for systems to communicate with each other. REST-compliant systems, often called RESTful systems, are characterized by how they are stateless and separate the concerns of client and server."*
>
> - Roy Fielding in 2000

Figure 1-32 highlights some of the REST principles.

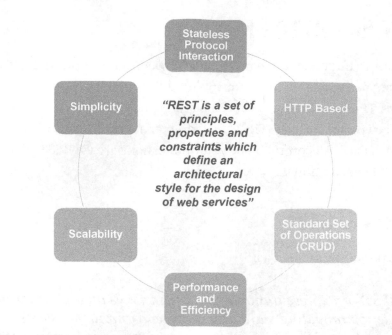

Figure 1-32. *REST guidelines*

As shown in Figure 1-32, REST is a set of principles that is constructed around being able to be stateless, to be HTTP-based, and to have a standard Create, Read, Update and Delete (CRUD) operation. To be able to have web-scale performance and efficiency, to be scalable, and to be generally simple, readable, and intuitive and client-server model based.

Let us go over some principles of REST.

Client-Server

Figure 1-33, illustrates a client server implementation in which a 5G NF (which is the client) is requesting the service from the server to be able to correlate to the aforementioned concepts of SBA. RESTful APIs are the means by which the SBA is implemented. This is where the two converge. As shown in Figure 1-33, in the 3GPP 5GC, the client is the consumer and the server is the producer of a particular service.

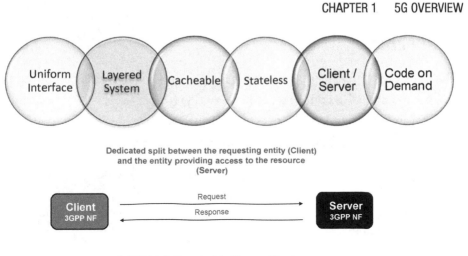

Figure 1-33. *Client server — REST*

Stateless

The next guiding principle of REST is that the server does not retain any information sent in the request and is therefore stateless.

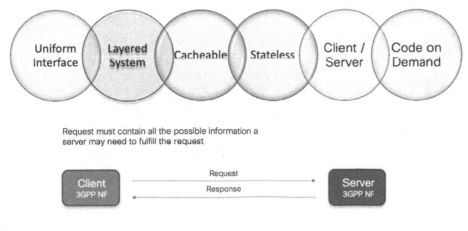

Figure 1-34. *Stateless — REST*

Cacheable

This guiding principle outlines the fact that the service consumer should be able to cache the contents of the response from the server for use later. This improves the efficiency of the application.

Figure 1-35 highlights the cacheable principle of REST.

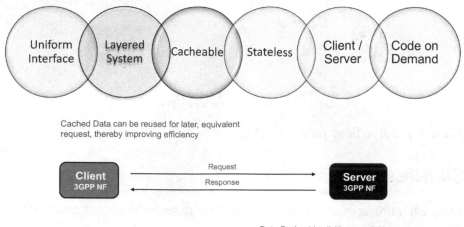

Figure 1-35. *Cacheable — REST*

Layered System

With this principle the client is totally abstracted from what is beyond the contacted server. As an example, to provide the service to the client the server may, in turn, need to contact other servers, but this is completely hidden from the consumer/client. This makes the architecture simple.

As an example, for user subscription data retrieval, the SMF will contact the UDM, which in turn may contact the UDR, but this is completely abstracted from SMF.

Figure 1-36 highlights the layered system feature of REST.

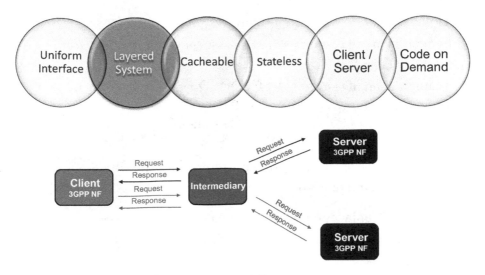

Figure 1-36. *Layered System — REST*

Uniform Interface

Uniform Interface REST principles are:

- Identification of resources: resources (documents, files, images) associated with a network service are uniquely addressed

- Manipulation of resources based on representation: resources can be updated by a client through a standard set of operations (HTTP Methods) – for example, CRUD

- Self-descriptive messages: messages must contain all the relevant information required by a server to fulfill the request

- Hypermedia as the engine of application state (HATEOAS): allows the client to learn, by means of hyperlinks within a response, which further action can be taken against the resource

Uniform interface is a closely followed guideline in 5GC implementation. All resources that are associated with a service are uniquely identified.

Manipulation of resources by HTTP2 are via a standard set of operations as follows:

> POST: requests the server to create a new resource

> GET: retrieves the resource addressed by the URI within the request

> PUT: replaces (completely) the resource addressed by the URI with the payload (JSON format) of the request

> PATCH: updates a resource (partially)

> DELETE: deletes the resource addressed by the URI in the request

The final REST principle is code on demand, in which the response from the server contains an executable code. This is not relevant in 5GC implementation and thus is omitted here.

Service-Based Interface in 5GC

Service-based interfaces are based on SBA.

Figure 1-37 shows the various SBI interfaces in 5G, and the table denotes the various NFs hosting them.

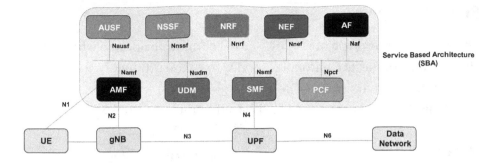

A Network Function can offer its NF services to other Network
Functions via an Open API (Application Programming Interface)

Figure 1-37. *SBI and REST in 5GC*

Figure 1-38 highlights some of the SBI APIs in 5G core network.

Specification	SBI API	Description
29.502	Nsmf	Session Management Services
29.503	Nudm	Unified Data Management Services
29.504	Nudr	Unified Data Repository Services
29.507	Npcf	Access and Mobility Policy Control Service
29.509	Nausf	Authentication Server Services
29.510	Nnrf	Network Function Repository Services
29.518	Namf	Access and Mobility Management Services
29.520	Nnwdaf	Network Data Analytics Services
29.522	Nnssf	Network Slice Selection Services
29.531	Nnef	Network Exposure Function Northbound APIs
29.572	Nlmf	Location Management Services
32.290	Nchf	Charging using Service Based Interface (SBI)

Figure 1-38. *SBI APIs in 5G*

Types of 3GPP API-Based Communication

There are typically the following types of HTTPv2-based communications:

Request/Response

This is the simplest type of HTTPv2-based communication in which the client simply requests a particular service from the producer—for example, a subscriber fetch from the UDM.

Figure 1-39 shows the 3GPP API-based request/response procedure.

Request / Response

A service Consumer (Client) can request a specific NF service from a service Producer (Server) (AMF requests subscriber information from UDM)

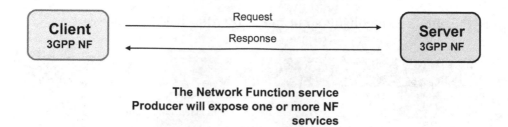

The Network Function service Producer will expose one or more NF services

Figure 1-39. *3GPP API-based request/response*

Request/Response with Notification

In this type of communication, the consumer additionally sends a callback URI to the producer, which is used by the producer to notify the consumer when certain triggers are met. In this example the SMF requests policy information from the PCF. It also includes the "notification URL" of the consumer endpoint so when certain trigger conditions are met, like revalidation time-out, the PCF can notify the SMF.

Figure 1-40 shows the request/response with notification procedures.

Request / Response with Notification

A service Consumer (Client) can request a specific
NF service from a service Producer (Server)
(eg. SMF requests policy information from PCF)
It also includes the "notification URL" of the
Consumer endpoint

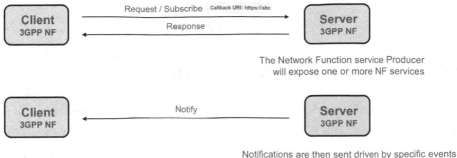

The Network Function service Producer
will expose one or more NF services

Notifications are then sent driven by specific events

Figure 1-40. *Request/Response with notification*

Subscribe/Notify

In this type of communication, the consumer can subscribe to
notifications from the producer via a callback URI. Hence when certain
events are triggered, the producer notifies the consumer. For example,
SMF can subscribe to NRF for notifications when other NFs go down.

Figure 1-41 shows the procedure for subscribe/notify.

Subscribe / Notify

A Consumer subscribes to a specific NF service
offered by the Producer. It includes the "notification
URL" of the Consumer endpoint

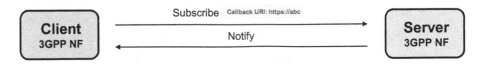

Producer notifies Consumer of the result of the subscription
Notifications are then sent periodically or driven by specific events

Figure 1-41. *Subscribe/Notify*

In the sections above we have touched upon the basic tenets of 5GC, how 4G evolved into 5G, the various use-cases in 5G, the various NFs, SBA- and API-based communication, and the various network identities.

In the upcoming chapters we will delve into further details of 5GC and its related concepts.

PDU Session Establishment

In this section we sum up the literature shared to this point and see how and what it takes for a PDU session to be established on a 5G device in NR conditions. We will do a step-by-step walk-through for a basic call set up.

1. After the UE is powered on and it completes its cell selection, UL and DL synchronize, and it receives the network settings via MIBs, it becomes ready to initiate a PDU session.

2. The UE sends a PDU session establishment request message, which is carried over the uplink NAS transport message.

3. The PDU session establishment request message contains the serving NSSA; this is the UE preferred network slice, or the network slice where the UE had been registered before. The DNN or the data network name (same as APN in 4G) is contained in this request. This gives information about the data service network that the UE wants access to. The UE also includes a PDU session ID, which, as discussed in earlier sections, is unique per PDU session and is generated by the UE.

Figure 1-42, Figure 1-43, and Figure 1-44 showcase the call flow for PDU establishment procedure in 5G.

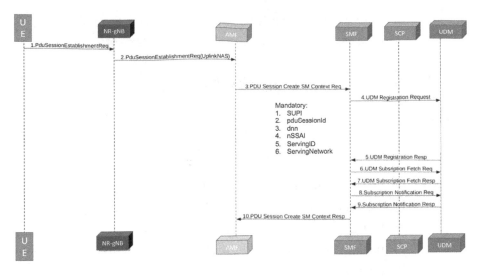

Figure 1-42. *Call flow for PDU establishment-1*

- The PDU session establishment request will
  have a request type, which can be one of "Initial
  Request" "PDU session handover" or "existing
  session" based on the situation of the UE. It also
  contains information on 5G session management
  capabilities, protocol configuration options (PCO),
  which defines various network parameters for
  the UE. The SM PDU DN requests a container to
  include authorization information to access data
  network. Based on the PDU establishment request
  type, the AMF will determine if it is a new PDU
  session or associated with any existing PDU session.

- If the NAS message does not have S-NSSAI
  information, then AMF selects the slice based on
  default configuration.

- If the NAS message doesn't contain DNN, then the default DNN as configured locally on the AMF is also selected.

- Now if the PDU request type is initial and the AMF does not have an association with the SMF for that PDU session ID, it sends Nsmf_PDUSession_CreateSMContextRequest to the SMF.

- As shown in Figure 1-42, the mandatory information supplied by AMF to SMF includes the SUPI, the PduSessionID that's sent by UE, DNN name, nSSAI, ServingID, **and** serving network details.

- The AMF selects the SMF based on the allowed NSSAI, plmn id, and TAI of the UE registered with NRF.

- SMF then communicates with UDM for registration of the UE, and it retries its subscription information and also subscribes to any notification.

4. UDM sends a registration response to SMF.

5. SMF requests UDM for the subscription fetch.

6. UDM responds to SMF with the subscription available.

7. A subscription notification request is sent to UDM to subscribe for any changes.

8. UDM responds with a subscription response.

9. Post successful registration and retrieval of subscription data of the PDUSessionCreateSMContextRes to the AMF.

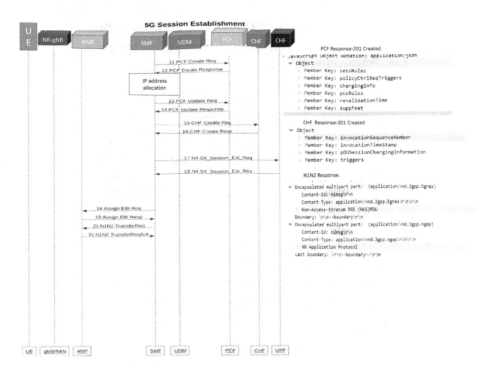

Figure 1-43. *Call flow for PDU establishment-2*

10. Next the SMF sends a "SM Policy Association create request" to the PCF.

11. The PCF responds with session rules, policyCtrlReqTriggers—which are triggers (e.g., ULI or RAT change)— charging information, PCC rules, revalidation time, and so on.

12-13. Next the SMF allocates the UE IP, then sends a policy update to PCF. It sends it the access type info of the UE, the Ipv6AddressPrefix, rattype, servingNetwork, UE TZ, and so forth.

14-15. The SMF also sends the CHF initial with invocation sequence number, timestamp, pdu session charging info, subscriber id, and so on.

16-17. Then the SMF sends the N4 session establishment to the UPF. During this process the SMF conveys the UE IP to the UPF along with all the traffic steering rules, packet detection, enforcement and reporting rules to be installed, such as PDR, QER, FAR, and URR. The UPF then notifies the SMF with UL GTP tunnel information.

18-20. After successful creation of a tunnel endpoint, the SMF sends Namf_Communication_ N1N2MessageTransfer with the tunnel endpoint information in N2 and PDU session details in the N1 container, inside an N2 message, AMF piggyback N1 PDU session establishment accept with NAS header with session parameters like QoS Rules, UE IP address, flows, SSC Mode, DNN, reflective QoS, and so on.

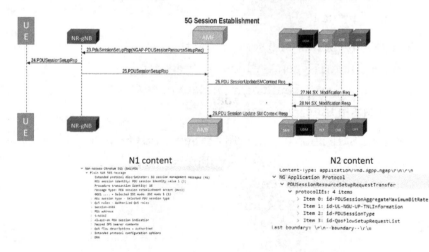

Figure 1-44. *Call flow for PDU establishment-3*

21-22. The AMF will then send a NGAP PDU session setup
request along with N2 parameter from SMF in the
aforementioned message with parameters, PDU
session ID, QFIs, QoS Profile, CN tunnel info, PDU
session type, and session AMBR. gNB will then
forward the N1 message to UE for setting of the PDU
session. After setting up the tunnel, gNB sends back
a N2 PDU session setup response to AMF.

23. AMF will then update the SMF about successful
tunnel setup by sending Nsmf_PDUSession_
UpdateSMContext_Request and receives response
from the SMF.

24-25. SMF sends an N4 modification request to the UPF to
set up user-plane resources for the downlink tunnel.
The UPF responds to the SMF with success, and the
SMF responds to AMD with PDU session update SM
context Resp.

This marks the successful setup of the PDU session.

In this chapter we have discussed an overview of 5G fundamentals,
network functions, and various 5G terminology, and we have gone through
a PDU session establishment call flow.

In the upcoming chapters we will dig deeper into the concepts of
mobile edge computing, 5G non-standalone concepts and deployment
strategies, 5G standalone concepts and deployment strategies, 5G packet
core testing strategies, automation strategies, and service provider
strategies.

CHAPTER 2

Multi-Access Edge Computing in 5G

Multi-access edge computing (MEC) is instrumental in meeting the challenging demands for 5G, especially for the 5QI needs from ultra-reliable low-latency communication (uRLLC).

The edge computing provides the possibility of hosting the application as well as the user plane for such applications that require low latency closer to the user at the edge from the traditional centralized data center.

MEC is an offering that can be leveraged not just by applications that have low latency requirements like autonomous vehicles, V2V, and V2X applications but also by applications that are regional and are restricted to a locality like stadium/sports arenas, shopping malls, and so on.

Although MEC is often regarded as a 5G-only offering, the reference architecture offered by MEC is technology-agnostic and can be leveraged by 4G network as well to host applications on the edge data centers to provide improved quality of service for applications that are delay-sensitive and region/location-specific. In such cases, the mobile network operators (MNOs) should take care to plan their network upgrade and migration of such applications from 4G to 5G.

MEC Architecture

A generic overview of an MEC architecture is as shown in Figure 2-1.

© Rajaneesh Sudhakar Shetty 2021

R. S. Shetty, *5G Mobile Core Network*, https://doi.org/10.1007/978-1-4842-6473-7_2

The MEC system architectures consist of a mobile edge host that includes mobile edge platform and virtualization infrastructure.

The mobile edge platform can provide these functionalities:

- service discovery to ensure that edge applications can identify the services that can be hosted or routed to the edge platforms;

- DNS management to help with the application discovery within the network; and

- traffic forwarding to forward the necessary data packets to the edge network.

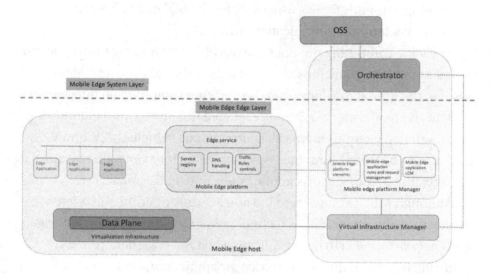

Figure 2-1. *MEC architecture*

In addition, the MEC architecture also includes modules for user portals, user applications, user application lifecycle management agents, as well as interfaces for communication between the modules.

A user application is an application run by the user terminal with capabilities to interact with the mobile edge system through the user application lifecycle management agent.

A user application lifecycle management agent allows initiation and instantiation of the terminal application request, termination of terminal application requests, and relocation or removal of user applications in the mobile edge system.

It also informs a terminal application of the state of a user application.

MEC Deployment

Figure 2-2 shows one of the deployment models where there are distributed data centers—that is, central data centers that host most of the 5G nodes, like AMF, SMF, UDM, NRF, PCF, and so on. 4G components like MME, HSS, PCRF, SAEGW-c, and so forth as well as components like IMS, DRA, and so on. In a typical deployment, the number of central data centers will be limited to approximately four to eight, depending on the geography of the coverage for the network.

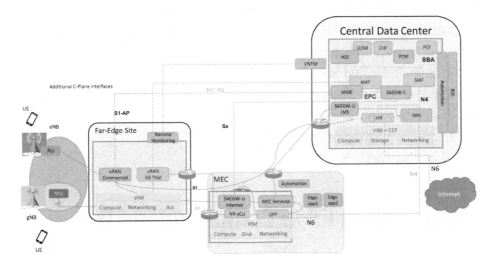

Figure 2-2. *MEC deployment with 4G and 5G nodes and distributed data centers*

Far edge computing nodes typically are very small data centers with not more than one or two computes hosted therein. Typically these data centers host only virtualized distributed unit (vDUs) that are connected to the repeater interface units (RIUs) on one end and virtualized central units (vCUs) toward the MECs.

Typically the far edge centers are 1000's in number, and multi-access edge computing nodes, sometimes referred to as regional data center (RDCs) are designed to be an aggregational level of hierarchy between the vDUs and the central data centers. MEC's / RDC's purpose is to provide first instances of MEC for 4G/5G applications that would improve the subscriber experience by providing easy, low-latency access to some services and Internet offload.

The MECs can host applications such as vCUs for both 4G and 5G radio, UPFs, SAEGW-u's, regional DNSs and edge application servers that can be cached at the edge.

In a typical deployment, the MECs can range anywhere from 100 to 400 MECs, depending upon the geography of coverage.

Traffic steering to the MEC components is a key design consideration for the operators. There are various methods to achieve this, and the SMF component in 5G and SAEGW-c component in 4G, which reside in the central data center, along with the help of the local DNS component, which resides in the MEC data center, play a vital role in traffic steering.

In addition to assigning the IP address to the UE, the SMF/SAEGW-c also provides the DNS information.

Multi-Access Edge Computing in 5G

Multi-access edge computing (MEC) compatibility toward 5G networks may involve:

- integrating the MEC data plane with the 5G system's for routing traffic to the local data network and steering to an application;

- an application function (AF) interacting with 5G control plane functions to influence traffic routing and steering, acquire 5G network capability information, and support application instance mobility; and

- the possibility of reusing the edge computing resources and managing/orchestrating applications and/or 5G network functions, while MEC still orchestrates the application services (chaining).

The user plane function (UPF) has a key role in an integrated MEC deployment in a 5G network. UPFs can be seen as a distributed and configurable data plane from the MEC system perspective. The control of that data plane—that is, the traffic rules configuration—now follows the NEF-PCF-SMF route. Consequently, in some specific deployments, the local UPF may even be part of the MEC implementation.

Figure 2-3 and Figure 2-4 shows how the MEC system is deployed in an integrated manner in a 5G network and illustrates UPF relocation as well as edge application server relocation due to UE mobility.

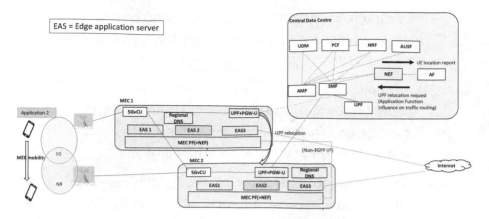

Figure 2-3. *Integrated MEC deployment in 5G network with UPF relocation*

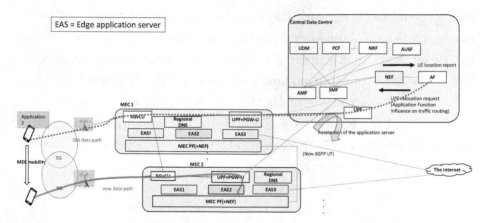

Figure 2-4. *Integrated MEC deployment in 5G network with application relocation*

Connectivity Models for Edge Computing

3GPP standards define three connectivity models to enable and realize edge computing.

Distributed Anchor Point

In this model, the PDU session anchor (PSA) realized by the means of a UPF stationed in one of the MECs is maintained common for all the user PDU traffic for a particular user. A single PSA will be maintained throughout without any breakouts. If the user equipment starts to move away from the MEC, then there is a possibility to have re-anchoring of this PSA (SSC mode 2 and SSC mode 3) to optimize the traffic routing for the UE.

Session Breakout

In this model, the PDU session has a PSA in a central site and one or more PSAs in the local site. Only one of them provides the IP anchor point. The traffic steering toward the different PSAs is performed using technologies/features such as UL classifiers and multi-homing.

During mobility of the UE, to optimize the traffic, the re-anchoring of the edge/local PSA can be performed.

Multiple PDU Sessions

In this mode, only specific PDU session/sessions are anchored by a UPF residing locally within the MEC called the PSA. For all other applications, the anchor point resides in the center. In other words, the UPF/PSA for the other PDU sessions reside in the central data center. UE route selection policy (URSP) can be used for steering the traffic to the local and central PSAs.

During mobility of the UE, to optimize the traffic, re-anchoring (SSC#2 and SSC#3) can be performed.

Figure 2-5 shows the three connectivity modes to realize the MEC.

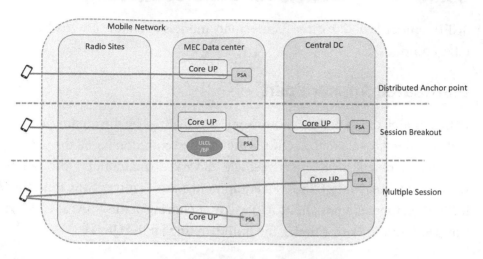

Figure 2-5. *Connectivity modes for edge computing*

Key Challenges with MEC

Selection of an Optimal Edge Application Server

In a large-scale deployment, there are typically multiple edge application servers that are similar in nature and are deployed in different RDCs.

All of these edge application servers normally have the same host name, and it is not possible for the UE/Application within the UE to be able to distinctly identify the edge application server by the host name.

Before UE/Application within the UE starts to connect to an edge application server, an UE/Application within the UE has to discover the IP address of a suitable application server (e.g., based on the location of the UE), so that the traffic can be locally routed to the optimal application server.

When a discovered application server becomes non-optimal, possibly because of UE mobility, then a new application server needs to be selected that is more optimal for the UE and will replace the old one.

To support efficient discovery of an edge application server (EAS), here are some considerations (as per TR 23.748):

- – Procedure for the UE to discover a suitable EAS based on the UE applications

- – Scenarios/conditions under which a UE needs to be aware of the EAS in the MEC and scenarios/conditions under which the UE need not be aware of the EAS in the MEC

- – Procedure for the discovery of an EAS and the information that needs to be used for the same and the information that can be obtained by such a discovery mechanism

Edge Relocation

One of the major considerations while planning and deploying MEC in 5G networks is the consideration for UE mobility and application server relocation. It is very important that the solution design ensures optimal usage of edge resources, especially if the mobility scenario is failing; if this happens, the purpose of moving the application toward the edge is defeated. 3GPP Rel-16 specifications already address some of these aspects, and the key scenarios to be further optimized/investigated are:

- • change of serving EAS without change of data network access identifier (DNAI; e.g., due to the serving EAS becoming congested or being in outage condition;this assumes an EAS IP address change);

- • change of the DNAI depending on the location of the UE to better serve the UE (this may imply an EAS IP address change, but in some cases, the old EAS may be kept as long as the UE transaction is not over); and

- potential improvements of the coordination of change of EAS and UPF (PSA) to support seamless change (e.g., preventing or reducing packet loss).

The triggers and functional entities that trigger the changes to support service continuity for the scenarios described here should be considered.

Network Information Provisioning to Local Applications with Low Latency

Examples of existing QoS information that may need to be exchanged quickly between network and application functions (e.g., edge application servers) include:

- The AF may subscribe to receive QoS congestion condition notifications.

- The AF may request 5GC to monitor QoS status (e.g., over-the-air and/or end-to-end data path) and receive QoS measurement reports.

Consecutive Traffic Steering in Different N6-LAN

One of the key challenges is to determine the procedure for steering the application traffic for processing at different locations (e.g., what traffic should be handled locally and what application needs to be steered to the central applications server).

In many cases, although there are application servers deployed on the edge, there is a need for a centralized application server for some part of its processing. For such edge computing use-cases:

- The UL traffic related to an application should be first sent to the application server residing on the MEC N6- (local application server [LAN] for local-processing and then further steered to the central application server N6-LAN based on the need.

- The DL traffic related to an application should be routed via the central application server N6-LAN and later steered to the local application server(s) in the MEC for local processing and finally provided to the UE.

Activating the Traffic Routing Toward Local Data Network per AF Request

In order to activate the traffic routing toward the local (access to) data network, the SMF should be configured with the requested DNAI. For Rel-16 ETSUN case, either SMF or I-SMF should be configured with the requested DNAI.

Study whether Rel-16 ETSUN solution is sufficient to support the aforementioned use-case and whether there is a gap.

The following 3GPP standard features support UPF chaining and control the local breakout decision flexibly to address the key issues stated earlier.

Solutions

Considering the number of key challenges stated earlier, the solution for these key challenges cannot be a single one; rather, there are multiple pieces of the solutions that need to be implemented or taken care of by the service providers to address the challenges.

Some of these key solutions are stated here.

Provisioning URSP config to the UE to Establish PDU for Edge Applications

In this solution, the URSP rules residing on the UE guides the UE to establish a PDU session before performing an application server discovery.

URSP resides on the UE statically or can be updated on the UE dynamically by PCF by means of UE policies dynamically.

The PCF receives the AF request message from the AF beforehand, and it should have the intelligence to determine the URSP rules based on the received information from, for example, the EAS IP address or FQDN and the location criteria.

During registration (initial or mobility), the UE may include the UE policy container in order to receive the URSP rules from the 5G core.

The application function can additionally subscribe for notifications from AMF for any change in the UE location (due to mobility) so that an updated URSP is sent toward the UE.

The PCF determines the URSP rules based on the policy requested by the AF. The URSP rules include parameters like DNN, S-NSSAI, and other relevant network parameters that can be used to match edge application traffic—for example, traffic from edge application clients installed on the UE to edge application servers.

The PCF can use policy clauses for the URSP rules that are specific for a particular edge DN.

Figure 2-6 explains the URSP policy configuration provisioning procedure.

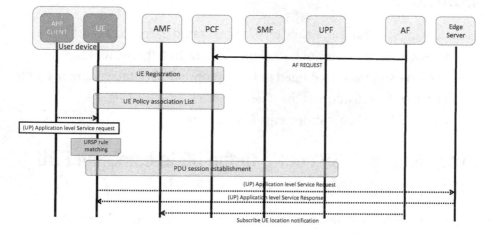

Figure 2-6. *Policy configuration provisioning procedure*

The AF logic should be enhanced to configure the edge service FQDNs on a session basis to the URSP rules or should, for example, include the FQDN or list of IP addresses of the EAS in the AF request.

Local DNS-Based Edge Server Address Discovery

As shown in Figure 2-7, for the edge server discovery during start-up, the UE initiates a PDU session establishment procedure when it detects a service requirement for an application that needs edge computing.

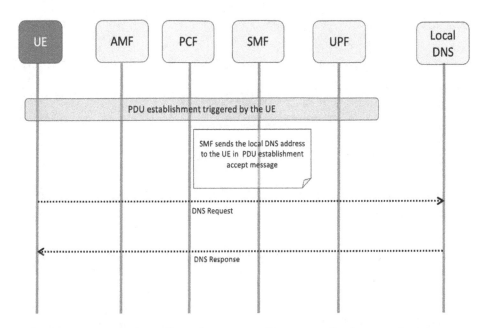

Figure 2-7. *Procedure for edge server discovery during service start-up*

In response to the PDU session request, the SMF sets up the session in the edge to enable access to the edge server. Additionally with the help of extended protocol configuration options (ePCOs) in the PDU session establishment, the accept message configures a local DNS address for the UE.

The application client within the UE triggers a DNS request to which the local DNS responds with the edge server's address. The address corresponds to the requested FQDN stored by the UE.

As shown in Figure 2-8, whenever the UE performs a service request procedure or the UE performs a handover procedure or a mobility registration, the SMF discovers the UE location by invoking Nsmf_PDUSession_UpdateSMContext with the AMF.

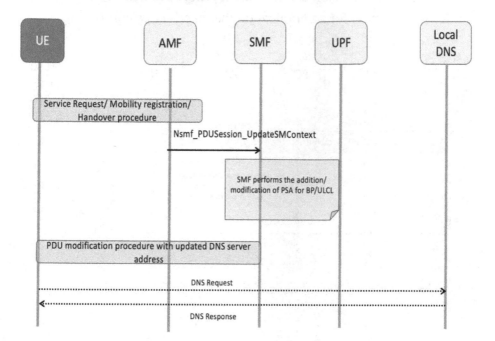

Figure 2-8. *Local DNS address provisioning procedure for ULCL or BP cases*

With this, the SMF is able to perform ULCL procedures—that is, the addition of the PSA and branching point.

Also based on the UE location, the SMF is able to determine the local DNS server address and sends it across to the UE in the ePCO via the PDU session modification command (as shown in Figure 2-8).

The UE stores/updates the DNS server address accordingly.

As shown in Figure 2-9, whenever the UE performs the service request procedure or the UE performs a handover procedure or a mobility registration, the SMF gets to know the UE location by invoking Nsmf_PDUSession_UpdateSMContext with the AMF.

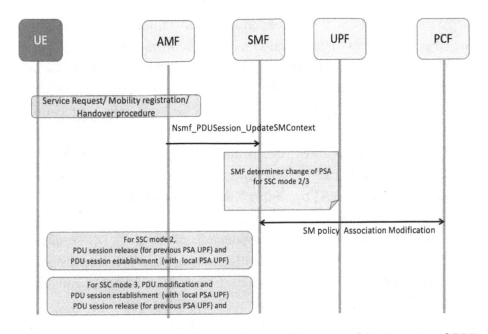

Figure 2-9. *Local DNS address provisioning procedure in case of SSC mode 2/3*

With this, the SMF can determine the change of PSA for SSC mode 2 and SSC mode 3. Additionally based on the UE location, the SMF is able to determine the local DNS server address and sends it across to the UE in the ePCO via the PDU session modification command (as shown in Figure 2-9). Additionally the SMF triggers the release of the PDU session for the old PSA UPF and the establishment with the new PSA UPF (as shown in Figure 2-9).

The UE stores/updates the DNS server address accordingly.

DNS Application Function

In this solution, the "session breakout" connectivity with the dynamic insertion of local PSA for edge computing is supported.

The DNS application function has the mapping table for the given user location and the FQDN application to a preferred PSA; it also includes the DNAI information and the corresponding subnet information for each of the N6 access points to the DN after network address translation (NAT).

During the session establishment procedure, the SMF is able to send the DNS AF address back to the UE in the ePCO field based on whether the UE sends a DNS request for the FQDN related to an edge application server.

The DNS AF also is able to determine a PSA for the UE based on its location and the application used. With the help of the PCF, the DNS AF is able to discover the PSA by adding N6 access location(s) as edns-client-subnet (ECS) option to the DNS request.

As shown in Figure 2-10, a UE application can trigger a DNS request with the application FQDN after the PDU session has been established. Since the application server is typically known by the domain name, there is a need for the translation of the domain name to IP address.

This query is sent to the DNS AF by the local DN to determine whether edge computing can be applied for the query from the UE.

The DNS AF verifies if there is an SLA for the application in place by looking for the application FQDN in the SLA-based translation table that it maintains:

    a)   If there is no match in the translation table, the DNS AF sends the DNS request to the MNO DNS, which shall resolve the FQDN.

b) If there is a match, the DNS AF retrieves the user location and with the UE Location and the FQDN, the DNS AF obtains the preferred locations for the N6 access to the DN for that application and the corresponding subnets (or full IP addresses), and one or more ECS options are added in the DNS query toward the MNO DNs as shown.

Only one ECS is selected and sent back to the UE as a response to the DNS query.

The UE is now able to send the application traffic to the indicated IP address in the DNS response message.

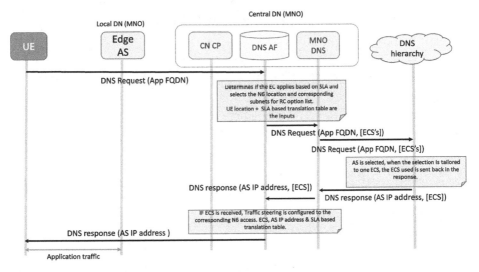

Figure 2-10. *High-level sequence diagram of EAS discovery and dynamic traffic steering in the DNS AF solution*

Discovery of Edge Application Server Based on DNS

In this solution, there are two possibilities:

1) If the DNS server is centrally deployed, it shall be responsible for all the FQDN resolution queries received by the UE. It is also required that the centrally deployed DNS server is aware of all the edge computing platforms and is able to query these edge DNS servers as needed.

2) If the DNS servers are locally deployed, then they are responsible for the FQDN queries resolution received from the UE into the IP address of an edge application server that is local to the DN.

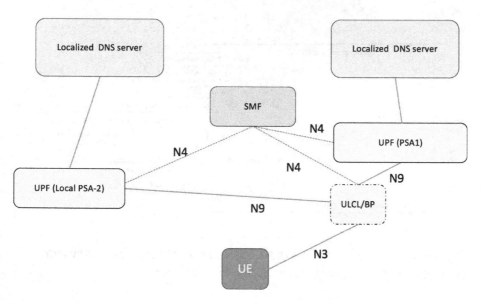

Figure 2-11. *Deployment options of DNS servers*

As shown in Figure 2-11, the solution uses the SMF as a DNS forwarder.

The SMF receives all the DNS queries from the UE and forwards the same toward the DNS server to resolve them and report back to the UE.

In the SMF, the FQDNs served by the edge application servers that correspond to each of the DNAIs can be either configured directly or sent to the SMF via AF (this is explained in the AF influence traffic routing procedure in the later sections of this chapter).

Additionally, the SMF can also have the mapping of the DNAI to the IP address for N6 as well as the address for the localized DNS server that is serving each of the DNAIs.

During the PDU session establishment procedure, SMF derives the PCC rules from the PCF.

These PCC rules can contain the FQDN served by the EAS for each of the DNAIs that is sent to the PCF via the AF.

The SMF selects a PSA (PSA1) for the PDU session and indicates PSA1 to perform DNS packet detection and forward the UE DNS query message to the SMF.

As shown in Figure 2-12, the UE initiates a DNS query toward the PSA1 UPF in the uplink and includes the FQDN of the requested application.

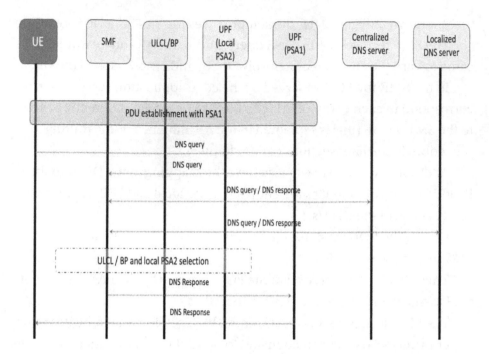

Figure 2-12. *Discovery of EAS based on DNS*

This query is forwarded by the PSA1 UPF to the SMF via the N4 interface.

The SMF is able to select the DNAI(s) that is suitable for the query based on the UE location and FQDNs served by the EASs.

The SMF can optionally decide to reroute the query to thee centralized DNS servers based on the IP address determined that is corresponding to the selected DNAI.

The query to the centralized DNS can contain the IP address and the ECS(s).

In response, the centralized DNS server provides the IP address of the EAS that should serve the FQDN (as per the ECS option and other local policies).

Based on the response received, the SMF may select ULCL/BP and a new PSA (local PSA2) for this PDU session based on the selected DNAI.

DNS response, including the IP address of the EAS, is sent back to the UE via the PSA1.

SMF Selection Based on DNAI

In this solution, the AF uses an AF influence traffic mechanism to activate the traffic routing toward the edge hosting environment.

The AF requests the information to be stored in the UDR as data set "Application Data" and data subset "AF traffic influence request information."

The UDR then notifies the PCF regarding the AF traffic influence, which the PCF sends across to the AMF.

As shown in Figure 2-13, during the PDU establishment procedure, when the UE sends the PDU establishment request message to the AMF, the AMF uses the DNAI/policy to select the SMF or the I-SMF along with the requested s-NSSAI and DNN by the UE.

The SMF then configures the I-UPF to route the DNS query message toward the edge hosting environment.

The AF traffic influence request information includes FQDN or DNS server address as traffic descriptor.

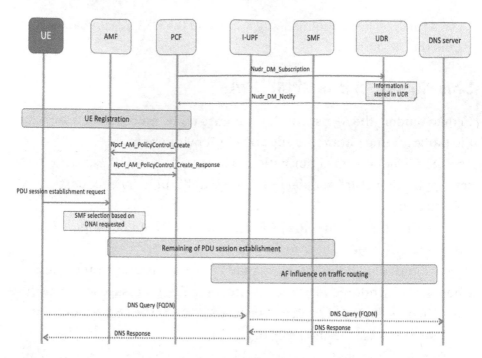

Figure 2-13. *SMF selection based on AF influence request*

MEC Toolkit for 5GC

Here are some of the features/use-cases that can leverage the MEC offerings to enable optimal usage of resources and help achieve the demanding 5QI requirements for some of the 5G applications/bearers.

1) uplink classifier branching point(ULCL/BP) usage.

2) IPv6 multi-homing

3) session and service continuity modes

4) AF influence on traffic routing

5) local LADN

Uplink Classifier Branching Point

The uplink classifier is a 5G feature/functionality that is mainly supported on the UPF.

The key target for the uplink classifier feature is to divert some of the uplink traffic received at the UPF from the UE to a local application server residing on MEC.

The traffic that can be diverted locally to the edge application server is determined by traffic filters that are provided to the UPF on the N4 interface by the SMF.

The control on when the traffic filter should be applied and removed for such traffic is completely decided by the SMF with the help of PCF and application function (AF).

After a PDU session establishment procedure is completed, the SMF can introduce an ULCL, which can be in the form of a UPF in the uplink data path of a PDU session.

There can be more than one ULCL introduced in the data path for a PDU session by the SMF, depending on the traffic filtering rules.

The UE need not be aware of the traffic diversion introduced by the SMF in the form of ULCL and is not impacted during the application/removal of the ULCL traffic rules.

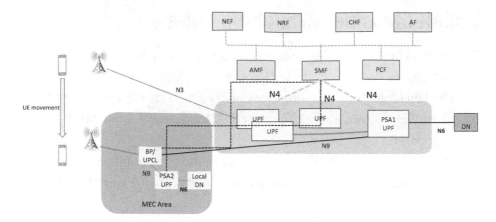

Figure 2-14. *Uplink classifier illustration*

Figure 2-14 illustrates the ULCL and how it can be used.

In Figure 2-14, the UE moves from the coverage region of one gNB to another, thereby moving closer to the MEC area shown in the figure.

The location of the UE is reported and is subscribed to by the SMF. In this case, the location reported maps to a particular DNAI, and this triggers the SMF to report the same to the AF.

Upon reception of the DNAI reported, the AF pushes rules toward PCF.

The SMF then pushes these rules to the I-UPF in the form of N4 rules.

This I-UPF now assumes the role of a BP (branching point)/ULCL and the PSA2, which provides access to the local MEC apps using NAT or secondary IP address.

The UPF supporting a ULCL can also support functionalities like traffic measurements needed for charging, traffic replication required for LI, and bit rate enforcement required to maintain the session AMBR while being controlled by the SMF.

Mobility with ULCL

As shown in Figure 2-15, the UE has an established PDU session already with a BP introduced in the MEC area 1, with some of the uplink traffic being redirected to the local DN via the PSAs UPF and the remaining traffic being terminated at the centralized DN via the remote UPF (PSA1).

When the UE moves to a region closer to MEC area 2 as shown, the location reported maps to a particular DNAI, and this triggers the SMF to report the same to the AF. This leads to pushing new PCC rules to the SMF via the PCF by the AF.

With these new rules, the SMF decides to change the ULCL/BP and the PSA2, thereby establishing the UPF and ULCL/BP.

The SMF also establishes a tunnel between the source ULCL and the target ULCL for exchange of data between the two to support session continuity during ULCL relocation. This tunnel is a temporary N9 forwarding tunnel between the source ULCL and target ULCL.

The N9 forwarding tunnel can be maintained until there is no active data being trasnferred between the source and the target ULCL for a configurable amount of time or until the AF instructs the SMF to release the old PSA.

While the N9 forwarding tunnel exists, the target ULCL UPF is configured with packet filters that enforce:

- uplink traffic from existing data sessions between UE and the application in the source local DN into the N9 forwarding tunnel toward the source ULCL

- any traffic related to the application in the target local DN is forced to go to the new local DN via the target PSA.

Finally the SMF updates the remote UPF for the downlink traffic with the target ULCL and also updates the target RAN for uplink traffic.

A new IPv6 prefix assignment is communicated toward the UE, and the SMF reconfigures the UE with the IPv6 prefix assignment for PSA1.

Once the traffic starts flowing through the new ULCL and is branched toward the PSA1 and PSA2 according to the traffic filters, the SMF releases the old ULCL UPF.

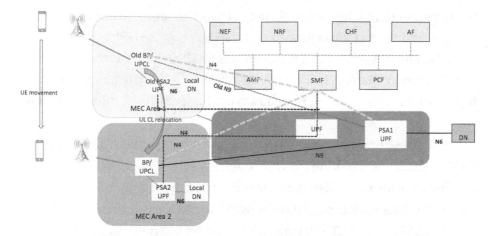

Figure 2-15. *Relocation of the ULCL due to mobility*

IPv6 Multi-Homing

There are scenarios wherein a particular PDU session is associated with multiple IPv6 prefixes; this is referred to as IPv6 multi-homing PDU session.

The characteristic of multi-homing PDU sessions is that there can be multiple PSAs through which the DN can access these PDU sesssions.

An examples of a typical IPv6 multi-homing session is shown in Figures 2-16 and 2-17.

Figure 2-16 illustrates a session continuity scenario where the N9 interface/BP is set up with a new anchor UPF (PSA2) before releasing the N9 interface with the old anchor UPF (PSA1)—in other words, make before break PSA relocation wherein the two PSAs are connected to the same DN.

Figure 2-17 illustrates the scenario where there are two different anchoring UPFs (PSA1 and PSA2) wherein PSA1 is connected to the centralized DN and PSA2 is connected to the local instance of the DN (within an MEC).

The different user plane paths leading to the different PSAs branch out at a "common" UPF, referred to as a UPF supporting BP functionality.

The BP is responsible for splitting the uplink traffic and forwarding it to different PSAs; in the downlink the BP is responsible for merging the traffic received from the two PSAs and sending them in one common stream toward the UE.

Some key notes on IPv6 multi-homing are:

- Multi-homing functionality is applicable only for IPv6 PDU sessions of IPv6 and is not applicable for IPv4 PDUs. The UE provides the indication on its support for multi-homing.

- The branching UPF can be controlled by the same or a different SMF, and it should be able to support charging, bit rate enforcement (maintaining the session AMBR) as well as LI functionalities—that is, it should be able to perform traffic measurement as well as traffic replication to support measurement and LI, respectively.

- The UPF insertion as a branching element can be performed during or post PDU establishment procedure orchestrated by the SMF. Similarly, the removal of the BP is decided by the SMF.

- N4 rules are passed on to the UPF acting as a branching point by the SMF to apply traffic filtering rules.

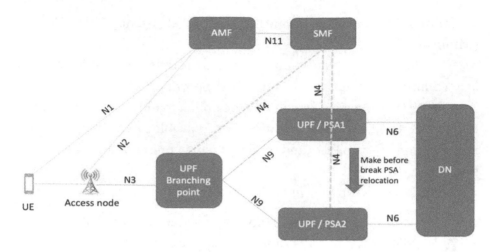

Figure 2-16. *Multi-homing PDU session ➤ service continuity case*

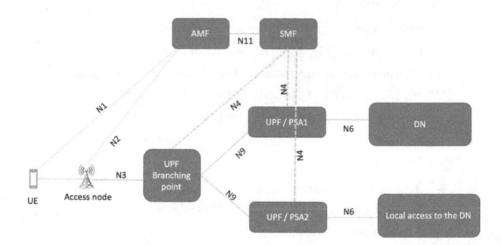

Figure 2-17. *Multi-homing PDU session ➤ local access to same DN*

Session and Service Continuity

Session and service continuity (SSC) support is introduced in the 5G system architecture to enable and support different levels of continuity requirements for the various 5G applications and the supported services from the UE.

With 5G, there is an introduction of three different SSC modes that can be associated with a PDU session.

SSC Mode 1

In SSC mode 1, the connectivity service provided to the UE in the form of an IP address is preserved even when the UE moves from one service area to the other.

SSC Mode 2

In SSC mode 2, the IP address as well as the PSA point that is associated with the UE can be released by the network because of mobility and other triggers before the addition of a new PSA point for the UE followed by allocation of a new IP address.

SSC Mode 3

In SSC mode 3, a new PSA point is established before removing the old session anchor point, thereby ensuring a better service continuity (in comparision to SSC mode 2). Similarly to SSC mode 2, the IP address in this mode is not preserved.

The SSC modes are explained with examples and details in the UPF selection criteria section of Chapter 4.

Selection of Session and Service Continuity Mode

The SSC mode selection policy is referred to within the SMF for applying a particular SSC mode for an application/group of applications that is being accessed for a UE.

During the PDU establishment procedure, the SMF queries the UDM for the user subscription information and, in response, receives a list of SSC modes that is supported by the UE. Apart from this, the SMF can also be configured with a default SSC mode that it can apply to any user tagged to a particular DNN for UEs trying to be associated with a particular s-NSSAI.

Based on the selection policy, in response to the PDU establishment request from the UE, the SMF sends across the list of allowed SSC modes toward the UE.

While choosing the appropriate SSC mode that should be configured for the UE, the data received from the UDM should have the highest preference and the locally configured values within SMF should be used only as fallback/backup.

The SMF also verifies whether the UE sent the SSC mode as part of either default SSC mode or allowed SSC mode in order of priority sent to the UE previously. A PDU session establishment reject is sent back to the UE with allowed SSC modes in the reject message. If the UE has not sent across the appropriate SSC mode in its request. If the SMF does not receive the SSC mode from the UE, then the default SSC mode in the order of above priority is chosen and used to establish a PDU session.

For the earlier deployment cycles for 5G, the UEs only support SSC mode 1; therefore, the usage and verification of SSC modes 2 and 3 are not considered.

However, with complex deployment where multiple application servers are residing locally on the MECs, it becomes very inefficient and impractical to have only SSC mode 1 support for all types of applications.

Figure 2-18 shows a use-case wherein the UE is moving across the regions that are served by different MECs.

During the PDU establishment procedure, as shown in Figure 2-18, the UE was served by the UPF as well as the application server that was residing on MEC1.

As the UE moves away from MEC1 and toward MEC2 and so on, since SSC mode 1 is the only mode supported by the UE, the anchor UPF for this UE still resides on MEC1, and the application server also resides on MEC1. However, as shown, the traffic path becomes complex, as there would be I-UPF residing on a different MEC transferring the uplink and the downlink data for the UE via the N9 interface all the way to the UPF on MEC1 and terminating on the application server.

This issue of suboptimal data steering can be avoided by use of SSC mode 2 or SSC mode 3 wherein the PSA for the UPF will be changed and hosted on the MEC that is closest to the UE, thereby providing the true benefits of MEC to the end-user.

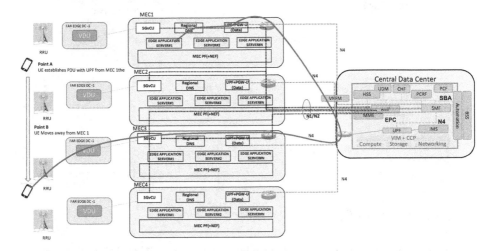

Figure 2-18. *Inefficient routing due to SSC mode 1 usage*

Figure 2-19 shows the call flow procedure for the SSC mode 2.

As shown, the UE is involved in UL/DL data transfer with UPF1 that is controlled by SMF1.

The SMF detects that the UE has moved into a location that is out of the coverage area for the UPF1. In this case, SMF1 and the UE session also should be transferred to another UPF that can serve better.

The SMF initiates a PDU session release toward the UE to re-establish PDU to the same DN.

Upon this, the UE performs a PDU establishment procedure wherein the SMF2 selects UPF2 as the anchor UPF for this session.

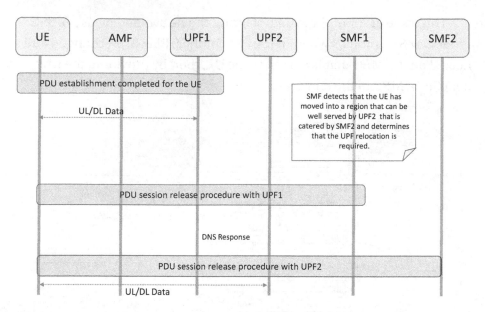

Figure 2-19. *Call flow for SSC mode 2*

Application Function Influence on Traffic Routing

An AF can influence the traffic routing in the 5G system by sending PCC rules to the SMF (via PCF) that helps the SMF decide on the local DNS servers where the applications should be steered. The AF requests also influence the UPF (re)selection and allow routing user traffic to a local access to a data network (identified by a DNAI).

In operator networks where the AF is not allowed to directly communicate with the SMF/PCF, NEF can be used to bridge this communication between the 5G nodes and the AF.

Figure 2-20 is an example of how an application function is instrumental in steering the user traffic toward different data centers based on their movement and how dynamically the uplink/downlink traffic can be controlled indirectly by the AF via the SMF.

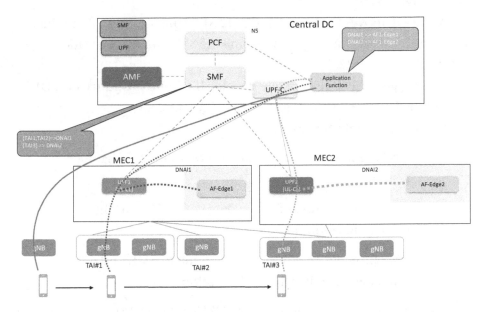

Figure 2-20. *AF influence on traffic routing with ULCL example case*

As shown in Figure 2-20, while in the region for gNB, the UE (which is not a part of any DNAI) establishes the PDU session.

During the session establishment, the AF sends across the traffic steering rules to the SMF with the DNAI list— in this case, DNAI1 and DNAI2.

The SMF subscribes to the location notification from the AMF for TAI or cell that maps to the DNAIs listed in the traffic steering rules.

As the UE moves out of the registered area into the region that is under TAI#1, there is a location notification that is triggered toward the SMF (due to its subscription).

With the location notification, the SMF is able to map the location to a particular DNAI—in this case, DNAI1.

The SMF initiates UPF ULCL with an appropriate UL offload filter and is sent across to the UPF1.

As the UE moves further toward the TAI#3, the SMF is again notified about the location change, and this time the SMF maps the location notification to DNAI2.

This triggers the SMF to delete the old ULCL and introduce new ULCL rules to the UPF2, which acts as the new ULCL node.

In the aforementioned example:

- DNAI represents the identity of a data center/edge center.

- AFs are only aware of which data center (DNAI) the local application servers are located.

- AMF provides the UE current TAI info to SMF, and AMF is not aware of the DNAI information.

- The SMF has a mapping from TAI/eNB to DNAI.

- AF provides SMF the rules as to which DNAIs, when reported, should result in local traffic breakout.

- AF also registers to be notified when UE enters or leaves specific DNAIs.

- The event notification of UE moving in and out of DNAI may be provided directly by the SMF to the AF or the SMF can communicate the same to the AF via the PCF.

CHAPTER 3

5G NSA Design and Deployment Strategy

The 5G core network framework is designed to make full use of the enhanced throughput and reduced latency that the new radio promises to provide.

3GPP provides two key solutions to realize the 5G networks:

1. **5G Non-Standalone (NSA):**
   In the 5G non-standalone solution, the service provider can leverage the LTE infrastructure (i.e., radio access as well as the core network, the evolved packet core [EPC]) to anchor for all mobility management and control plane-related aspects for a session and integrate the same with new radio (5G NR) to provide better coverage and enhance the throughputs for the exisiting users, thereby enabling the operators to provide 5G services to the end user within a short time and at a significantly lower cost.

© Rajaneesh Sudhakar Shetty 2021
R. S. Shetty, *5G Mobile Core Network*, https://doi.org/10.1007/978-1-4842-6473-7_3

2. **5G Standalone (SA):**

    In the 5G standalone solution, an all new 5G packet core needs to be introduced with many new network functions and newer capabilities within those functions inherently built within it.

    As the name suggests, the SA architecture is comprised of a new radio (5G NR) connected to a 5G core network and working as a standalone entity together without the need to leverage the 4G network elements for and functional support to the end-users.

The 3rd Generation Partnership Project (3GPP), which is the global telecommunications standards organization, released its initial delivery of NSA NR new radio specifications for 5G in late 2017. Efforts were carried on throughout 2018 to complete documenting the entire set of 5G standards.

This set of initial standards was highly focused around enabling various mobile operations to take an early leap into the 5G world.

These standards enabled use of 5G NR with the existing LTE-SAE core infrastructure (NSA), which is used to bridge the transition from the traditional 4G network into a 5G network.

The 5G NSA is popularly embraced by various telecom service providers to support the enhanced broadband use-case. This would enable the operators to leverage the benefits of the 5G NR with their existing 4G core. It is often used as the architecture for initial deployments of 5G using the existing 4G networks.

NSA, also called an EN-DC, was standardized in the 3GPP Release 15 in December 2017. This also enforces the fact that an LTE anchor is necessary for control plane operation like session admission, authentication, mobility management, and so on.

Use of 5G NSA is beneficial to the operators in accelerating their transition toward 5G, as it allows the reuse of their existing LTE network elements with a few changes to accommodate the 5G use-cases.

The call flows for 5G NSA are very similar to 4G, with some NSA-specific IEs added.

Out of the use-cases for 5G, eMBB is the use-case that is prioritized and often catered to with the use of NSA. uRLLC is the second-most commonly catered-to use-case by 5G NSA.

Therefore, the mobile operators would be able to get a chance to be the fastest to rollout 5G and get a much-needed technology and market advantage. This would also help operators to leverage 5G spectrums to enhance capacity in their networks while leveraging the use of their current 4G core infrastructure.

Many mobile operators have already rolled out NSA in their networks as of April 2020. This would give them an opportunity to be an early adapter to 5G devices.

There are many deployment options of NSA that have been identified, out of which the most commonly and widely used is Option3/3x for the initial migration path. We will discuss these options in the chapter under the upcoming sections.

Evolution of the Network from 4G to 5G Non-Standalone

Figure 3-1 shows a standard 5G NSA control and user plane separation (CUPS)-based deployment, wherein a 5G-capable user's equipment is connected to the 4G EPC network via the 5G NR for the data path and the 4g eNB for the signaling path.

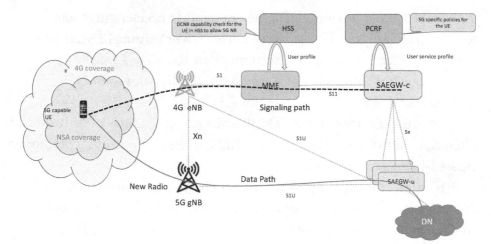

Figure 3-1. *5G NSA (CUPS-based) network topology*

An important part/concept in the aforementioned topology is **CUPS,** which entails the separation user plane (data path) from the user plane (control path). We will deliver further details of this concept in the upcoming sections. However, for an initial understanding, we can take an example of a gateway node like **serving gateway** (SGW) or **packet data network gateway** (PGW) in the 4G world. These nodes traditionally process both control and user plane data; however, in the world of CUPS, the control and user plane have been separated into two different nodes **functionally split with** an interface between them called **"Sx" interface**.

The 5G NSA architecture, which is also known as EN-DC architecture, leverages a feature called **dual connectivity** to achieve higher throughputs. This is made possible by using the 5G NR for packet data network (PDN) connection—that is, for user plane data transfer to and from the Internet while continuing to use the legacy 4G network for signaling and controling the PDN connection.

We will discuss CUPS and the various feature changes required in NSA, including the dual connectivity feature, in detail in the coming sections of this chapter.

Dual Connectivity

Dual connectivity (DC) is used when a device is served radio resources by two different network access points, such as an eNB and gNB. In addition, each network access point involved in DC for a device may assume different roles. This feature is an important step, as it enables one of the early 5G options.

Figure 3-2, represents a high-level architecture for dual connectivity.

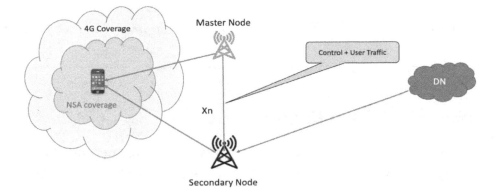

Figure 3-2. *Dual connectivity*

There are different flavors of DC, as shown in Table 3-1.

The main differentiating factors for each of these dual connectivity modes are:

- – the master node

- – the secondary node

- – the core network to which these nodes are connected

Table 3-1. *Dual Connectivity Options*

Name	Abbr.	Master	Secondary	Core
New Radio Dual Connectivity	NR-DC	gNB	gNB	5GC
E-UTRA – NR Dual Connectivity	EN-DC	eNB	en-gNB	EPC
NG-RAN – E-UTRA-NR Dual Connectivity	NGEN-DC	ng-eNB	gNB	5GC
NR – E-UTRA Dual Connectivity	NE-DC	gNB	ng-eNB	5GC

New Radio Dual Connectivity

This is when there is a DC between two gNBs and the core network that these gNBs are connected to is the 5G Core, hence called NR-DC. NR-DC is deployed typically when the secondary gNB is a small cell. This essentially implies that the UE will have the option of connecting with two gNBs.

Multiple Radio Access Technology Dual Connectivity

Table 3-1 identifies the various DC options.

When the service provider adopts LTE as a potential option for DC along with 5G, a number of different connectivity options exist between the device and the core network, which is known as multi-radio access technology–dual connectivity (MR-DC). Some of the options are listed as here.

1. **E-UTRA–NR Dual Connectivity**

   E-UTRA–NR dual connectivity (EN-DC), in which
   the device connects to a master eNB (MeNB) and
   a secondary gNB (SgNB). With this configuration,
   the master node will be connected to the EPC, with
   SgNB connecting to the MeNB via the X2 interface.

2. **NG-RAN–E-UTRA-NR Dual Connectivity**

   With this option, the next generation eNB (ng-eNB)
   is used as the master RAN node within a NG-RAN–
   E-UTRA-NR dual connectivity (NGEN-DC) scenario.
   In this example, the ng-eNB connects to the 5G
   Core, with a gNB acting as the secondary node.
   Connectivity between the master ng-eNB (Mng-
   eNB) and the SgNB is based on the Xn interface.

3. **NR–E-UTRA Dual Connectivity**

   Similar in concept to NGEN-DC, Figure 3-3 outlines
   the architecture for NR-E-UTRA dual connectivity
   (NE-DC). With this approach, a gNB serves as the
   master RAN node, connecting to the 5G core. The
   secondary RAN node is an ng-eNB, which connects
   to the MgNB via the Xn interface.

Architecture

Early adoptions of 5G technology will predominantly be based on NSA,
whereby the EN-DC model of DC is used. The EN-DC architecture is
outlined Figure 3-3, which shows the eNB acting as a master node and the
en-gNB acting as the secondary node.

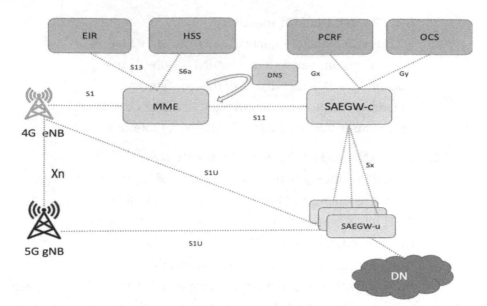

Figure 3-3. *NSA architecture*

Migration Options

In the earlier part of this chapter we discussed that the NSA 5G network solution is an intermediate solution/phase leveraged by many service providers on their network migration journey from 4G to 5G SA network solution.

The deployment transition from 4G to 5G SA will need to pass through different phases of migration, and these phases/migration paths will vary from one service provider to another. For some service providers, the radio network upgrade from eNB to gNB NR is planned earlier than the core network upgrade from EPS to 5G core, and in some other operators, the 5G core network upgrade is planned before the radio upgrade from eNB to gNB NR.

Figure 3-4 shows some of the different options of deployment and also highlights some of the popular migration paths for transitioning from a 4G network to a 5G network.

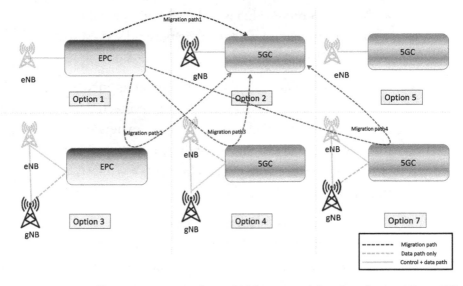

Figure 3-4. *Different migration paths for transitioning from 4G to 5G*

As shown in Figure 3-4:

- Option 1 is a standard LTE deployment option where the eNB is connected to the EPC and the calls are served by eNB for both the data and control planes.

- Option 2 is an SA 5G deployment where the NR (gNB) is connected to the 5G core and provides both data and control plane connections to the UE.

- Option 5 has the 4G eNB connected to the 5G core.

- Option 3 has multiple flavors (i.e., option3, option3a, and option3x), which are discussed in the next section. In this option, there are both 4G radio (i.e., eNB) and 5G radio (i.e., gNB) connected to the 4G core network (i.e., EPC) with an Xn interface between the two to exchange signaling as well as data between themselves. Another key aspect to option 3 is that the eNB acts as the master node—that is, the eNB maintains the signaling connection with the core network (S1-MME) for the UE in this option.

- Option 4 is similar to option 3, with the difference being that the two radios (gNB and eNB) are connected to the 5G core network instead of the 4G core network. Also the gNB acts as a master node and maintans the signaling interface with the core network for the UEs that are connected.

- Option 7 again has different flavors to it (i.e., option7, option7a, and option7x), and as shown in Figure 3-4, it is very similar to option 4, with the difference that the eNB acts as the master node for this option, maintaining the signaling connection for the UEs with the core network.

Some of the popular examples for migration paths seen across service providers are:

4G (Option1)_ ➤ 5G NSA (Option3x) ➤ 5G SA(Option2)
4G (Option1) ➤ 5G NSA (Option 7x) ➤ 5G SA (Option2)
4G (Option1) ➤ 5GNSA (Option4) ➤ 5G SA (Option2)

Option 3/3a/3x

As discussed in the earlier sections, there are three variants to option 3: option 3, option 3a, and option 3x.

Due to the fact that the eNB is the master node, it supports S1-MME connectivity to the EPC. However, in the case of option 3a and option 3x, both the eNB and the gNB could support user plane connectivity via S1-U. For control between the master and secondary nodes, the Xn reference point is utilized. Finally, to support split bearers and also data forwarding, the Xn-U reference point could be used between the MeNB and en-gNB.

Figure 3-5 outlines the user plane bearer core network connectivity options for when EN-DC is in operation. It is possible for the secondary en-gNB to have its own user plane connection to the core network as well (e.g., IMS bearer) or for the data bearer when the UE is not in the 5G NSA coverage region. Figure 3-5 also includes the RAN bearer splitting options.

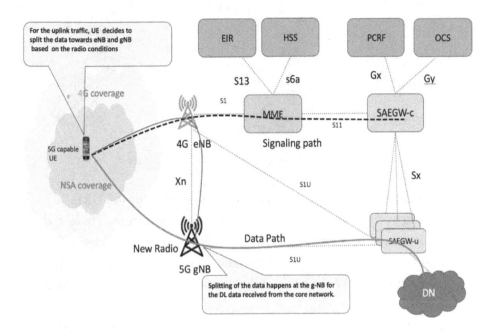

Figure 3-5. *User plane connectivity via S1-U for M-eNB as well as S-gNB*

Option 3a

With respect to the RAN "options" that were initially proposed for 5G, options 3a and 3x are alternative configurations to the original option 3 (whereby the RAN is configured for EN-DC operation). The difference is essentially the user plane connectivity; with option 3a, the RAN is configured for EN-DC with support for secondary cell group bearers.

Figure 3-6 illustrates option 3a.

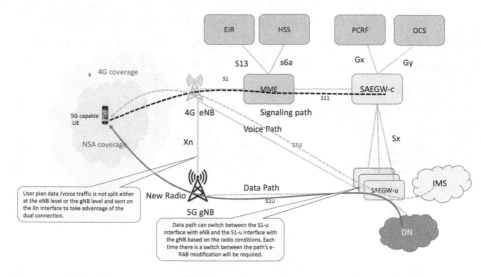

Figure 3-6. *Illustration of option 3a*

As shown in Figure 3-6, the signaling connection for the UE is maintained by the eNB with the 4G core network. When the UE is in the 4G coverage region, the data path for the UE is maintained with the 4G network—that is, the active S1-u interface for the data transfer for this case is between the SAEGW-u and the 4G eNB for all downlink as well as uplink data.

When the UE moves toward the 5G NSA coverage region, the eNB detects that the UE is capable of receiving and sending data via the NR (gNB), and an e-RAB modification procedure is triggered to remove the data path between SAEGW-u and eNB and add a new S1-u data path between the gNB and the SAEGW-u as shown.

There is a possiblity that the UE is served by two separate PDU connections at the same time (one via the eNB for IMS and another via the gNB for data, as shown).

Another important aspect of option 3a is that though there is an Xn interface between the eNB and the gNB, it is leveraged only for exchanging signaling procedures between the two entities, and in this option the data will not be split by either the gNB or the eNB and sent on the Xn interface.

Option 3a is not as popular as option 3x for these reasons:

- For the initial phase of deployment, during mobility, there can be many handovers for the UE between the 4G and 5G NSA coverage regions; this will mean that the UE will need to switch its data path from eNB to gNB and vice versa that many times, leading to inefficiency.

- Option 3a does not allow the possibility to load-share between the gNB and eNB by splitting the data and sending it across the Xn interface.

Option 3x

Option 3x is very similar to option 3a with the enhancement that the Xn interface can be used not only for signaling exchange but also to split the data and send from the gNB to the eNB to leverage the DC advantage of the UE capability.

With option 3x, the RAN is configured for EN-DC with support for secondary cell group split bearers.

Figure 3-7 illustrates the deployment of option 3x.

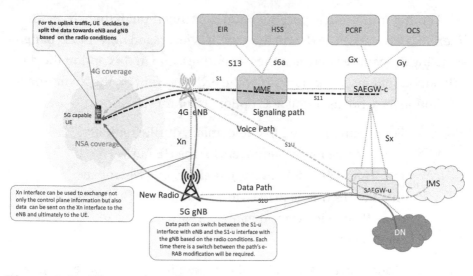

Figure 3-7. *Illustration of option 3x*

As shown in Figure 3-7, the eNB acts as a master node in option 3x, and the gNB, acting as a secondary node, has only the S1-u connection with the 4G core.

When the UE moves toward the 5G NSA coverage region, the eNB detects that the UE is capable of receiving and sending data via the NR (gNB), and an e-RAB modification procedure is triggered to remove the data path between SAEGW-u and eNB and add a new S1-u data path between the gNB and the SAEGW-u.

Unlike option 3a, in option 3x, the Xn interface between the eNB and the gNB can be leveraged to exchange both the signaling messages as well as data between the two nodes.

The gNB in option 3x can split the data and send one stream of data directly to the UE on the 5G air interface and send another stream of data to the UE via the Xn interface, which can be sent to the UE via the 4G air interface by the eNB, thereby leveraging the DC functionality to achieve higher throughput.

The splitting of data on the gNB can be a vendor-specific logic and can be based on multiple factors like buffer usage on the scheduler and radio conditions of NR for the UE, BLER, and so on.

Data splitting on the uplink is purely determined by the UE based on the radio conditions and can be sent either to only gNB, eNB, or both.

Similarly to option 3a, there is a possiblity that the UE is served by two separate PDU connections at the same time (one via the eNB for IMS and another via the gNB for data, as shown).

Due to the enhanced processing capability of a en-gNB versus an eNB, option 3x is a popular bearer-splitting option for service providers as opposed to using an master cell group (MCG) split bearer approach, which would mean the eNB would have to perform the data splitting.

Option 3

In option 3, as shown in Figure 3-8, there is no connection between the gNB and the 4G core network.

All the data either in the uplink or downlink are tranmitted through the gNB, which acts as a master node.

Depending on the NSA radio conditions experience by the UE, the eNB can split the user plane data in the downlink and send it to the gNB via the Xn interface so that the gNB can transmit the data to the UE on the 5G air interface.

The logic for splitting the data is purely vendor-specific and can be based on radio conditions experienced by the UE, the data buffer in the 4G eNB scheduler, congestion conditions of the eNB, and so on.

Since the higher bandwidth provided by the gNB is not fully leveraged by this option, and more data will need to be sent on the Xn interface to improve the throughput provided to the user, this is not a very popular option.

However, under mobility conditions where the UE moves to and from into the 5G NSA coverage region, there is no need for the constant eRAB modification procedure, thereby improving the signaling efficiency and improved quality of experience for the UE.

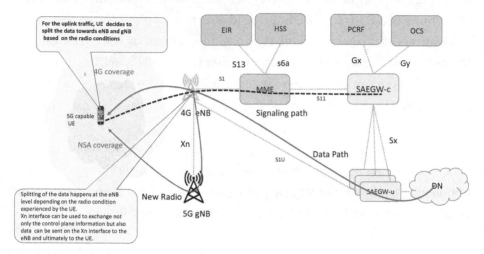

***Figure 3-8.** Illustration of option 3*

Control and User Plane Separation

CUPS implies the separation of control and user plane of the EPC nodes. This brings in the enhancements to user in the changes to split the control and user plane in the SGW and the PGW of the EPC.

With this advancement, adding capacity to scale and operating the network becomes very flexible. The control and user plane nodes can be added independently of each other. Hence any additional thoughput requirement would translate to adding of user plane resources only maintaining the control plane as it is. This addition can be done completely independently of existing deployment and would not be subject to service interruption during this expansion.

This CUPS can be designed to have centralized or distributed control plane and user plane. The functional split takes care of not affecting any functionality of SGW and PGW. Hence all the existing features of SGW and PGW are retained with CUPS.

User data traffic has been increasing multifold year over year during the past decade. The use of smart phones with high-definition screens suitable for video streaming, gaming, and so forth have contributed to this significantly. The use of tethering from mobile devices to serve as hotspots has made high-speed internet available to PCs, anytime and anywhere; this has also contributed to a high amount of data usage derived from the mobile packet core network.

To add to this, there is a very high quality of experience focus for end-users and lower latency is a key performance indicator (KPI) that is closely pursued by the service provider. CUPS solves both of these challenges remarkably.

The high demand for throughput can be added incrementally as needed by mere additions of user planes, saving costs in areas of hardware, software, and deployment. The virtualized EPC also has a significant role in this, as the EPC software can now be deployed on commercial off-the-shelf hardware and is no longer dependent on expensive proprietary hardware that would require millions to deploy to add a few tens of gigabytes of data.

The latency can be further reduced by moving the user plane to the edge and close to the UE. This would directly reduce hops and hence provide latency, significantly improving the quality of experience of the users.

In a nutshell, CUPS provides the following:

- It reduces latency. This is achieved by intelligent user plane selection based on proximity of the eNB. With this, the user plane closest to the base station can be chosen, and hence the number of hops in the service provider IP core is saved. This results in improving latency.

- CUPS is a transition path to the 5G architecture by separating the control and user planes and gives out an early adoption path to the service providers.

- Any capacity expansion can be easily accommodated with low cost and no service interruption. The addition of user planes is complelely independent of control planes; hence more user planes can be added to the existing control plane, saving costs for the operator.

- The operator can identify high-density pockets in a region, which demands higher throughput and selectively adds user planes there to cater to the demand, keeping the control plane centralized. This results in significant savings.

- CUPS leverages the concepts of software-defined networks, which reduces the dependency on hardware and ushers in the prospects of automation, reducing the time to deploy new nodes.

CUPS Architecture

Since CUPS splits the control and user planes, it brings in one new Sx interface, which connects the two. This new interface is based on packet forwarding control protocol (PFCP). Similarly to GTP-c the transport for PFCP is the user datagram protocol (UDP).

The interface between SGW-c and SGW-u is called Sx-a, the interface between PGW-c and PGW-u is called Sx-a, and for a combined interface between SPGW-c and SPGW-u, the interface is called Sx-ab.

Figure 3-9 illustrates the interfaces that are associated with CUPS.

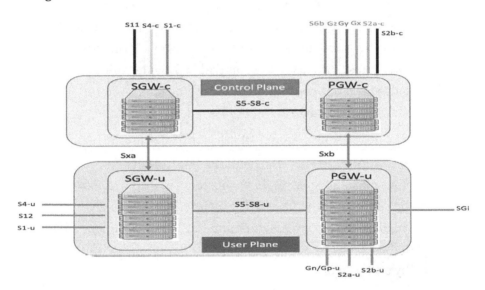

Figure 3-9. *Interfaces associated with CUPS*

Following are the key aspects of CUPS.

- The CUPS control plane function serves to terminate all the control signaling messages or the control plane protocols like diameter, GTP-c, PFCP, and so forth.

- The control plane node can interface with multiple user plane functions, and conversely the user plane can interface with multiple control plane nodes.

- Consider a use-case when the UE is serviced by a control plane, for a particular APN (say, the "internet") the control plane an select a user plane; for the same UE for a different access point name (APN; say "IMS"), the control plane may select a different user plane. Hence the same UE can be connected to the same control plane and different user planes.

- The control plane node is the brain for decision making and gives directions to the user plane function to provision rules for traffic steering and packet detection and inspection. It provides actions to the user plane to forward, drop, duplicate, or buffer packers. It provides QoS rules to the user plane and also provides the rules for usage reporting that would be later used for charging and so forth.

- The user plane supports all the 3GPP features of lawful interception: policy and charging control (PCC), charging, and so forth; however, it's also important to be agnostic of the underlying technology. Just to give an example, user plane function (UPF) is unaware of bearer concept; for UPF it is just GTP tunnels identified by endpoints.

- The UPF measures the traffic and reports to the control plane in the form of usage reports. The online and offline charging is supported, as it was in 4G, and there is no impact on the same.

- The GTP-u tunnel identifier F-teid is allocated by UPF and conveyed to the control plane.

- Also as a migration strategy, a legacy PGW, SGW can be replaced by a CUPS node without affecting any connection to the current legacy nodes.

- The selected protocol for the Sx interface is PFCP. It is based on UDP, and it was selected as it was easy to implement on forwarding devices, had low latency, and had the support for all existing 3GPP features and ease of maintenance, among others.

- Once the control plane and the user plane come up and is configured, an Sx association is set up between the control and user plane functions. The control plane would need to mandatorily support the initiation of Sx establishment; however, the initiation of Sx establishment is optional for user planes.

- When the Sx is established, the control plane informs the user plane about critical information, like user IP pools, and configuration relating to the upkeep and operation of the Sx link. It can also support a PFD configuration push in which all the packet static rules and so forth can be pushed to the user plane.

- The Sx procedures are categorized into two main types: the node-related procedures and the session-related procedures.

Figure 3-10 shows some highlights for the PFCP node procedures.

PFCP Node Related Procedures

PFCP Association Setup Procedure	• The PFCP Association Setup procedure is used to setup a PFCP association between a CP function and a UP function
Heartbeat Procedure	• CP or UP function may send a Heartbeat Request each other to find out if the peer is alive
Load Control Procedure	• Load control enables the UP function to send its load information to the CP function to adaptively balance the PFCP session load across the UP functions according to their effective load.
Overload Control Procedure	• Overload control enables a UP function becoming or being overloaded to gracefully reduce its incoming signaling load by instructing its peer CP functions to reduce sending traffic
PFCP PFD Management Procedure	• It used by the CP function and UP function to provision Packet Flow Descriptions for one or more Application Identifiers.
PFCP Association Update Procedure	• The CP function initiates the PFCP Association Update procedure to report changes to the PFCP association to the UP function
PFCP Association Release Procedure	• The PFCP Association Release procedure is used to terminate the PFCP association between the CP Function and the UP Function
PFCP Node Report Procedure	• The PFCP Node Report procedure is used by the UP function to report information to the CP function which is not related to a specific PFCP session

Figure 3-10. *PFCP node procedures highlights*

- As seen in Figure 3-10, the node-related procedures are related to the establishment of the PFCP-based Sx connection, the operational maintenance, and the deletion of the same.

- The session-related procedures are related to each PDN session and directly map to a UE session. All the dynamic traffic steering rules received from PCRF are sent to the UPF for a particular UE via these procedures. When a UE is disconnected, this session is deleted via the Sx deletion procedure.

- Only the UE session is established and deleted when the UE attaches or detaches. The Sx link remains up throughout and is not interrupted unless it's a planned activity or network disruption.

Figure 3-11 highlights a few PFCP session procedures.

PFCP Session Related Procedures

PFCP Session Establishment Procedure	• The CP function initiates the PFCP Session Establishment procedure to create a PFCP session for a PDN connection.
PFCP Session Modification Procedure	• The PFCP Session Modification procedure is used to modify an existing PFCP session or to configure a new rule, to modify an existing rule or to delete an existing rule etc.
PFCP Session Deletion Procedure	• The PFCP Session Deletion procedure is used to delete an existing PFCP session between the CP function and the UP function.
PFCP Session Report Procedure	• The PFCP Session Report procedure is used by the UP function to report information related to the PFCP session to the CP function.

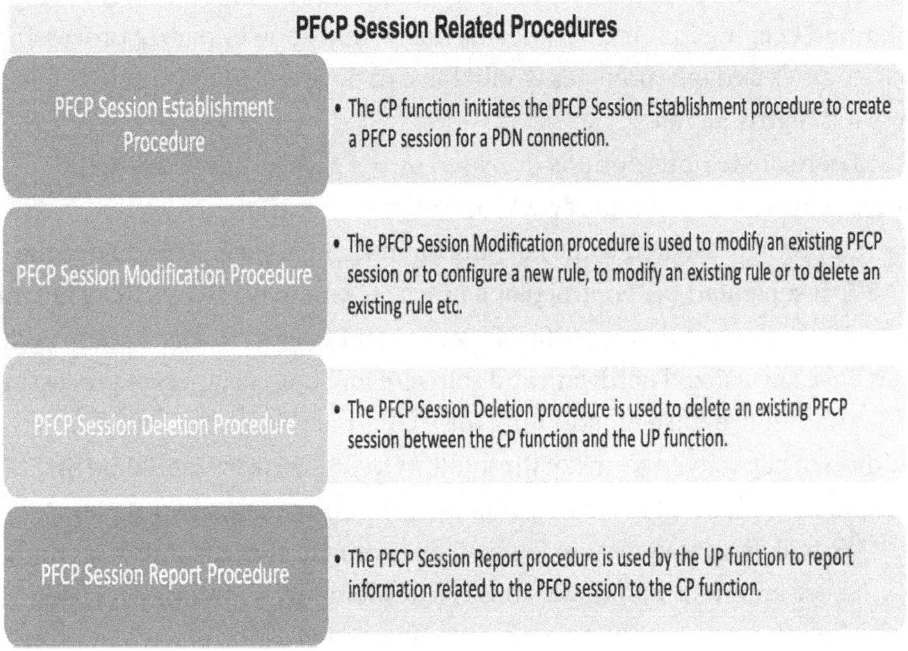

Figure 3-11. *PFCP session procedures highlights*

Legacy-Based NSA and CUPS-Based NSA

The operators have various options to implement NSA.

NSA on Legacy vs CUPS

The first and most common approach is to continue with DCNR support on legacy monolithic 4G gateways. However, this would require the gateway vendors to be able to support higher packet processing data rates that would be on par with 5G data rates. This is often a challenge for most vendors as the legacy platforms used to support 4G data rates were not planned keeping in mind 5G speeds; hence high-power packet processing capabilities and technologies would have to be adopted to be able to cater to such high data rates.

There are various options provided by the gateway vendors to the service providers to support NSA; one of them is CUPS.

CUPS was designed while keeping in mind high-speed UEs, hence the CUPS. It separated the control plane function, which involves a lot of lengthy decision making and processing of signaling messages. The user plane nodes can have specialized hardware and software for super fast packet processing.

Another use-case for adopting the CUPS-based solution was that addion of capacity in terms of throughput to the network would be as simple as addition of more user planes with the existing control plane.

We will delve deeper into capacity planning in the upcoming sections.

There are two major flavors of cups implementation that are mostly based on use-cases and latency requirements. Let's look at each of them.

Co-Located CUPS

This is a gateway solution in which the legacy SGW and PGW is split into control plane and SGW-c, PGW-c, SAEGW-c and user plane nodes SGW-U, PGW-U, and SAE-GWU. All these control and user plane components are physically located in the same data center.

The control and user plane gateways are all typically virtualized VM-based gateway functions. With the advancement of network function virtualization (NFV) and rapid adoption of virtualization by all gateway vendors and most service providers, implementation and migration to CUPS is now very speedy.

Co-located CUPS is often selected by the service provider, as it is easiest to rollout and fits in smoothly with the existing IP core network that the operator had planned to support the 4G solution.

Additional consideration on IP core design to reduce latency between control and user plane functions need not be considered in this case, as both are physically located in close proximity in the same data center and the Sx communication wouldn't need to go multiple hops over the service provider IP core.

Centralized CUPS hence simplifies and consolidates operations and interfaces to surrounding control elements.

Servicability is achieved, as the upgrades to control and user planes in the network can be independent of each other, hence leading to minimal disruption of traffic during maintenance.

Figure 3-12 illustrates the high-level architecture for a co-located CUPS solution.

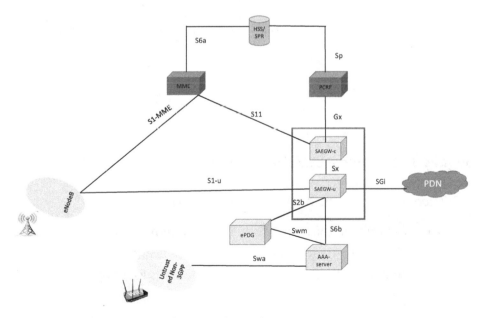

Figure 3-12. *Co-located CUPS-based solution*

Remote CUPS

This is a gateway solution in which the legacy SGW and PGW are split into control plane and SGW-c, PGW-c, SAEGW-c and user plane nodes SGW-U, PGW-U, and SAE-GWU. All these control and user plane components are physically located in the different data centers.

Figure 3-13 illustrates the high level architecture for a remote CUPS solution.

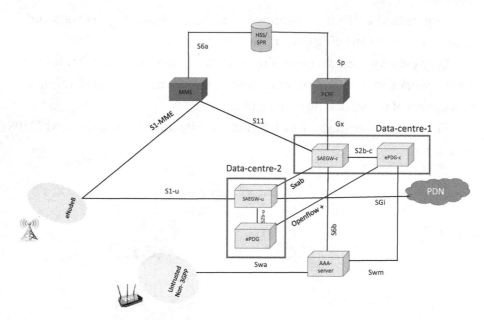

Figure 3-13. *Remote CUPS illustration*

There can be two further types of remote CUPS:

- Centralized remote CUPS: This is implemented by placing the control planes in a central location (data center) and distributing the user planes into many locations (data centers).

- Distributed remote CUPS: This is implemented by placing both control and user planes in a distributed manner across many locations (data centers).

Irrespective of the the type of remote CUPS, there are some very niche use-cases that can be realized with the help of this type of solution—for example, the edge use-case—in which a user plane is located as close to the UE as possible to achieve low latency.

The operator can further decide to implement use-case-based optimization and use of user plane. Since CUPS can be compelely implemented on commercial off-the-shelf hardware, the operator may choose to select the use of faster and more expensive processors for user planes serving some mission-critical applications or high-speed UEs, and for lighter use-cases (such as voice calls), a much cheaper hardware can be used. This flexibility of choosing the hardware based on the applications help the operators save a lot of CAPEX.

Since the operators can now save a lot of investment that would otherwise go in procuring expensive proprietary hardware, they can choose to invest in building more redundancy and fault tolerance.

Since the control and user plane functions are now separate, an outage in the user plane will not affect the control plane function. Also since the user plane for different APNs can be separated, the failure of one user plane won't impact the traffic on other unimpacted APNs.

As discussed in the previous sections, capacity can be added on both control and user planes independently now by mere addition of more servers, thereby breaking off the shackles that came with the monolithic architecture where this differentiation was impossible.

The backhaul can be better utilized by remote CUPS in which the application is brought closer to the user plane function.

A classic use-case of implementing remote CUPS is that of a university campus where thousands of students are present all the time. This is where a service provider can choose to place hundreds of user planes to deal with the high volumes of traffic, while keeping the control plane to a centralized location.

Conversely, in rural areas where there are vast farmlands and population density is less, a few user planes can be leverged to serve large population, all the time leveraging the same centralized control plane that serves both dense and spare areas, thereby utilizing its resources optimally with minimum idle time.

NSA Call Flows

Initial Attach Considerations

For an NSA call, it is required to have a UE that supports dual connectivity with new radio (DCNR). Activation of EN-DC occurs once the device has attached to the 4G network, specifically due to the fact that EN-DC can only take place once security at the master eNB has been established. However, the 4G attach procedure is still affected by the operation of EN-DC in the network.

Figure 3-14 illustrates a high-level attach procedure between the UE and MME with dual connectivity.

NAS Attach Request : Dual Connectivity with NR flag set in the UE Network Capability IE

                                                                              MME

NAS Attach Accept :
MME may also choose to decline EN-DC operation by setting the "Use of Dual Connectivity with NR is Restricted" flag

Figure 3-14. *Attach with DC*

The non-access stratum (NAS) attach request message will contain the UE network capability information element, which lists the various network capabilities that the device supports. One of these capabilities is "Dual Connectivity with NR," which will be set if the device supports EN-DC. Therefore, the mobility management entity (MME) will be aware that the device is EN-DC capable, although this does not mean EN-DC will actually be used. For example, the MME may set the "Use of Dual Connectivity with NR is Restricted" flag in the attach accept, which would prevent EN-DC from being used. The Dual Connectivity with NR flag will assist the MME in choosing an appropriate P-GW for EN-DC operation.

Note that the eNB will be informed that the device supports EN-DC during the attach process, once the device has conducted an initial attach with the network (hence, the MME has the UE capabilities stored). In particular, the S1AP Initial UE Context Setup message contains the UE radio access capability information for the E-UTRA, which will contain an indication that EN-DC is supported. As such, the eNB will attempt to establish EN-DC operation as soon as it is feasible to do so in the network (typically when security has been established and the device is in radio coverage of a qualifying en-gNB, assuming all other limiting conditions are met, such as cell restrictions).

With respect to the tracking area update procedure, the same concepts apply in that the device will use the same technique to advertise support for EN-DC. Likewise, the network may decline the use of EN-DC by using the same flag in the tracking area update accept.

Figure 3-15, Figure 3-16, and Figure 3-17 together shows the attach call flow for a DCNR UE.

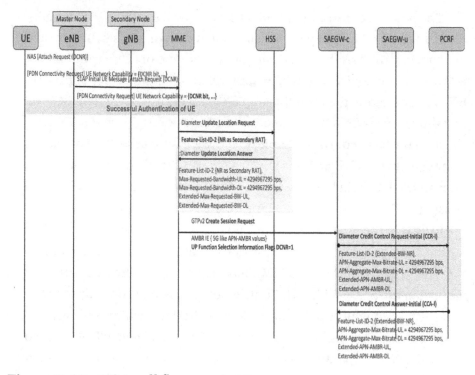

Figure 3-15. *NSA call flow — part 1*

Let us get into further details of the NSA-based attach procedure in a step-by-step manner.

1. The UE will send an attach request with the DCNR bit set as shown in Figure 3-14. This bit is a part of the UE network capability IE. This message is sent to the M-enB.

2. The M-enB then sends the initial UE message with the attach request containing this DCNR bit set within an NAS container to the MME.

3. The MME then starts the UE authentication procedure with the help of home subscriber server (HSS). This procedure is the same as the traditional UE authentication procedure in 4G.

4. After the authentication procedure the UE performs a location update with "NR as the secondary RAT" set in the "Feature-List-ID-2." This is sent by the MME to the HSS as a part of the update location request.

5. The HSS responds with an update location answer with Feature-ID-List2 "NR as Secondary RAT" along with the enhanced bit rates for the user, which can be leveraged with the new radio to deliver higher 5G-like speeds. Hence it is important that the UE has also subscribed for the enhanced 5G plan to be able to leverage its new radio for higher speeds. The HSS responds **back** with Max-Requested-Bandwidth-UL, Max-Requested-Bandwidth-DL **along with the new parameters** Extended-Max-Requested-BW-UL, Extended-Max-Requested-BW-DL.

6. If the UE has no subscription for NR or is not authorized to receive DCNR services, then the HSS will in that case send subscription-data with "Access-Restriction" carrying "NR as SecondaryRAT NotAllowed."

7. The MME then sends a create session request message with the extended APN-AMBR values in existing AMBR IE to the PGW via SGW. The extended APN-AMBR values are used to support the higher bit rates for 5G speeds.

8. PGW sends credit control request-initial (CCR-I) to policy and charging rules function (PCRF). To communicate to PCRF about the dual connectivity with new radio, it sends "Extended-BW-NR" feature bit in "Feature-List-ID-2." The PGW also sends "APN-Aggregate-Max-Bitrate-UL," "APN-Aggregate-Max-Bitrate-DL," and the extended bandwidth values in new AVPs "Extended-APN-AMBR-UL" and "Extended-APN-AMBR-DL."

9. PCRF then responds with credit control answer-initial (CCA-I) with the"Extended-BW-NR" feature bit in "Feature-List-ID-2." PCRF also sends "APN-Aggregate-Max-Bitrate-UL," "APN-Aggregate-Max-Bitrate-DL," and the extended bandwidth values in new AVPs "Extended-APN-AMBR-UL" and "Extended-APN-AMBR-DL." PCRF offers the same extended APN-AMBR values requested by policy and charging enforcement function (PCEF) or modify the extended APN-AMBR values.

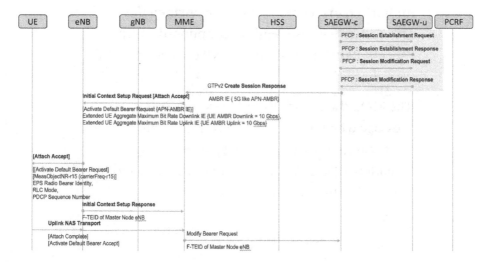

Figure 3-16. *NSA call flow—part 2*

10. PGW enforces the extended APN-AMBR values accordingly as sent by PCRF and sends the extended APN-AMBR values in existing IE "APN-AMBR" in the create session response message.

11. If the implementation is CUPS-based, then the PGW control plane executes an additional step of session establishment with the user plane and communicates with the user plane the bit rates it has received from PCRF. Upon successful response, it then sends the create session response to the MME.

12. MME then processes the UE-AMBR value and sends an "Initial Context Setup Request" message after populating and sending the IE's "extended UE aggregate maximum bit rate downlink" and "extended UE aggregate maximum bit rate uplink," providing an AMBR max value of up to 10 Gbps.

13. MME also can leverage the existing APN-AMBR IE to send a value up to 65.2 Gbps and use the new IE "extended APN aggregate maximum bit rate" for values above that and send it in the attach accept message.

14. The eNB then sends initial context setup response.

15. As executed in legacy 4G call flow, the MME then sends modify bearer request to the SGW with the S1-U FTEID.

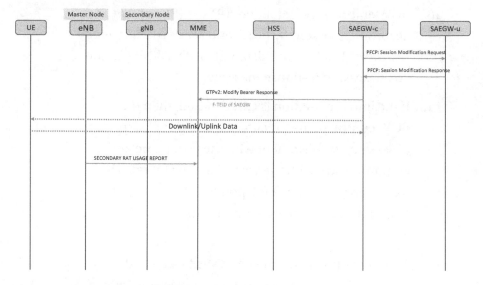

Figure 3-17. *NSA call flow—part 3*

Deployment Considerations

The service provider needs to keep a large number of key considerations in mind in order to design a robust network that is able to perform to its expected capacity. It is often observed that operators often spend a lot to re-design their networks because of weak intial planning. The following key considerations would help to adequately plan the transition to an NSA-based network.

Some of the key considerations that a service provider should have in mind while deploying a 5G NSA network are listed here.

- Device strategy and APN planning for NSA

- Gateway node selection

- User plane selection criteria

- MEC strategy

- Charging in NSA

- Secondary node addition/deletion

- Automation consideration

- Lawful interception (LI)

- IP pool planning

- Redundancy considerations

Apart from this, there are a few challenges that an operator faces due to the basic NSA architecure.

In the remaining sections of the chapter, we will discuss these deployment considerations and the challenges a little more in detail.

Device Strategy and Access Point Name Planning

The strategy to onboard or upgrade devices would go hand-in-hand with the radio and core network deployment/upgrade plan. For most service providers, there would be an existing 4G network that would be supported by the existing 4G devices. A natural migration path for those service providers would then be to move to the NSA-based deploymment as explained in detail in the preceding sections. To support dual radio, enhanced bit rates for NSA, and additional features brought in by NSA, the UE would need to be updated. Many new 4G UEs that have been launched over the past 2 years have had the support needed to access dual radio, and hence a simple software update would make those devices ready for NSA deployment. It is important that the NSA devices are backward compatible with legacy 4G and 3G networks.

However, the 5G SA devices would need to support a whole range of new features, starting with supporting mmWave bands. The voiceover NR-related features would support network slicing-related features and Sub6GHz bands. In addition to this it is expected to also be backward-compatible with NSA, legacy 4G, and 3G networks.

137

Since the 5G UE is expected to support so many new requirements, the time to develop, test, and launch these UEs is also time-consuming.

The first generation of 5G UEs have already been launched commercially in some parts of the world, but a lot of work is still pending to integrate the full feature set.

Therefore the device strategy for most operators would be in tandem with their network transition path from 4G Legacy ➤ 5G NSA ➤ 5G SA.

The access point names, in NSA would remain similar to 4G legacy. The key APNs allocated to accessing internet, IMS for voice and video calls, and so on as well as the APNs connected to roaming, mobile virtual network operators (MVNOs), corporate customers, and so on would be exactly the same as 4G legacy. Hence it is expected to be a smooth transition in this regard between legacy and NSA.

Gateway Node Selection

The operator network will have a mixture of legacy 3G/4G nodes, and 5G support both functionally and performance-wise can be present only on some S/PGW nodes. With this it becomes crucial for the service provider to design a gateway selection logic so that the applications that need high speed can be routed to the CUPS-based gateways.

Therefore the requirement should be that the MME should always be able to select 5G-enabled GWs for 5G-capable devices.

Figure 3-18 illustrates the gateway selection scenario.

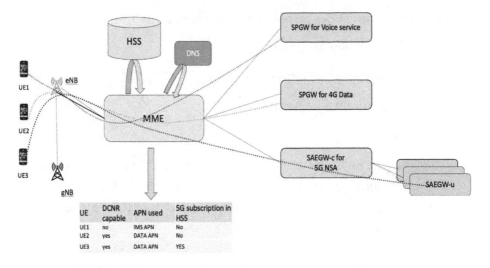

Figure 3-18. *Gateway selection example in a hybrid deployment*

As shown in Figure 3-18, which is indicative only and is not necessarily the only/optimal design for deployment, the MME may select a 5G-enabled S/PGW based on various parameters, including:

– UE capability

– UE subscription

– Gateway node capability

– APN (if different APN is used for 5G NSA and 4G)

Additionally if there is a UE usage type (UUT) subscription for a UE, it can also be used for a gateway node selection.

When a UE that is DCNR-capable attempts to register with an APN that is reserved for 5G NSA and the HSS subscription for the UE confirms that it is 5G NSA-subscribed, then the MME performs a query to the DNS server to select gateway nodes that can support 5G NSA users (preferably nodes with higher throughput capabilities)

Here is a sample DNS response to the query from MME:

x-3gpp-sgw:x-s5-gtp+**nc-nr**

x-3gpp-pgw:x-s5-gtp+**nc-nr**

x-3gpp-pgw:x-gn+**nc-nr**

x-3gpp-pgw:x-gp+**nc-nr**

After the gateway selection, the MME/SGSN sets the DCNR flag in "UP Function Selection Indication Flags IE" over S11/Gn for CUPS to indicate SAEGW-C to select SAEGW-U optimized for NR. It is ignored in a non-CUPS deployment.

User Plane Selections

CUPS brings in a lot of flexibility and options for criteria in selection of SGW-U and PGW-U. This flexibility was missed prior to EPC Release 14. These flexibilities offered by CUPS provides the real value and savings to the operator.

SAEGW-U is selected by SAEGW-C, and there can be many considerations while selecting the user plane. Some of the consideration parameters that the control plane can use for selecting the user plane node are

- APN and the user plane group that is reserved for a particular APN.

- Gateway dynamic node: The gateway dynamic load can be on the APN level or on the node level itself.

- Location of the user plane with respect to the UE location (for some of the applications that are delay-sensitive, it makes sense to select an user plane on the MEC that is located closer to the UE).

- UUT: If the service provider environment is such that the user plane groups are configured based on the UUT subscription of the UE.

– Static capacity of the user plane: Within a particular user plane group, the user plane selection can be based on the relative static capacity of the UE to ensure equal load distribution among user plane nodes within a user plane group.

Figure 3-19 represents some, but not necessarily all, the considerations that can be used by the operators for the user plane node selection.

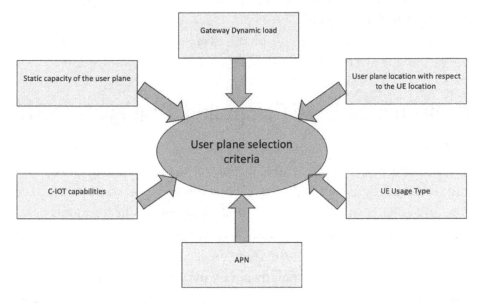

Figure 3-19. *User plane selection criteria*

Challenge 1: No Dedicated Gateway Reserved in the Network for 5G NSA Users

Often, during the design of NSA, there is a tendency to leverage the existing 4G CUPS deployment architecture and upgrade only the radio with NR, and some of the operators might not consider having separate gateway nodes for the 5G NSA users.

This design approach can have the advantage that the operator can save cost by not reserving dedicated gateway nodes for the NSA users. However, when the user plane has sessions from UEs that are 4G only and NSA-capable UEs, there is a possibility that the NSA users, when in the NR coverage, can consume higher bandwidth, thereby starving the 4G-only UEs.

There should be a good balance between the impact to the existing 4G users and the hardware cost/resource utilization while considering one of the aforementioned options.

Fair usage policy can be considered to ensure that there is no UE starvation due to a few high-usage users within a user plane node.

Multi-Access Edge Computing Strategy for NSA

MEC moves data center functions closer to the end-user at the edge of the network and away from the core. This improves application response time and reduces the amount of data traversing the transport network between core and edge. Distributing the UPF to the edge results in additional cost. Therefore, implementations typically deploy the UPF in the same EDC as other MEC servers, as well as the xhaul devices.

Mobile SPs can choose their own NFV infrastructure (NFVI) implementation to host the UPF in MEC. MEC needs routing back to the main data center to link the control plane functions.

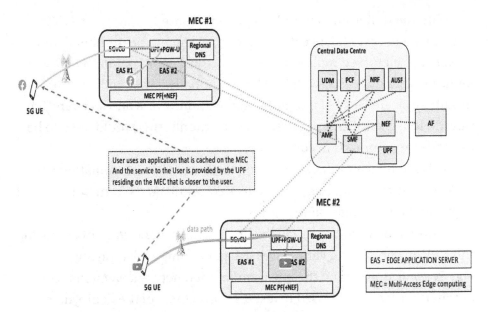

Figure 3-20. *Multi-access edge computing in a 5G deployment*

Role of Automation

The operator space is moving away from traditional old school deployment techniques wherein a large number of engineers were required for building and upkeep of 3G and 4G networks, which impacted both CAPEX and OPEX.

The adoption of virtualization was a game-changer for all service providers. That greatly helped in reducing CAPEX costs, which enabled service providers to use cheaper COTS hardware. The next area of optimization was to reduce the cost in terms of time and resources to actually deploy a network. This problem was solved by automation.

Investment in automation frameworks has helped operators reap golden benefits in terms of CAPEX and OPEX. Automation can be used in every aspect of deployment and maintenance.

With the shift from monolithic appliance-based gateways to COTs hardware and cost-effective data center equipment, the number of total servers has increased multifold. Hence the number of points of hardware faults also has increased with it. Whereas initially it was sufficient to monitor a single piece of monilithic gateway hardware and software, it is now no longer enough to do that since the monitoring would need to be expanded to hundreds of components.

This has thus introduced the need for automation. Automation can be leveraged to monitor and co-relate alarms and faults from hundreds of components to a single pane of glass.

Automation frameworks can be built right from the stage of deploying the NFV, to onboarding various VMs, to generating and applying Day-N configurations on the newly onboarded network elements. The automation can also be used to test the correctness of the deployment by running test calls and checking for the results to detect any missing configuration or faulty equipment.

Therefore, automation should be adopted by the service provider as a culture rather than an option.

With a fully automated framework, the end-to-end deployment of a network can be done in minutes as compared to the days and weeks required by a legacy-based system.

We will explore deeper into the automation prospects in the upcoming chapters.

Role of Analytics

Network analytics has been a topic of interest over the last few years. It can provide a lot of value to the service providers in terms of analyzing the current health of the system. It helps with analyzing the overall capacity of the network and also greatly helps in predicting the future capacity needs to plan expansion of networks.

Network analytics can be divided into multiple categories; some of them are related to user behavior, some are related to market trends, and some can throw light on performace of a particular network element or a hardware equipment.

Some of the analytics use-cases that can help the service providers in making various decisions pertaining to their network planning are as follows:

1. Analytics of plot graphs that depict the overall usage of the network, the existing usage vs the planned capacity

2. Analytics of plot graphs that depict the call failure rates and also which can be correlated to a cause or network equipment

3. Analytics of plot graphs that depict the handover success rates and also causes of failure, if any

4. Analytics of plot graphs that depict the user behavior in terms of TCP vs UDP traffic usage; possibility of optimization of TCP or UDP by bringing the content closer to the user (NSA use-case)

5. Analytics of plot graphs that would show the concentration of users in a particular geographical location; this again can be used to plan NR small cells or user planes

6. Analytics of plot graphs to show hardware failure rates.

7. Analytics of plot graphs to show the percentage of high-speed UEs in an area, which would again be used as feedback to plan user plane expansion

8. Analytics of plot graphs to show usage per APN, which can be used to plan user plan expansion per APN.

In addition to the above use-cases, the operator can leverage analytics to evaluate the performance of equipment from various vendors and use it as feedback for enhancements and so on.

Radion Access Network and Transport Implications

In addition to RAN changes and implementing NRs and UEs, transport expansion needs to be considered, as there would be cases where traffic cannot be offloaded at the cell site. The 5G transport should be very sensitive to latency. Especially with the introduction of Cloud RAN, it is expected that this traffic will have to be transported through the fronthaul to a pre-aggregation site where virtualized baseband unit (vBBU) is located. Placement of the virtualized central unit (vCU) and virtualized distributed unit (vDU) will have an impact on the network speeds. The same network serving as a 4G backhaul may be 5G midhaul, depending on the vCU placement.

Fronthaul bandwidth and latency requirements can be very demanding depending on the radio split used, which is outside of the scope of this document. However, a possibility that existing transport facilities may not be able to serve the new network has to be taken into consideration and addressed.

Therefore, for the reduced latency and high-throughput demands brought in by the 5G use-cases, the transport network needs to be scaled and updated accordingly. Techniques like differentiated services codepoint (DSCP) marking on packets to help prioritize as well as planning a faster network by adopting the latest network models is key to support the 5G use-cases.

In addition to this, because virtual RAN and cloud native-based core network have further disaggregated the network function, security is a key design aspect that needs to be kept in mind.

Advanced secure tunnels in addition to enhanced access control lists (ACLs) would need to be adopted to ensure the communication is safe from extenal attacks.

QoS and Charging in NSA

NSA supports all the existing nine QoS class identifier (QCIs) that was supported in legacy LTE. Hence all the existing use-cases and applications would be inherently supported in NSA. However, as we know by now, NSA will support faster speeds with the help of NR. To support this there need to be enhancements to the QoS parameters to support the higher speeds.

Since NR theoretically supports up to 20 Gbps in the downlink and up to 10 Gbps in the uplink, a few changes have been done in the NSA core to accommodate this. If the device is dual-radio capable, the PGW would notify PCRF with the **"Extended-BW-NR"** field. It will request extended bandwidth from the PCRF when it detects a dual-radio-capable UE via the **"Extended-APN-AMBR-UL/DL"** in CCR message to the PCRF. The PCRF then responds with a CCA and fills in the value of these fields. Similarly PGW requests values of **"Extended-Max-Requested-BW-UL/DL"** and **"Extended-GBR-UL/DL"** for maximum bit rate (MBR) and guaranteed bit rate (GBR) values on Gx and Gy (PCRF and OCS)

In addition to this, some 5G requirements of low-latency communication are also supported by the support of QCI 80, which is non-GBR, and dedicated bearers with QCI 82 and 83, which is ideal to support industrial automation cases. Therefore in NSA there is a support for some of the 5G QCI in addition to the nine standard 5G QCIs.

As far as charging and usage reporting goes, the eNB informs the usage uplink and downlink data volume of secondary RAT type, PGW, which is responsible for reporting usage of this secondary RAT type via Gz and Rf CDRs (offline reporting).

Accounting functionality is undertaken by the SGW and the PGW, the eNB reports the secondary RAT usage data information, which is then included in messages on S11 to SGW and S5/S8 interface to the PGW. The PGW then sends Rf records or charging data records (CDRs) to the radius accounting servers or charging gateway function as configured. The reporting of UL/DL volumes is done on a per-EPS-bearer basis for a particular time interval.

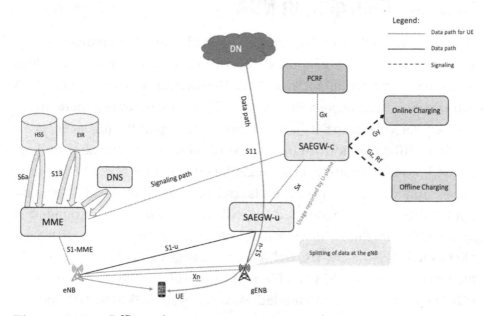

Figure 3-21. *Offline charging representation for 5G NSA*

As explained for supporting Gz, a new sequence of containers defined in PGWRecord/SGWRecord for PGW-CDR/SGW-CDR to support RAN secondary RAT usage data reporst on the Gz interface.

```
RANSecondaryRATUssageReport    ::= SEQUENCE
  --
{
    dataVolumeUplink              [1] DataVolumeGPRS,
    dataVolumeDownlink            [2] DataVolumeGPRS,
    rANStartTime                  [3] TimeStamp,
    rANEndTime                    [4] TimeStamp,
    secondaryRATType              [5] SecondaryRATType OPTIONAL
}
```

Figure 3-22. *Gz AVPs to support 5G charging*

To support Rf accounting, the grouped RAN-Secondary-RAT-Usage-Report AVP (AVP code 1302) is introduced to support secondary RAT usage data report values.

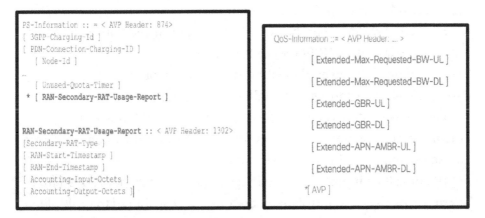

Figure 3-23. *Rating function (RF) accounting support for 5G UEs*

A charging challenge with CUPS is the requirement to report on usage data from the UP. The control plane already has an established mechanism for this activity, and Gy/Gz interfaces supporting charging are well-defined from the control plane node. In addition to that, with the user plane not having direct communication with the OCS/OFC systems, usage data from the user plane has to be reported via the Sx interface ot the control plane and ultimately to the OCS/OFC.

Charging in NSA is an operator's requirement on usage reporting and can be unclear. For example, should subscribers be charged higher rates for NR vs LTE? How would the interoperator charging reconciliation work based on usage of NR data?

One of the biggest challenge when it comes to online charging for a user using the NSA services differentially based on the usage of secondary RAT (i.e., gNB vs primary eNB for uplink and downlink data transfer) is determining precisely when the user is using the secondary node.

Challenge 2: Non-Adaptive IP Pool Allocation

The introduction of virtualized 5G NSA and SA networks into service provider space brings in unparalleled scope for operators to expand the capacity of their networks and onboard a large number of subscribers in their networks with rapid turnaround time.

Service providers may choose to deploy centralized control planes but highly distributed UPFs (edge use-case). With automation and NFV-based deployments, user planes could be spun up on demand to cater to dynamic spikes for throughput in different regions.

Hence user planes can be added (or removed) with regard to utilization of resources, such as compute CPU, port utilization, memory, and so on, managed by closed-loop automation.

IP pool allocation is a key challenge in CUPS. Since pools need to be carved out by the control plane nodes to be distributed to multiple-user plane nodes. A centralized control plane is responsible for IP pool allocation to each of these user plane groups.

All user planes in the pool are given the same size of IP pool chunk by means of static configuration in the control plane (user plane selection can be based on APN/DDN or TAI, etc.). When a new user plane is added, it is allocated a similar pool chunk size as the other associated user planes. This is acceptable when there is an availability of pools chunks; however, when there is a condition where the pools in the control plane are close to being exhausted, even if a new user plane is allocated to reduce the load, the control plane wouldn't be able to assign chunks, as it may not have a large enough chunk available to allocate to that user plane, and hence the user plane wouldn't be able to share the load.

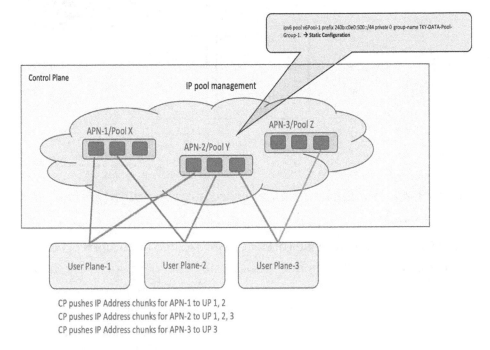

Figure 3-24. *IP allocation by the control plane*

Intelligent distribution and utilization of the pools is of utmost importance for maximum performance of the solution. Overutilization can cause service impact and underutilization, and skewed distribution of IP pools by control planes can cause overallocation in some user planes and starvation in others.

Figure 3-25 shows one such algorithm that provides a fair usage of IP pool allocation.

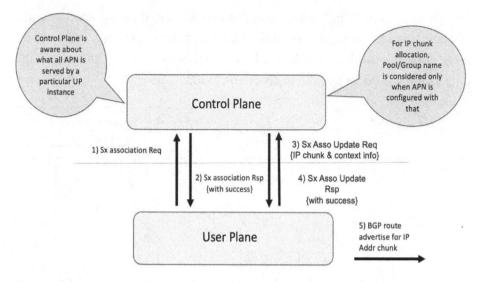

Figure 3-25. *IP chunk allocation procedures by control plane*

Typically all user planes in the same user plane group are given the same size of IP pool chunk by means of static configuration in the control plane. When a new user plane is added, it is allocated a similar pool chunk size as the other associated user planes.

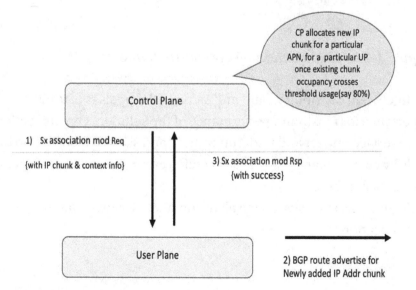

Figure 3-26. *IP chunk replenishment by control plane*

Similarly unused chunks are withdrawn from the user planes by the control plane.

Since the chunk size is constant, there is a possibility where the control plane shall not allocate IP chunks to a user plane upon a request because of pool exhaustion on the control plane. This can lead to a call-drop situation. Also if a new user plane is added to the group, there can be a situation where there are no chunks available on the control plane to allocate it to the request from the new user plane, as shown Figure 3-27.

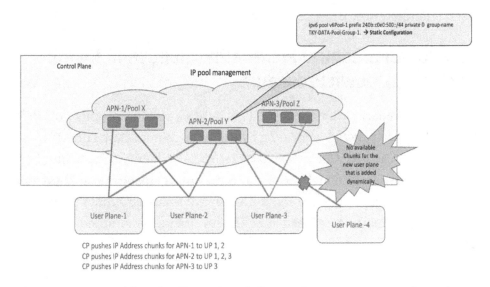

Figure 3-27. *IP chunk allocation failure when a new user plane is introduced in load conditions*

Although the situation looks like a total congestion situation, in reality, there is a possibility to accommodate more users by optimizing the allocated chunk size to the existing user planes, as there are many unused IPs/IP chunks in the other user planes that can be reused here.

Thus we see the need to have an adaptive pool chunk allocation algorithm in the control planes by which the control plane can assess the current usage of IP pools and allocate adaptively in a ramp-up or ramp-down manner to be able to cater to dynamic IP pool allocation requests.

Adaptive IP Pool Chunk Allocation

We need an adaptive pool chunk allocation algorithm in the control plane, which enables the control plane to assess the current usage of IP pools and allocate adaptively in a ramp-up or ramp-down manner to be able to cater to dynamic IP pool allocation requests.

Many service providers have experienced service loss and drop in KPIs due to non-availability of IP chunks in CUPS (especially for service providers using IPv4 pools). The IP pool is finite resource, and it has to be used efficiently between all user planes.

Enable CUPS Control Plane with Adaptive IP Chunk Size Ramp-Down Procedure

Consider a scenario when the control plane has a specified number of "IP Chunks" defined and it is allocating to user plane groups based on APN/DDN services hosted. Due to high usage such as an increase in the number of subscribers attached to the user plane, the control plane doesn't have new chunks, and it has to ration or reduce the size of available chunks so that it can allocate to existing user planes or any new usere plane added to support growth.

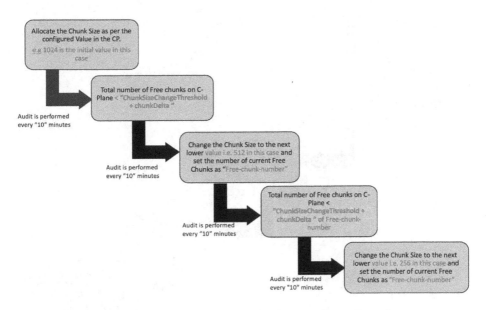

Figure 3-28. *Adaptive chunk size calculator algorithm for downgrade case*

Enable CUPS Control Plane with Adaptive IP Chunk Size Ramp-Up Procedure

Consider the scenario when the control plane has a specified number of "IP Chunks" defined and it is allocating to the user plane group based on APN/DDN services hosted. Due to less usage by the user plane, such as a decrease in the number of subscribers attached to the the user plane, the control plane can optimize the number of chunks and size of the chunk itself.

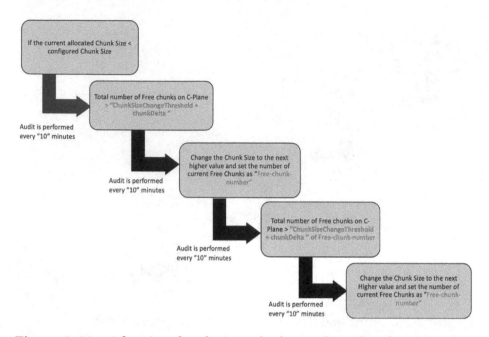

Figure 3-29. *Adaptive chunk size calculator algorithm for upgrade case*

The UPF should be facilitated to recalculate the chunk size and free up the chunks back to the control plane by a means of parameter passing through the Sx interface. User planes monitor subscriber sessions and calculate requirements of the anticipated "IP chunk" and notify the control plane. The user plane re-calculates the chunk size from the allocated pool or requests an additional "IP chunk" from the control plane by requests on the SX interface.

The aforementioned algorithms, once implemented in CUPS, will solve the problem encountered in customer networks.

Challenge 3: Frequent Secondary Node Addition and Deletion Can Cause Bad Quality of Experience and Signaling Storm

During the initial phase of deployment of 5G SA and 5G NSA, the 5G cell coverage will clearly be a subset of 4G coverage, and for an area of 4G coverage, there can be multiple 5G cell coverage.

For 5G NSA, the most popular mode of deployment is option 3x, where the core network is from 4G, wherein the 4G eNB acts as the MeNB and the 5G gNB acts as the SgNB. Figure 3-30 represents the mode of operation for an option 3x deployment.

The 5G frequency range is divided into two main parts: sub6Ghz and mmWave 5G.

A sub-six-band 5G technology will be able to cover a larger geographical area for 5G coverage but will not be able to provide higher speed downlink. A mmWave 5G technology will be able to provide very high downlink speeds but at the cost of less geographical area coverage. The path loss is very high for mmWave 5G, and chances of multipath reception for such waves is less; therefore, there are very high chances for frequent addition and deletion/modification of secondary node for UEs within the coverage region for mmWave 5G, or for 5G NSA in a situation when, for example, the user is indoors and the 5G transmitter is outside, there is a very high possibility that the UE will have varying RSRP received by the 5G cell and results in very frequent addition/deletion of the secondary node.

This pattern of UE/network behavior can result in:

1) Signaling spike on the RAN as well as core network due to frequent addition and deletion of the secondary

2) Bad QoE for the user, as there is a fluctuating radio condition and there are way too many retransmissions and switches in the path of downlink/uplink data transfer

3) Impact on UE battery performance due to frequent switching between single and dual streams of data

Before getting into the details of the possible solution for the aforementioned problem statement, let us try and understand the criteria for secondary node addition and deletion.

Secondary Node Addition Criteria:

Figure 3-30 shows the procedure for secondary node addition for an option 3x deployment

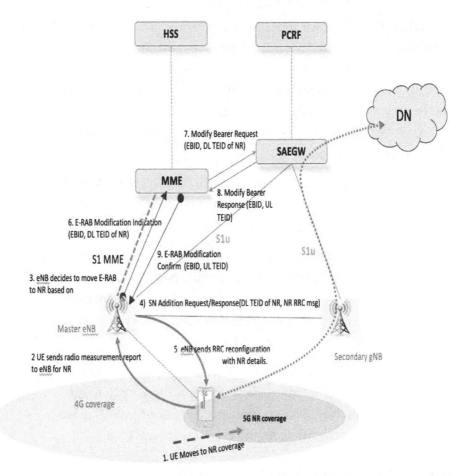

Figure 3-30. *Secondary node addition procedure for NSA option 3X*

The pre-condition to the procedure shown Figure 3-30 is that the RRC reconfiguration message when UE is connected in the 4G network has the B1 event and thresholds configured so that UE can report measurement when the NR measurement criteria are met.

When the UE moves from the 4G coverage area to an area where it experiences a good RSRP for the NR coverage and the B1 measurement reporting criteria is met on the UE end, it reports the B1 event toward the MeNB, and the secondary node addition procedure occurs as explained in the earlier NSA call flow section of this chapter.

As shown Figure 3-30, some of the key steps for secondary node addition procedure are:

- The trigger for the addition of a secondary node is always the UE sending the B1 measurement report to the MeNB for the 5G NR cell.

- After receiving the measurement report, the MeNB decides to move the E-RAB to the NR based on some criteria that is vendor-proprietary (e.g., some of the considerations can be experienced RSRP value for the 4G cell, PDCP buffer utilization, etc.).

- The eNB will perform a SN addition request on the X2 interface, and upon successful addition it will trigger an E-RAB modification procedure toward MME to move the S1-u bearer from the eNB toward the gNB.

Secondary Node Deletion Criteria

The secondary node deletion procedure can be triggered either by the MeNB or by the SgNB, depending on which of the two nodes detects the UE release first.

Figure 3-31 explains the procedure for secondary node deletion in both the cases.

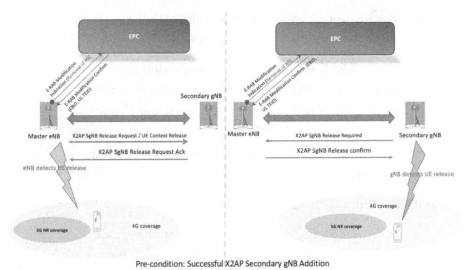

Figure 3-31. *Secondary node deletion procedure*

To be able to address the challenge of frequent addition/deletion of the secondary node to the NSA system, a few design considerations are required as a solution.

1. The method to identify UEs that are performing secondary node addition/deletion/modification at an unusual/alarming rate

   This can be done by means of KPIs as a part of central self-organizing network (SON) structure or can be a count maintained at the eNB/gNB level to identify whether any UE connected to an eNB/4G cell for a long time has been involved in multiple secondary node addition/deletion procedures.

   This method can be further enhanced to verify whether the frequent addition/deletion of the secondary node for the UE/set of UEs is for a particular eNB-gNB pair to identify any coverage issue for the UE.

2. The method to restrict/regulate such UEs to perform secondary node addition/deletion/modification

    Upon detection of the UEs that are performing an alarmingly high number of secondary node addition/deletion procedures, there should be some mechanisms at either the central SON level or at the gNB level to restrict these UEs from further adding/deleting the secondary node.

The trigger for restriction can be:

1. SON-based trigger restricting the secondary node addition for either some set of UEs or secondary node additions for a few gNBs to a particular eNB based on the statistics;

2. eNB calculated based on the number of switches made by a UE over a period of time and restrict the dual bearer addition; or

3. the core network (MME) can trigger restriction of the secondary node addition method (e.g., OVERLOAD START message on the S1AP interface) and can be used as a trigger for secondary node addition restriction.

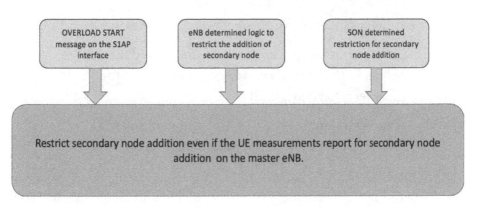

Figure 3-32. *Some of the triggers to restrict secondary node addition for a UE or a cell pair*

This can result in the following benefits:

– Enhanced QoE for the users by restricting frequent switch of S1U path between the master and secondary node Bs

– Reduces the signaling overhead (signaling storm) in the air interface as well as the S1AP interface and, subsequently, packet core signaling

– Can help in identifying coverage gaps/non-optimized radio network planning by patronizing UE behavior for a particular pair of MeNB and SgNB

Redundancy

One of the most invaluable features of CUPS-based NSA is the inherent ability to cater for a fault-tolerant and resilient network solution. Redundancy can be achieved on a CUPS-based NSA solution at multiple levels, thus hence making it a highly available solution.

The redundancy can be very broadly classified into two broad areas:

1. Local redundancy: This is where the redundancy is built in the same location geographically as the gateway is located.

2. Geo redundancy: This is when redundancy is built in a different location from where the gateway is located.

Using the above two principles, a lot of resiliency can be built in CUPS as it inherently removes the single point of failure and distributes it into the contol and user planes.

The control and user planes can, in turn, be designed to be highly available in an active-active or an active-standby manner.

Each control plane can also have multiple user planes; hence, the failure of one user-plane will not necessarily lead to service interruption. These user planes can again have 1:1 or n:m redundancy.

In the virtualized world, the data back plane of the legacy applicance-based systems is now brought out into leafs and spine-based data centers. The failure of the back plane itself, which was again a single point of failure, has been eliminated. In this case, redundancy of the data plane can be planned by the operator with a lot of flexibility from having redundant ports at the server level to redundant leafs and spines and top routers. Hence, the operator has a go-as-you-like option to plan their network based on their specific requirements and cost constraints.

Lawful Intercept Implications

In countries where LI is required for data traffic, additional provisions need to be made because user traffic is bypassing the control plane node entirely, and additional X3 interface is needed on the user plane. Figure 3-33 depicts LI as part of the CUPS architecture.

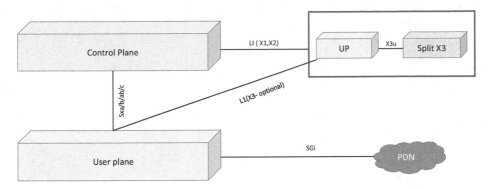

Figure 3-33. *LI architecture for CUPS*

The high-speed LI solution on CUPS user plane has the following steps:

- LI traffic of intercepted subscribers is handled by the user plane.

- The user plane duplicates the intercepted subscriber's packets and adds X3 headers.

- These intercepted packets are sent on the various TCP connections toward the LI mediation server.

- There are multiple TCP connections toward a given LI mediation server from a user plane.

- The flows for a single high-speed UE are sent over multiple TCP connections.

- A single quintuple flow of high-speed UE is always sent in a single TCP connection, thus avoiding any ordering/ re-assembly issues.

In the earlier sections, we have gone over the details of NSA design and the various aspects of deployment. In the upcoming chapters, we go into further detail about 5G SA key concepts, details about MEC, testing strategies, and more.

CHAPTER 4

5G SA Packet Core Design and Deployment Strategies

In this chapter, as a part of the introduction, we will discuss the various components of the 5G core network and compare them with their 4G equivalent components.

The highlight of the chapter is to introduce the reader to the various design challenges and the design/deployment considerations that are required for deploying an effective 5G standalone (SA) network

To conclude, we will discuss the redundancy options within a 5G SA network.

5G Core Network Introduction

The network function architecture of 5G systems based on 3GPP specifications is shown in Figure 4-1.

R. S. Shetty, *5G Mobile Core Network*, https://doi.org/10.1007/978-1-4842-6473-7_4

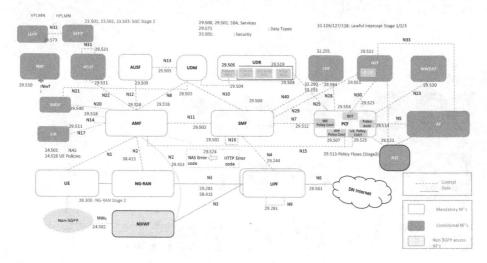

Figure 4-1. *5G SA core network architecture with 3GPP specification references and mandatory NFs marking*

Introduction to various network functions and their key functionalities are discussed in detail in the section "Overview of the Network Functions" in the Chapter 1.

As shown in the 5G SA core network architecture in Figure 4-1, there are a few network functions (NFs) that are mandatory for any 5G deployment, and some of the network functions can be optional/conditional.

The NFs that are mandatory/bare minimal for any 5G core network deployment are:

- next generation radio access network (NG-RAN)

- access and mobility mManagement function (AMF)

- session management function (SMF)

- user plane function (UPF)

- authentication server function (AUSF)

- unified data management (UDM)

- unified data repository (UDR)

- policy control function (PCF)

The bare minimal setup with the network functions mentioned here can be used for a small-scale demonstration of 5G functioning or to demonstrate some proof-of-concept (PoC) setup.

Consider that for any commercial deployment there will be additional complexity to the network with the introduction of the following:

- network slicing

- implementation of different 5G use-cases (refer to Chapter 1 for use case details)

- redundancy and esiliency

- capacity planning

- roaming and handover scenarios

- interworking with other 3GPP networks

- monitoring and debugging requirements

The network architecture will change accordingly, and the scale and interactions between the NFs will also change depending on these factors.

In the further sections of this chapter, we will discuss some of the key design considerations while designing a 5G SA core network and some of the best practices around the same.

Before discussing the various design considerations, it is important to have a comparison between the network functions in 5G core vs the 4G core network elements.

Table 4-1 tries to describe the different nodes that are a part of 5G core network, their description, and an equivalent/similar network element in 4G network.

Table 4-1. *Mapping of 5G Network Elements with the 4G Core Network Elements*

Node	Description	Similar function in EPC
AMF	access management function	MME
SMF	session management function	SGW, PGW-C
UPF	user plane function	PGW-U
PCF	policy control function	PCRF
NRF	NF repository function	partly DNS
	discovery of network functions	
	communication with network functions	
NEF	network exposure function	SCEF
NSSF	network slice selection function	n/a
AF	application function	e.g., IMS
AUSF	authentication server function	AAA, Radius
UDM	unified data management	HSS/HLR
N3 Interwork	in order to enable WiFi calling with 5G core	ePDG

Figure 4-2 shows the comparison between the core network components in 4G vs the core network components in 5G.

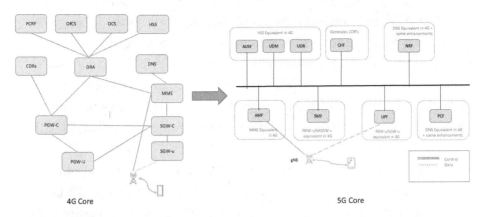

Figure 4-2. *4G core network component mapping to 5G core network components*

Design Considerations for a 5G Core Network Deployment

There are many aspects that have an impact on the design of a 5G core network.

Some of the key considerations/design aspects are listed here.

- Devices

- 5G SA slicing considerations

- Node selection

- Interworking with 4G/5G NSA

- Redundancy considerations

Devices

Device capability and planning the 5G network around the device is a very important design consideration that the operators will need to have, especially during their early phases of 5G deployment.

Many of the 5G devices are capable to support the sub-6GHz spectrum but cannot support the mmWave frequencies. This needs to be kept in mind, especially with the radio network and network slice planning.

UE capability to support voiceover new radio (VoNR) is another important factor that will act as a key input toward planning the voice support for the 5G SA core (i.e., IMS or emergency call support) for UEs in 5G network.

Typically, in the early stages of 5G SA deployments, all UEs will perform evolved packet system (EPS) fallback to a 4G network for any IMS (voice) or emergency-related services. EPS fallback procedure will be discussed in detail in the **5GSA-EPC/NSA interworking** section of this chapter.

In the early stages of deployment for many operators, there will be a combination of 4G, 5G NSA, and 5G SA networks all co-existing and with a significant amount of coverage overlaps.

It becomes extremely important for the operators to have proper planning as far as devices, and their provisioning is considered to ensure that the end-users (UEs) are mapped according to their capabilities and provisioning on the network.

Figure 4-3 provides a very high-level mapping for different UEs with different UE capabilities and subscriptions and how they should be considered in the network design.

Some operators might consider upgrading (firmware) the NSA UEs to SA UEs and have a uniform provisioning wherein the SA users are able to access the NSA-specific nodes and vice versa.

Figure 4-3 shows the logic that should reside on MME for allowing/ blocking a subscriber based on the UE capabilities and the HSS subscription.

| | | UDM / HSS subscription | | |
		5G SA	5G NSA	4G
UE Capability	5G SA capable	• [5GC UPF] Allowed and preferred • [EPC UPF] Allowed (but not preferred) • [NSA UPF] Block	• [5GC UPF] Blocked • [EPC UPF] Allow (but not preferred) • [NSA UPF] Allowed and preferred	• 5GC UPF] Blocked • [EPC UPF] Allowed and preferred • [NSA UPF] Blocked
		• 5GC PGW-c] Allowed and preferred • [EPC PGW-c] Allowed (but not preferred) • [NSA PGW-c] Blocked	• 5GC PGW-c] Blocked • [EPC PGW-c] Allowed (but not preferred) • [NSA PGW-c] Allowed and preferred	• 5GC PGW-c] Blocked • [EPC PGW-c] Allowed and preferred • [NSA PGW-c] Blocked
	5G NSA capable	• [5GC UPF] Allowed but not preferred • [EPC UPF] Allowed and preferred • [NSA UPF] Blocked	• [5GC UPF] Blocked • [EPC UPF] Allowed (but not preferred) • [NSA UPF] Allowed and preferred	• [5GC UPF] Blocked • [EPC UPF] Allowed and preferred • [NSA UPF] Blocked
		• 5GC PGW-c] Allowed but not preferred • [EPC PGW-c] Allowed and preferred • [NSA PGW-c] Blocked	• 5GC PGW-c] Blocked • [EPC PGW-c] Allowed (but not preferred) • [NSA PGW-c] Allowed and preferred	• 5GC PGW-c] Blocked • [EPC PGW-c] Allowed and preferred • [NSA PGW-c] Blocked
	4G	• [5GC UPF] Allowed but not preferred • [EPC UPF] Allowed and preferred • [NSA UPF] Blocked	• [5GC UPF] Blocked • [EPC UPF] Allowed and preferred • [NSA UPF] Allowed but not preferred	• [5GC UPF] Blocked • [EPC UPF] Allowed and preferred • [NSA UPF] Blocked
		• 5GC PGW-c] Allowed but not preferred • [EPC PGW-c] Allowed and preferred • [NSA PGW-c] Blocked	• 5GC PGW-c] Blocked • [EPC PGW-c] Allowed and preferred • [NSA PGW-c] Allowed but not preferred	• 5GC PGW-c] Blocked • [EPC PGW-c] Allowed and preferred • [NSA PGW-c] Blocked

Assumptions: 1) All UE's are 4G capable   2) 5G SA subscription and 5G NSA subscription are independent
3) 4G subscription is a default fallback subscription

Figure 4-3. *UE capability vs subscription mapping for a network with 4G, 5G NSA, and 5G SA setups*

As shown Figure 4-3, not just the UE capability but also the user subscription is considered for network node selection for a particular subscriber.

In this example:

– The 4G subscribers are not allowed to use the nodes that are specifically reserved for 5G SA or 5G NSA (PGW control plane [PGW-C] and UPF).

– Use of 4G nodes are allowed for all the UEs; however, it is not preferred for use by the 5G SA and 5G NSA users with corresponding subscriptions.

- 5G NSA users are not allowed to use the nodes reserved for 5G SA.

- 5G SA users are allowed to use the 5G NSA-specific nodes but are not preferred.

These classification and design considerations are important because with the introduction of 5G SA, there are newer elements in the 4G core introduced (i.e, SMF+PGW-C and UPF + PGW user plane [PGW-U]) that can technically cater to 4G, 5G NSA, and 5G SA. The traffic offloading between these nodes should be based on load, capability, and subscription as a best practice.

Also considering there are high chances of UEs moving between the RATs of 4G and 5G, it is important to plan for session continuity for such UEs.

Session continuity without the loss of quality of experience (QoE) for UEs will require the UEs to be mapped to the right nodes in 4G domain, keeping their 5G capabilities into consideration.

We will discuss more about session continuity in the *5G SA-EPC/NSA Interworking* section of this chapter.

5G SA Slicing Considerations

5G network slicing enables operators to configure virtual network instances and stitch them together, instantiated automatically and optimized to meet specific functional requirements of a subscriber or application. Network slicing requires optimal deployment of user requirements and network functions and resource exclusivity on end-to-end 5G infrastructures to provide desired quality of service.

In order to instantiate and design a network slice it is important to bring together the business requirements, network resource availability, user equipment subscription, and operator policies.

Network slicing can be achieved in various ways, depending on 5G network functions such as network slice selection function (NSSF), user equipment route selection policy (URSP), slice or service type (SST), and slice differentiator (SD), which need to be carefully planned to achieve desired outcome.

Single-Network Slice Selection Assistance Information

To uniquely identify a network slice, 5G defines a single-network slice selection assistance information (S-NSSAI) comprised of:

- SST: This will define the expected behavior of the network slice in terms of specific features and services. Standardized SST values include enhanced Mobile Broadband (eMBB), ultra-reliable low-latency communication (URLLC), and massive internet of things (MIoT).

- SD: This is optional information that complements the SST and is used as an additional differentiator if multiple network slices carry the same SST value.

Figure 4-4 shows the composition of S-NSSAI.

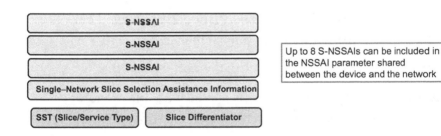

Figure 4-4. *S-NSSAI composition*

Here are some of the common terms used w.r.t NSSAI while design/ deployment of use-cases are:

- Configured NSSAI (configured on the UE SIM): NSSAI provisioned to the UE applicable to one or more public land mobile networks (PLMNs; max 16 stored in UE). Default configured NSSAI is provisioned by home PLMN (HPLMN).

- Requested NSSAI: NSSAI provided by the UE to the serving PLMN during registration

- Allowed NSSAI: NSSAI provided by the serving PLMN during a registration procedure, indicating the S-NSSAI values the UE could use in the serving PLMN for the current registration area (max 8 stored in UE).

- Subscribed S-NSSAI: Configured in unified data management (UDM). S-NSSAI based on subscriber information, which a UE is subscribed to use in a PLMN (one or more are marked as a "default" S-NSSAI[s]).

- Supported S-NSSAI: S-NSSAI configured by operations, administration, and maintenance (OAM) in radio access network (RAN) or received in the next generation (NG) setup response message from access and mobility management functions (AMFs). (This is a concept in RAN.)

- Home S-NSSAI: S-NSSAI value of the home network

A network slice instance can be asssociated with one or more S-NSSAI's and also one s-NNSAI can be associated with one or more network slice instances.

NSI-ID

This is used when slices are configured with the same slice ID.

The NSI-ID is also called a sub-slice ID.

The NSI-ID is returned by the NSSF for the AMF to query from the NF repository function (NRF) to select the specific session management function (SMF).

The NSSF returning the specific NSI-ID for a particular slice ID is implementation-dependent (perhaps based on load).

Table 4-2 provides the 3GPP definition of NSI-ID with the attributes.

Table 4-2.

Table 6.1.6.2.7-1: Definition of type NsiInformation

Attribute name	Data type	P	Cardinality	Description
nrfId	Uri	M	1	This IE shall contain the API URI of the NRF to be used to select the NFs/services within the selected Network Slice instance.
nsiId	NsiId	O	0..1	This IE may be optionally included by the NSSF. When present, this IE shall contain the Identifier of the selected Network Slice instance

NSSF's Role in Network Slice Selection

Although NSSF is not a mandatory network function for 5G SA deployments, there are two main use-cases where NSSF plays a very important role.

1. When AMF cannot serve all the requested slice IDs

2. When there are two slices with the same Slice IDs

Scenario 1: When AMF cannot serve all the requested slice IDs

Figure 4-5 shows a deployment where there are two different slices with slice IDs 1 and 2. The core network slice design is such that not only are SMF and user plane function (UPF) components for these two slices different but also AMF and NRF components are different for both these slices.

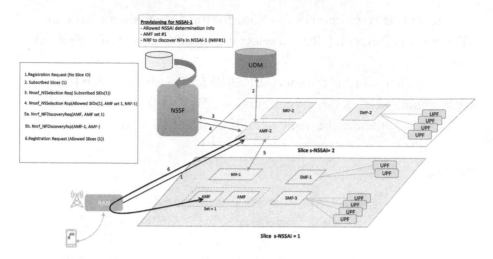

Figure 4-5. *Multiple AMFs serving different slices*

Note   Not all NFs are shown in Figure 4-5, and only impacted NFs are shown.

AMF-2 is configured as the default AMF for the gNB serving the cell where the UE tries to register itself.

In such a deployment scenario, consider a UE registration case.

1) Typically, as a part of registration procedure, UEs send an initial UE message toward the gNB with the below parameters.

   – Requested NSSAI

   – Tracking area identity (TAI)

   – PLMN-ID

   Within the gNB, there is a mapping between the requested NSSAI vs the connected AMFs that support the NSSAI.

In this case, UE sends an initial UE message to the gNB with either no slice information (i.e., no requested NSSAI) or the UE sends an initial UE message to the gNB with a NSSAI that is unknown to the gNB (i.e., there is no mapping in the gNB for the requested NSSAI vs connected AMFs).

Upon receiving such an initial UE message, the gNB is configured to send the registration request message to the default AMF (AMF-2, configured in the gNB).

2) Upon receiving such a registration request message, the AMF-2 queries the UDM to fetch the subscripiton details for the UE.

One of the subscription details for the UE is the subscribed NSSAI for the UE with the default NSSAI. In this example, the UE is subscribed to slice ID =1.

3) Once the AMF receives the subscription details for the UE, if the UE is subscribed to NSSAI, that is not served by the AMF. It sends an Nnssf_NSSelection Req to the NSSF to get the details of the AMF to which the registration request message should be forwarded. This is represented by the message "Nnssf_NSSelection Req (Subscribed SIDs{1})" in the aforementioned example.

4) The NSSF typically has the data corresponding to the UE and the AMF and NRF details that should serve the UE. NSSF sends these data in the response to AMF as Nnssf_NSSelection Rsp (Allowed SIDs{1}, AMF set 1, NRF-1) in the aforementioned example.

5) With these details received from the NSSF, the AMF-2
   now sends a Nnrf_NFDiscoveryReq to the NRF that
   was specified in the Nnssf_NSSelection Rsp by the
   NSSF. This is represented below.

   The step 5a wherein AMF-2 sends Nnrf_
   NFDiscoveryReq(AMF, AMF set1)to NRF-1 in the
   above example.

   In reponse the NRF-1 sends the Nnrf_NFDiscoveryRsp
   message back to the AMF-2 with the details for the AMF
   requested in the Nnrf_NFDiscoveryReq message. This is
   represented by Step5b in the earlier example where the
   NRF-1 provides Nnrf_NFDiscoveryRsp(AMF-1, AMF-3).

6) With the details received from the NRF-1, the AMF-2
   decides to directly reroute to target AMF or the reroute
   via NG-RAN message based on its possibility to reroute
   the NAS message to the target AMF.

If the infrastructure allows the AMF to reroute the NAS message to the
target AMF directly, then the AMF goes ahead and does that. If not, then
it reroutes the NAS message via NG-RAN wherein it will include the target
AMF address.

This is represented by step 6 in the earlier example, where the AMF
sends the registration request {Allowed Slices(1)}.

Scenario 2: When there are two slices with the same slice IDs

Figure 4-6 is an example where there are three different slices wherein
the core network slice design considers two of the slices with the same
NSSAI IDs (i.e., NSSAI=2) but different sub-NSI IDs (i.e., NSI=1 and
NSI=2).

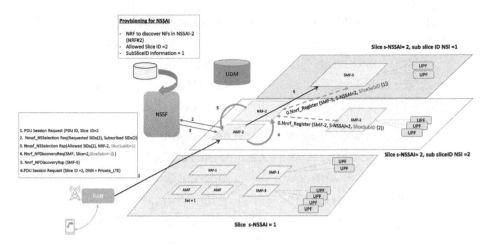

Figure 4-6. *Multiple slices with same slice IDs*

Note   Not all NFs are shown in Figure 4-6, and only impacted NFs are shown.

For slices with different NSSAI values, the AMF and the NRF components are exclusive, and for slices with the same NSSAI IDs the NRF and AMF components are common; however, the SMF and the UPFs are different for all the slices.

In such a deployment scenario, consider a PDU session establishment case.

1) The earlier scenario assumes that the registration procedure for the UE is completed with the AMF and other NFs corresponding to the slice with slice ID NSSAI=2.

   When the gNB sends the PDU session establishment request message to the AMF corresponding to the SliceID2, the PDU session establishment request message consists of TAI, PLMN-ID, and NSSAI parameters; in this example, the NSSAI value is 2.

2) When the AMF receives the PDU session establishment request with NSSAI=2, it is configured to contact the NSSF and sends Nnssf_NSSelection request message to the NSSF with the requested slice ID and the subscribed slice ID for the UE. It is represented by step 2.

3) NSSF is preconfigured by the provisioning tool such that it sends a response back to the AMF with the details of the NRF to discover NFs in the requested NSSAI, allowed slice IDs, and sub-slice ID information. This is represented by step 3 in Figure 4-6 where the NSSF sends back Nnssf_NSSelection Rsp (Allowed SIDs{2}, NRF-2, SliceSubID=1) in response to the AMF.

4) With these details received from the NSSF, the AMF now sends a Nnrf_NFDiscoveryReq to the NRF-2. In the earlier example, this is represented by step 4, wherein AMF sends Nnrf_NFDiscoveryReq(SMF, Slice=2,SliceSubId=1) to NRF-2.

5) In response the NRF-2 sends the Nnrf_NFDiscoveryRsp message back to the AMF with the details for the SMF to which the AMF should send the PDU session establishment request message. This is represented by step 5 in the earlier example, where the NRF provides Nnrf_NFDiscoveryRsp (SMF-5).

6) The AMF forwards the PDU session establishment request from the UE to SMF-5. SMF further processes the message and allocates appropriate UPF resources for the UE. This is represented by step 6 in the earlier example.

Apart from the use-case and the application-specific slicing explained in Chapter 1, there are some more aspects that need to be considered while designing a slice. They are mentioned here.

Dimensioning

It is important to understand how many users in the network will be using a particular slice on average as well as during peak and the number of network components needed to design a slice.

Some of the slices based on the applications they cater to can be user plane-heavy (e.g., eMBB slice). In such cases, it is required to consider more UPFs while designing the slice and relatively fewer SMFs/AMFs.

Some other slices catering to applications like IoT may require more signaling capacity and less user plane capacity. In such cases there will be dedicated signaling components like AMFs for these slices and they need to be dimensioned based on the TPS.

Network Functions Planning per Slice

By definition, the minimum exclusive network function that can define a slice is UPF; however, in most of the deployments, SMFs and UPFs are a part of a slice.

While designing the slices, it is also important to keep in mind the type of slices that are being planned.

For example, even if the introduction of a new slice does not impact the capacity of some of the elements like charging function (CHF), UDM, policy control function (PCF), and so on, some slices like mobile virtual network operator (MVNO) slices prefer to have their own NFs within their slice to ensure segregation of traffic and also better control over the different components of the slice.

Some other slices might want to have only some network functions as CHF and PCF within their slice to maintain policy and charging for users accessing their slice but would prefer to have a common UDM, authentication server function (AUSF), AMF, and so on.

Figure 4-7 provides an example of a typical deployment with three slices, where the first slice is a default slice and the other two slices correspond to private LTE use-case and MVNO use-cases.

In the private LTE slice, the slice-specific components as listed are SMF, UPFs, NRF, PCF, and CHF. The components within the slice will register themselves with the NRF dedicated to the slice. The rest of the components are shared with the default slice life (e.g., AMF, UDM, UDR, AUSF).

For the MVNO slice, Figure 4-7 shows that all the components are exclusive and no components (except NSSF) are shared with the default slice.

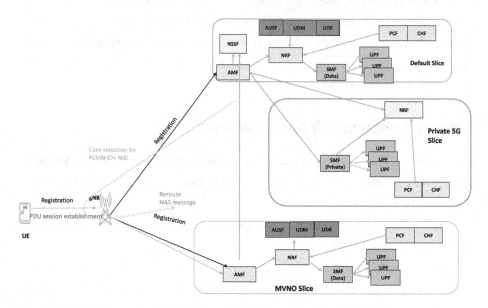

Figure 4-7. *Example deployment for three slices with different NF layout*

Slice Orchestration and Lifespan

It is also important to consider lifespan of a slice.

Not all slices are permanent and not all components within the slice are fixed. Some of the slices—especially enterprise slices—can vary often, and design should take into consideration such dynamics to ensure that the creation/deletion of slice does not impact the users in another slice.

Node Selection

One of the key considerations/topics when it comes to designing the 5G SA core network is the node selection criteria.

Because 5G SA flows a service-based architecture (SBA) and most of the interfaces between the network functions are service-based interfaces (SBIs), it is possible for any network function to interact with any other network function theoretically.

Since the number of NFs in a 5G core network are higher in number when compared to 4G, and since there are additional NFs such as service communication proxy (SCP), NRF, security edge protection proxy (SEPP), and so on, it is important to design the flow of communication between the NFs in a manner that is optimal and secure.

The next section will discuss a few key nodes and their selection criteria depending on the deployment/design of the 5G SA core network.

AMF Selection by 5G Access Node (gNB)

The AMF selection functionality should be supported by the gNB.

AMF selection is defined in clause 6.3.5 AMF discovery and selection of 3gPP specification TS 23.501.

Typically a gNB will be connected to multiple AMFs via the N2 interface, and based on the incoming request from a UE an appropriate AMF node is selected for procedures like registration, PDU session establishment, and so on.

In simpler 5G core network deployment—especially during the initial phases of 5G enrollment—AMFs are common for all the slices and can serve all the slices. The gNB selection criteria for choosing the right AMF for a UE request becomes simpler, as all AMFs should be able to handle the request from the UE and there is no need for the AMF to forward/redirect the requested message to another AMF.

However, with complex deployment with multiple slices and different AMFs serving different slices, the AMF selection criteria on the gNB becomes a little more complicated.

On the gNB side there will be a need to have a mapping for the requested slice by the UE vs the AMFs that can support the requested slices. There also needs to be a configuration of a default AMF, which the gNB will choose when the UE sends a request to the gNB with an unknown slice ID or no slice ID.

Similarly, on the AMF side, the AMF will need to check the slice ID in the requested message and determine if it can serve the slice or will need to forward the request to another AMF that is a more suitable node.

The gNB selects an AMF set and a candidate AMF from the AMF set under the following circumstances:

- when the UE provides neither the 5G-S-TMSI nor the globally unique AMF ID (GUAMI) to the gNB

- when the UE provides 5G-S-TMSI or GUAMI but the routing information (i.e., AMF identified based on AMF set ID, AMF pointer) present in the 5G-S-TMSI or GUAMI is not sufficient and/or not usable (e.g., UE provides GUAMI with an AMF region ID from a different region)

- when AMF has notified the gNB that it is unavailable (identi- fied by GUAMI[s]) and no target AMF is identified

- when gNB has detected that the AMF has failed

- when AMF region ID and AMF set ID are derived from GUAMI

- when the requested NSSAI is from the UE

- for lcal operator policies

- for load balancing across candidate AMF(s) (e.g., considering weight factors of candidate AMFs in the AMF set)

When the UE accesses the gNB with a 5G-S-TMSI or GUAMI that identifies more than one AMF (as configured during N2 set-up procedure), the gNB selects the AMF considering the weight factors or priority (if configured).

When 5G-S-TMSI or GUAMI provided by the UE to the gNB contains an AMF set ID that is usable, and the AMF is identified by AMF pointer that is not usable (e.g., AN detects that the AMF has failed) or the corresponding AMF indicates it is unavailable to the gNB, then the gNB uses the AMF set ID for selecting another AMF from the AMF set considering the aforementioned factors.

Note   Typically the UE selects the RAN based on PLMN selection and access network selection.

AMF Selection by Another AMF to Forward Requests from gNB

Typically, the AMF can query the NRF to discover the AMF instance(s) to forward the request. However, for complex deployments, there is a good possibility that the NRF may not have the details of the target AMF, as it is registered against another NRF in the network.

In such cases, the AMF will need to query the NSSF to first determine the NRF details to which the NFDiscovery-request can be sent from the AMF. Then based on the response from the NRF, the request can be forwarded to the target AMF.

To discover the target AMF instance(s),the source AMF can use the below parameters:

- AMF set ID

- AMF region ID

- target location information

- S-NSSAI(s) of allowed NSSAI

The AMF selection function in the AMF selects an AMF instance as described here:

- Use GUAMI, TAI to discover the AMF instance(s).

- NRF provides the NF profile of the associated AMF instance(s).

- If the associated AMF is unavailable due to AMF planned removal, the NF profile of the backup AMF used for planned removal can be provided by the NRF.

- If the associated AMF is unavailable due to AMF failure, then the NF profile of the backup AMF used for failure can be provided by the NRF.

- If no AMF instances related to the indicated GUAMI can be found or AMF pointer value used by more than one AMF is found, a list of NF profiles of candidate AMF instances in the same AMF set is provided by the NRF.

- The NF profile may contain priority TAI(s) and other relevant information.

NRF Selection

For a simpler deployment, a NRF will cater to all the slices and will have all the NFs registered with it.

However, for complex deployment scenarios, AMF will need to determine the right NRF depending on the slice ID requested by the UE and send a NFDiscovery request.

For a case with multiple slices, the NSSF can provide the NRF details to the AMF.

Figure 4-8 shows a generic flow for discovery requests between any network function and the NRF.

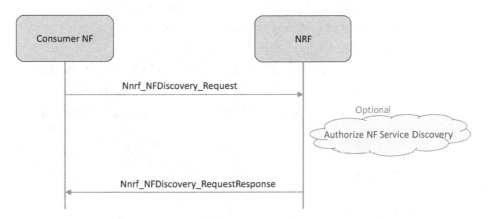

Figure 4-8. *Call flow for NFDiscovery*

AUSF/UDM Selection by AMF

The AMF/UDM discovers the AUSF from the NRF by sending Nnrf_ NFDiscovery_Request and includes the UE's routing indicator as per 6.3.4 section of Spec 23.501 AUSF discovery and selection.

Routing indicator is included in subscription concealed identifier (SUCI)/subscription permanent identifier (SUPI) to route signaling to specific AUSF/UDM.

AMF with the help of NRF needs to route traffic with routing indicator to the same AUSF/UDM.

SMF Selection by AMF

If the AMF is serving all the slices and there is a common NRF within the 5G network to which all the network functions (i.e., SMFs) from all the slices are registered toward, then the SMF selection procedure in AMF can be very simple.

189

The AMF can refer to the NSSAI received by the gNB and can internally have a mapping of SMF that can cater to the corresponding NSSAI.

With the SMF information, the AMF can either send the request directly to the SMF or get the SMF details from the NRF via NFDiscovery procedure and send the request toward the SMF.

For deployment with multiple slices and multiple NRFs within the network, the SMF selection by the AMF cannot be local to the AMF.

Figure 4-9 shows the flow for the SMF selection for such a scenerio.

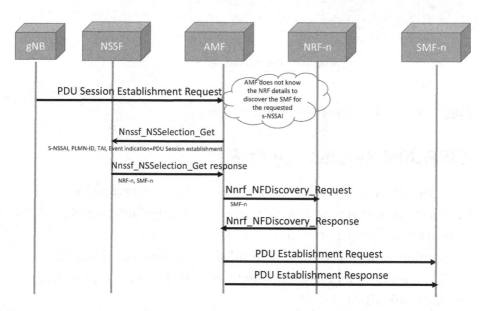

Figure 4-9. *PDU session establishment with network slice selection*

As shown in Figure 4-9, the AMF receives a request from the gNB (e.g., PDU session establishment request with s-NSSAI).

If the AMF does not know the NRF details that need to be contacted for the particular s-NSSAI received, it sends a Nnssf_NSSelection_GET message to get the NRF and SMF details to which it can forward the PDU establishment request message.

From the response received from NSSF, the AMF is now able to contact the right NRF (in this case, NRF-n) to perform an NFDiscovery request procedure to get the details for SMF-n.

SMF Selection by MME

Initial attachment over LTE or 5G to LTE iRAT scenarios require the MME to discover and select the S5-C IP address on the appropriate SMF.

The MME will use the mechanism defined in 3GPP TS 29.303 for DeCOR to determine the IP address of the SMF S5-C interface based on the UE usage type (see section 5.12.1.2 "Selecting a Node Supporting a Particular Network Capability Within a Dedicated Core Network").

As defined in RFC 3958, the MME will send a query to the DNS using the APN as the domain name. The DNS server will respond with a list of all NAPTR, SRV record, and RR records that are related to this APN, which may include different records for a service depending on the UE usage type. Following is an example for such a DNS configuration, providing a different record for the UE usage types 1 and 2:

```
web.apn IN NAPTR 100 100 "s" "x-3gpp-pgw:x-s5-gtp:x-s8-gtp" ""
nodes._pgw
web.apn IN NAPTR 100 100 "s" "x-3gpp-pgw:x-s5-gtp+ue-1.2:x-s8-
gtp+ue-1.2" "" _nodes._smf
```

The DNS will then respond to a query for the "net.apn" with multiple NAPTR records for this APN query (plus the corresponding SRV and A/AAAA records), as shown here from a sample output:

```
Answer            :
  Name            : net.apn.epc.mnc111.mcc123.3gppnetwork.org.
  TTL             : 300
  Class           : IN
  Data Length     : 97
  Type            : NAPTR
```

```
Order             : 100
Preference        : 100
Flags             : s
Service           : x-3gpp-pgw:x-s5-gtp+ue-1.2:x-s8-gtp+ue-1.2
Regexp            :
Replacement       : _nodes._smf.epc.mnc111.mcc123.
                    3gppnetwork.org.

Name              : net.apn.epc.mnc456.mcc123.3gppnetwork.org.
TTL               : 300
Class             : IN
Data Length       : 83
Type              : NAPTR
Order             : 100
Preference        : 100
Flags             : s
Service           : x-3gpp-pgw:x-s5-gtp:x-s8-gtp
Regexp            :
Replacement       : _nodes._pgw.epc.mnc111.mcc123.
                    3gppnetwork.org.
```

The MME will now parse all the received NAPTR records and select the resulting IP addresses based on the service and the UE usage type that it retrieved from the home subscriber server (HSS), and in the aforementioned example would choose the SMF for usage type 1 and 2 and the PGW for all other values.

PCF Selection by AMF

AMF communicates with the PCF to derive the AM policies and the UE policies for the UE.

It performs this action through the following principles:

- For simpler deployments, PCF information is configured locally in the AMF.

- For deployments with slices, AMF uses the NRF to discover the candidate PCF instance(s) for a UE. AMF selects a PCF instance based on available PCF instances obtained from the NRF.

As a backup, there can always be a local configuration on the AMF so that the AMF can fall back to the configured PCF when:

- there is no answer from the NRF, or

- candidate PCFs are not available.

PCF and CHF Selection by the SMF

The SMF communicates with the PCF to derive the SM policies for a session from the UE.

Typically for a simpler deployment, the PCF information is configured locally in the SMF.

However, for a complex deployment with multiple slices, the SMF will need perfrom a NFDiscovery procedure with NRF to determine the PCF details that can be contacted by the SMF.

As a backup, there can always be a local configuration on the SMF so that the SMF can fall back to the configured PCF when:

- there is no answer from the NRF, or

- candidate PCFs are not available.

As a part of network optimization to avoid multiple queries to UDM from different PCFs to fetch the policies for a particular UE/session, it is possible to ensure that the AM-PCF, UE-PCF, and SM-PCF can be forced to be the same.

If UE registers in 5GS, the AMF can use the same PCF for AM-PCF and UE-PCF. After selecting AM-PCF/UE-PCF, the AMF can signal this selected AM-PCF in PDU session setup signaling to the SMF. By doing so, the NRF lookup for SM-PCF may be avoided.

When the UE is in EPS, there is no AMF, and SMF (+PGW-C) chooses the SM-PCF instance.

Later when the UE moves to NR/5GS, AMF would independently select AM-PCF/UE-PCF, and SMF would stay with the SM-PCF chosen when the UE was in EPS.

The SMF performs CHF selection by determining the CHF address during PDU session establishment.

- Typically the PCF shall provide one or more CHF addresses as part of the PCC rule.

- CHF selection can also be based on NRF discovery for an SMF.

- UDM-provided charging characteristics can be used for CHF selection by the SMF.

- For simpler deployments, local configuration of CHF on the SMF can also be used for CHF selection by SMF, or the local configuration can be used as a fallback by the SMF in case any of the aforementioned CHF selection procedures fail.

UPF Selection by SMF

UPF selection is one of the key aspects of the core network design.

In 5G, considering the fact that there can be central as well as edge data centers, UPF selection can be based on many factors, such as:

- The location of the end-user (i.e., the AMF) may send the UE location to the SMF, along with the notification, for UPF selection.

- Application used by the user (if the application is cached on the edge or central data center

- 5QI for the PDU session

- Capacity on the edge vs center, etc.

If the UPF is co-located with the SMF, then the SMF shall select the UPF based some vendor proprietary algorithm (e.g., round-robin).

When the UPF is in a regional data center (RDC) near the UE and the DNN allows for remote UPF selection, the UPF selection mechanism will be different.

Table 4-3 descibes some of the parameters that can be considered by the SMF for UPF selection.

Table 4-3. *UPF Selection Criteria*

Use Cases	Description
Load Control	UPF's dynamic load.
	UPF's relative static capacity among UPFs supporting the same DNN.
Node Location	UPF location available at the SMF.
User Location	UE location information.
FFS	An appropriate UPF can be selected by matching the functionality /features required for the UE.
Basic	Data Network Name (DNN).
Basic	PDU Session Type (i.e. IPv4, IPv6, IPv4v6, Ethernet Type or Unstructured Type) and if applicable, the static IP address/prefix.
SSC	SSC mode selected for the PDU Session.
FFS	UE subscription profile in UDM.
MEC/LADN	DNAI as included in the PCC Rules
Option	Local operator policies.
Slice	S-NSSAI.
Basic	Access technology being used by the UE.
	Information related to user plane topology and user plane terminations, that may be deduced from: AN-provided identities (e.g. CellID, TAI), available UPF(s) and DNAI(s);
	Information regarding the user plane interfaces of UPF(s). This information may be acquired by the SMF using N4;
	Information regarding the N3 User Plane termination(s) of the AN serving the UE. This may be deduced from AN-provided identities (e.g. CellID, TAI);
ULCL	Information regarding the N9 User Plane termination(s) of UPF(s) if needed;
MEC/LADN	Information regarding the User plane termination(s) corresponding to DNAI(s).

One of the methods to select a remote UPF is that the SMF assigns a virtual APN to the PDU so a different UPF group can be allocated to the PDU.

5G core solution can support multiple UPFs to cover different services as explained in the Chapter 3. In such cases, dynamic UPF (i.e., single UPF or multiple I-UPF) along with A-UPF selection logic is required. Selection logic can be done internally by SMF or using the discovery function from NRF.

As a part of the session management procedure, there are cases wherein a PDU session can use single or multiple UPFs for an SMF.

Figure 4-10 shows different cases/combinations of UPF selection where there are one or multiple UPFs between the gNB and the DN.

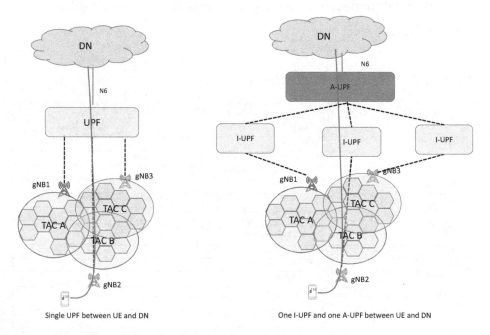

Figure 4-10.   Different combinations for UPF selections

Note   The details of UPF selection are described in clause 6.3.3 of TS 23.501. The number of UPFs supported for a PDU session is unrestricted.

UPF Selection Logic for UE Mobility

During mobility, there is a high chance of discontinuity between the A-UPF and I-UPF.

3GPP standards allows three modes of session and service continuity (SSC) as shown here.

1) SSC Mode1

In SSC mode 1, the UE continues to use the initially allocated A-UPF by the SMF during the PDU session establishment procedure.

Here the IP address allocated by the UE is retained even when the UE has mobility outside the area where the UPF can serve.

The diagrams in Figure 4-11 show the UPF selection logic in SSC mode 1.

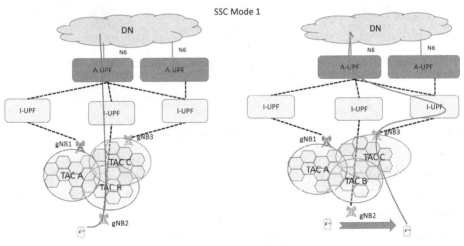

I-UPF changes due to mobility of the UE but the A-UPF does not change

Figure 4-11. *UPF selection logic in SSC mode 1*

2) SSC Mode2

In SSC mode 2, the UE will be forced to perform A-UPF reselection as it moves from one coverage area to another both of which are served by two different sets of UPFs.

Here the IP address allocated by the UE during the PDU session establishment cannot be retained, and there will be an impact on the session continuity as the UE will be prompted to perform a session reconnect that can result in a service disruption of up to 300 ms.

The diagram in Figure 4-12 shows the UPF selection logic in SSC mode 2.

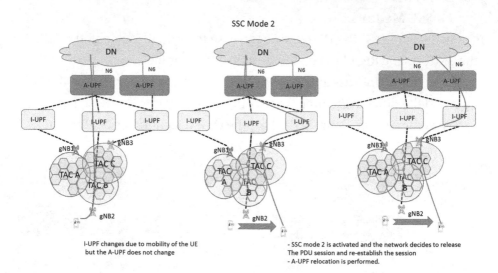

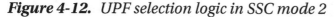

Figure 4-12. UPF selection logic in SSC mode 2

3) SSC Mode3

This mode is similar to the SSC mode 2 except that the UE is capable of dual registration; therefore, the UE session re-establishment happens with the new A-UPF before releasing the old PDU session.

SSC mode 3 with a multi-homed scenario is also possible.

The diagram in Figure 4-13 shows the UPF selection logic in SSC mode 3 with multiple PDU session mode 3.

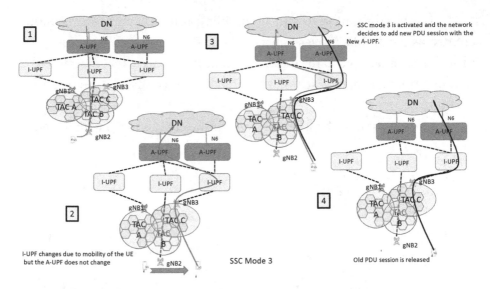

Figure 4-13. *UPF selection logic in SSC mode 3 with multiple PDU sessions*

Interworking with 4G/5G NSA

Interworking procedures between EPS and the 5G core network ensures that an end-user can have a seamless transition between 4G and 5G network by preserving its IP address, thereby avoiding any interruption to applications.

3GPP has defined two options for interworking between 5G core network and EPS:

- – N26-based interworking

- – Interworking without N26

N26-Based Interworking

In N26-based interworking, there is a signaling interface between AMF and MME, which is called the N26 interface.

This interface is used to transfer mobile's authentication and session context as the mobile moves between the two systems. This scheme provides seamless (<300 ms interruption time) mobility to a mobile's IP session and thus enables seamless mobility to voice sessions between 4G and 5G.

Figure 4-14 shows the interworking between 4G and 5G with the N26 interface.

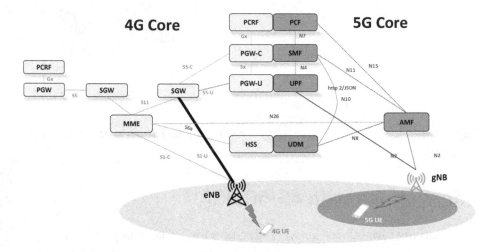

Figure 4-14. *N26-based interworking between 4G and 5G*

Some of the key integrations that have to be in place for N26-based interworking are listed here

- MME and AMF should be connected through the N26 i nterface, and one of the two (MME/AMF) performs the registration procedure with HSS + UDM and also maintains the context for the UE.

- The UDM and HSS should be able to interconnect with each other and exchange the subscription data for the UE when the UE moves between 4G and 5G.

- To ensure this, the PGW-C + SMF combo node should be able to maintain mapping between the PDN connection and PDU session-related parameters, including:

  - APN to DNN mapping

  - APN-AMBR to session AMBR mapping

  - QoS mapping in 4G to 5QI mapping in 5G

  - PDU session type mapping

- The PCRF and the PCF should be able to exchange UE-related policies between themselves to provide seamless mobility between the 4G and 5G networks.

- For seamless handover between the 4G and 5G networks, it is important to provide IP address continuity. To ensure this, it is important that the PGW-C + SMF node and the PGW-U + UPF node remain the same when the UE moves between 4G and 5G.

We will discuss various design options to ensure the right node selection in both 4G and 5G networks to ensure seamless mobility between the two technologies.

During the attach procedure in the 4G network, when the UE provides its capability indication for the 5G network, the MME stores the information.

With this the MME queries the HSS to get the subscription capabilities for the UE and selects a PGW-C + SMF combo node that can also serve the 5G network as SMF.

Similarly the SMF + PGW-C selects a UPF + PGW-U combo node.

The UE provides a 5G PDU Session ID (a parameter that is needed when UE will move to 5G) during the IP connection setup. During the IP connection setup, the SMF + PGW-C provides 5G QoS parameters to the UE for the UE to use when it moves over to 5G.

When the UE initiates handover by providing radio measurements to the eNB, based on the radio measurements the eNB knows that the target cell is a gNB and initiates an intersystem handover via the MME and the AMF. The UE's context is provided to the AMF via the N26 interface between the MME and the AMF.

The UE subsequently moves to the 5G cell and the UE's IP connection now is via the gNB and UPF + PGW-U. The PDU session ID and the 5G QoS parameters are used now for the UE's IP connection in 5G.

Interworking Without N26

As the name suggests, there is no N26 interface between the AMF and MME.

When the mobile moves between EPS and 5GS, it may need to be re-authenticated (as the new system does not have the security parameters of the UE).

For a mobile that is capable of only single registration, this could result in interruption time of around 800 ms to 3 seconds, as the mobile will need to perform a registration onto the 4G/5G network during mobility.

For UEs that are dual-registration-capable, they can simultaneously receive and transmit on the 4G and 5G networks. These mobiles can pre-register in the target system and get authenticated before it moves its data session to the target system, thus interruption time may be reduced to about 800 ms. However, dual receive/transmit mode has significant impact on the UE battery consumption and requires mobile to monitor for paging on both 4G and 5G radios at the same time.

To ensure session continuity, there will be some changes required on the HSS. UDM maintains the session in both MME and AMF until the time that the UE is able to successfully transfer the PDU session.

On the 5G network, the AMF indicates to the UE, during initial registration, that interworking without N26 is supported. A similar indication to the UE can be provided by the MME to indicate as well in the 4G network.

The dual-registration-capable UEs can use this indication to register to the 4G network as well as 5G network to minimize the service interruptions.

Dual registration UEs can selectively decide to move PDN connections and PDU sessions.

Figure 4-15 shows interworking between 4G and 5G without an N26 interface.

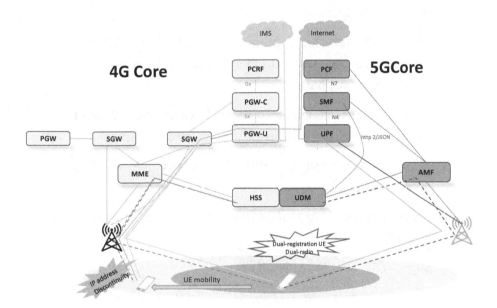

Figure 4-15. *N26-based interworking between 4G and 5G*

Impact Analysis on EPC due to N26 Interface

To support 4G/5G SA interworking, the following components of EPC are impacted.

MME

- N26 interface needs to be implemented.

- Handover parameters related to 5GC as well as RAT type of 5G needs to be supported by the MME.

- S11/S5: Determine 5GC interworking indication to SGW/ PGW based on N1 mode support, subscription data, and network configuration.

- S6a: Handle new subscription data "CN Type restriction," updated RAT type restriction for NR, per APN level 5GC interworking support.

- MME should be capable of discovering AMF using 3-octet tracking area code (TAC) at EPS to 5G core handover.

- MME will need to support EPS fallback for voice as well as emergency calls.

- Support the 5G SA-specific cyphering and integrity protection algorithms (UASC).

- Support 5G-specific APNs, if any.

- Support nc-nr flag from DNS/DCNR flag from the UE.

DNS

- Configure the network-capability as "smf" to support the selection of a PGW-C/SMF for 5G UEs.

- Additional gateway selection criteria for 5G SA UEs based on their slice subscription

- New APN queries for 5G SA, if any

- NRSRNA handling

SGW

- Support to handle MMEs 5G core interworking indication from the S11 interface if the indication is set to indicate that the UE supports 5G, and the PDN connection supports interoperation with the 5GS. SGW carries this identification to the PGW through the S5/S8 interface.

- S5-C interface implementation with PGW-C/SMF

- s5-U interface implementation with PGW-U/UPF

Table 4-4 shows the call flows that will have interactions between 4G and 5G core networks and the network elements within EPC/5G core that will be impacted because of the call flow.

Table 4-4. *Impacted Nodes in 5G/4G Core Because of Interworking*

Requirement Type	E2E call Flow name	RAN	EPC	5GC
Interworking with EPS	Interaction with PCC	gNB , eNB	PGW-C, HSS, DNN, PCRF, MME	SMF, PCF , NRF , UDM, AMF
	Mobility Restriction	gNB , eNB	PGW C, HSS, DNN, PCRF, MME	SMF, PCF , NRF , UDM, AMF
	PGW Selection	gNB , eNB	PGW-C, HSS, DNN, PCRF, MME	SMF, PCF , NRF , UDM, AMF
	PDN connection establishment	gNB , eNB	PGW-C, HSS, DNN, PCRF, MME	SMF, PCF , NRF , UDM, AMF
	Network Configuration	gNB , eNB	MME	AMF
Handover Procedures	5GS to EPS handover using N26 interface	gNB , eNB	MME, SGW, HSS, PCRF DNS	AMF, PGW-c+SMF, PGW-u+UPF, UDM , CHF
	EPS to 5GS handover using N26 interface	gNB , eNB	MME, SGW, HSS, PCRF DNS	AMF, PGW-c+SMF, PGW-u+UPF, UDM , CHF
	Handover Cancel	gNB , eNB	MME, SGW, HSS, PCRF DNS	AMF, PGW-c+SMF, PGW-u+UPF, UDM , CHF
Idle Mode Mobility	5GS to EPS Idle mode mobility using N26 interface	gNB , eNB	MME, SGW, HSS, PCRF DNS	AMF, PGW-c+SMF, PGW-u+UPF, UDM , CHF
	EPS to 5GS Mobility Registration Procedure (Idle and Connected State) using N26 interface	gNB , eNB	MME, SGW, HSS, PCRF DNS	AMF, PGW-c+SMF, PGW-u+UPF, UDM , CHF
	EPS to 5GS Mobility Registration Procedure (Idle) using N26 interface with AMF reallocation	gNB , eNB	MME, SGW, HSS, PCRF DNS	AMF, PGW-c+SMF, PGW-u+UPF, UDM , CHF
Impact to EPS procedures	E-UTRAN Initial Attach	eNB	MME, HSS, DNS, SGW, PGW-C +SMF	-
	Tracking Area Update	eNB	MME, HSS, DNS,	-
	PDN Connection Request	eNB	MME, HSS, DNS, SGW, PGW-C +SMF	
	Registration procedure	gNB , eNB	MME	AMF
	UE Requested PDU Session Establishment procedure	gNB		AMF, PGW-c+SMF, PGW-u+UPF, UDM
	UE or Network Requested PDU Session Modification procedure	gNB		

4G/5G Interworking Design Considerations

Problem Statements

1) Proper Network Element Selection During UE Mobility from 4G to 5G

5G core with slice design and architecture in place provides the flexibility to choose the core network elements for a user based on the user's slice subscription and the application mapping to the slice that the user requests during PDU establishment request.

This mechanism ensures that the desired QoE for the PDU session is met and the network elements are planned and utilized efficiently based on the type of application used by the user.

However, in the 4G network, when UE executes an initial attach to the EPC, UE and MME are not aware of the slicing concept and cannot select a proper network (EPC or 5GC) and network slice. This can prevent a 5G-capable UE from seamlessly handing over from a 4G to 5G network.

A specific mechanism to select a proper network is required.

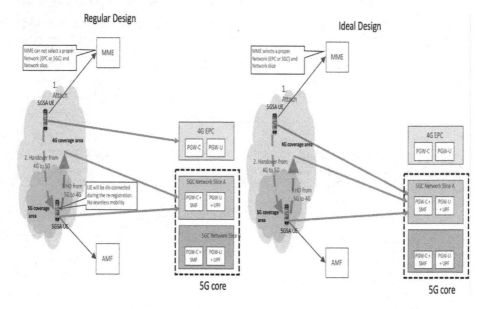

Figure 4-16. *4g/5g interworking regular design vs ideal design*

2) 5G NSA UE Traffic Offloading

Prior to the deployment of 5GC, the EPC would serve 4G UE and 5G (NSA) UE. However, considering that the 5GC will have 5GC SMF/UPF as well as EPC PGW features (i.e., PGW-C and PGW-U), it is important to design the 5GC in a manner that it can provide the operators the flexibility to plan the traffic offloading of NSA UEs based on the capacity and load status on the EPC node.

Figure 4-17 shows an ideal 5GC design that considers 5G NSA UE traffic offloading capability vs a design without NSA consideration.

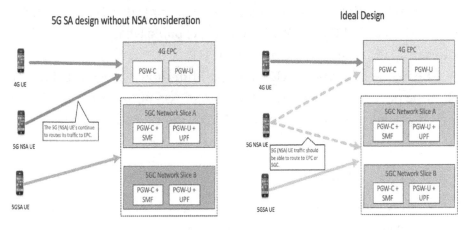

Figure 4-17. *5G NSA traffic offloading design - Regular vs ideal*

3) Overlapping NSA and SA Coverage

The radio of 5G NSA and 5G SA can be the same/similar, and there can be many instances where there are overlapping coverage areas for 5G NSA and the 5G SA.

In many cases, the same gNB can be connected to the 4G core as well as 5G core to cater to the secondary RAT addition for NSA users and handover to the 5G SA users.

Considering that many of the 5G UEs and subscriptions can have 5G NSA and 5G SA subscriptions in place, there is a need to plan and prioritize one over the other in these overlapping instances.

Fallback upon failure and the type of services that are used by the user should also be considered in such cases for planning for efficiency.

Solution: UE Capability Subscription and APN Mapping

UE capability subscription and APN mapping can act as one of the solutions to the considerations mentioned in the previous sections. As a part of this solution, new APNs are introduced for 5G users for data usage, which is different from the normal 4G users APN for the same service.

Introducing the 5G SA nodes will bring in additional changes to the 4G network in terms of logic that will be required on MME/DNS to select the right node (i.e., SAEGW/PGW) for a 5G SA-capable UE trying to establish a connection in 4G with an appropriate APN.

The new network/node selection algorithm should consider at least the following parameters to ensure seamless interworking in a situation where the UE makes a movement from 4G to 5G coverage area and vice versa.

- UE capability (4G/5G NSA/5G SA)

- UE subscription

- APN used by the UE (not just the default but also all possible APNs that can be selected by the UE)

- N26 interface support between MME and AMF

In this method:

- If the MME receives update location accept (ULA) from HSS with allowed APN for the UE as "5G-DATA-APN" and the UE is 5G-capable and NRSRNA flag is set (allowed), then the MME along with DNS selects the 5G PGW-SMF (combo) instead of the 4G SAEGW nodes, provided the requested APN by the UE is 5G-DATA-APN.

- If the requested APN by the UE is "4G-DATA-APN" and even if the ULA received from the HSS suggests that the UE is allowed to use "5G-DATA-APN," then the MME along with the DNS will select the 4G SAEGW/PGW nodes instead of the new 5G PGW-SMF combo node.

- If the requested APN by the UE is "5G-DATA-APN" and if the ULA received from the HSS suggests that the UE is not allowed to use "5G-DATA-APN," then the MME will reject the attach/TAU request from the UE.

- If the requested APN by the UE is "4G-DATA-APN" and if the ULA received from the HSS suggests that the UE is allowed to use "4G-DATA-APN," then the MME will select the 4G SAEGW/PGW nodes.

Table 4-5 shows an APN-based enhancement to the 4G network logic of selection of gateway nodes (i.e., SAEGW/PGW) for the UE based on the UE capability, UE subscription, and APN used by the UE, assuming there is an N26 interface between the MME of the 4G network and the AMF of the 5G network.

Note N26 interface is considered to exist between MME and AMF for the aforementioned logic.

4G-DATA-APN and 5G-DATA-APN are used only for illustration; in reality the logic can be extended to any APN/DNN names.

Table 4-5. *Gateway Selection Logic Enhancement in 4G*

UE capability	UE subscription	APN selected by the UE	SAEGW selection logic on MME
5G SA capable	5G Subscription	4G Data APN	SAEGW in EPC
		5G Data APN	S-GW in EPC P-GW in 5GC (new combo node)
5G SA capable	4G subscription	4G Data APN	SAEGW in EPC
		5G Data APN	Attach / TAU Rejected
4G Capable	5G Subscription	4G Data APN	SAEGW in EPC
		5G Data APN	S-GW in EPC P-GW in 5GC (new combo node)
4G Capable	4G Subscription	4G Data APN	SAEGW in EPC
		5G Data APN	Attach / TAU Rejected

Figure 4-18 illustrates the explained logic for a UE in 4G and 5G network coverage area when it initiates registration with different APNs/ DNNs.

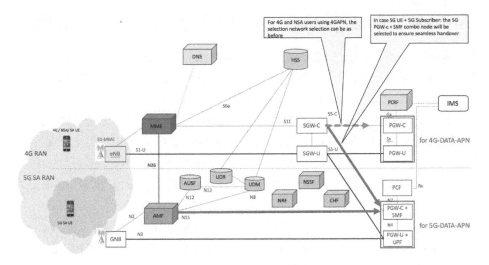

Figure 4-18. *Proper slice corresponding node selection for 5G UEs in a 4G network*

With this solution, there is a good chance of selecting the right 5G PGW/SMF node in a 4G network to ensure seamless transition when the UE makes mobility from the 4G network to the 5G network.

In complex deployment scenarios where there are multiple slices in the 5G network and the S-NSSAI mapping on the 5G network can lead to different slice selections or multiple slice selection, the UE capability subscription and APN mapping solution might not result in a very accurate selection of the 5G PGW/SMF node in the 4G network.

In such cases, default slice node selection on the 4G network might be required to reduce the complexity, and session continuity will need to be maintained for such users when they move from 4G to 5G coverage area and vice versa.

Voice and Emergency Services Support/Design in 5G

Similarly to voiceover LTE (VoLTE), in 5G, the voice services in 5GS over NG-RAN (VoNR) will continue to be IMS-based, meaning the 5GS needs to be connected to IMS core to support VoNR.

For VoNR, in Release-15, 3GPP has agreed to continue with diameter-based Rx interface for the PCC interface between PCF in 5GC and P-CSCF in IMS core in order to not impact IMS. SBI between proxy-call session control function (P-CSCF) in IMS and PCF in 5GC is planned in Release 16.

The IMS core needs to be connected to 5GC to offer IMS-based voice services to 5G users. The key challenge for VoNR introduction is that the same IMS core is connected to both EPS (Rx connectivity to PCRF) as well as 5GC (Rx connectivity to PCF).

VoNR service requires support in the UE, RAN, and 5G core network. To get the right quality of service for voice, there is a need for careful optimization and tuning of the radio network. Most of the operators will plan and introduce VoNR in their networks in steps.

There are two main options that the oeprators choose to support voice services in their 5G network.

Voiceover NG-RAN (VoNR)

To support VoNR, 5GS must be able to support required QoS handling for IMS signaling as well as dedicated bearer handling to support voice. The UE, gNB, and 5GC must support VoNR. The 5GC must be connected to IMS core as well. Additionally, 5G RAN as well as 5GC must be dimensioned, configured, and optimized to handle IMS signaling as well as dedicated bearer for voice to ensure good quality voice.

Considering the smaller cell size of 5G radio and limited coverage in the operator's network, it is unlikely that the operators will have a large-scale 5G deployment with VoNR coverage.

One of the important aspects to match the required quality of experience for the end-user is voice service continuity between 5G and 4G.

Services similar to single-radio voice call continuity (SRVCC) in voice service continuity between 5G and 3G/2G CS domain is a part of 3GPP study item for Release 16. Therefore call continuity cannot be guarenteed if there is no VoLTE coverage bordering the 5G network.

EPS Fallback for Voice

Considering that for many operators, VoNR at the initial stage of 5G network deployment cannot be supported for voice, the option for supporting voice for such operators is IMS voice service via EPS fallback to support voice service.

During the voice session establishment procedure, 5GS will move the UE to EPS via inter-RAT handover or redirection mechanism, where the call setup will continue to be established.

If the UE is capable of dual registration, it can continue to receive the non-voice service services on the 5G network and fallback to the 4G VoLTE network only for IMS-related services.

With EPS fallback, 5G NR needs to support IMS call setup signaling, even though it does not need to support dedicated voice bearer setup for voice. During the SIP registration phase the call is moved to EPS. Voice call then continues in EPS.

In comparison with the VoNR service, since EPS fallback involves a handover or redirection to LTE from 5G, the call setup time will be longer.

EPS fallback with N26 interworking support is preferred, as it can provide better user experience than non-N26 interworking. Without N26 interworking support, seamless service continuity for any non-voice session that may have been present at the time of voice session establishment cannot be provided, resulting in bad user experience. Additionally, the call setup time is longer when N26 interworking is not supported.

EPS fallback is described in TS 23.502 clause 4.13.6.1.

IMS DNN needs to connect to the IP Multimedia Subsystem (IMS) core over New Radio (NR) so that Mobile originated (MO) and Mobile Terminated (MT) calls can be signaled and then moved to EPS for the bearers.

To allow for EPS fallback feature, during the registration the AMF needs to get the VoPS homogeneous support indication, as shown in the flow in Figure 4-19.

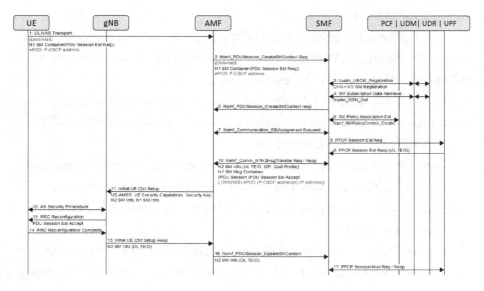

Figure 4-19. *IMS PDU establishment*

Figure 4-20 shows the high-level call flow procedure for an EPS fallback procedure.

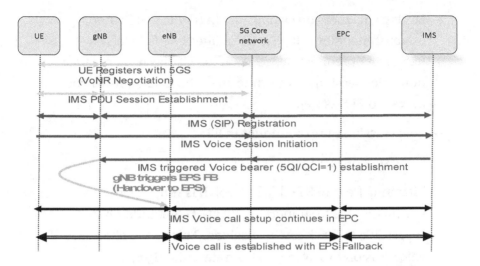

Figure 4-20. *High-level call flow for an EPS fallback procedure*

Following is a very high-level procedure for the EPS fallback.

- During the registration procedure, the UE indicates the support of IMS voice to the AMF and the AMF sends back the 5GS support for voice in response.

- The UE performs the IMS PDU session establishment procedure toward 5GS to obtain an IP address for the IMS session as well as IP address of the P-CCSF.

- The UE performs IMS registration via 5GS.

- An IMS voice session (either originating or terminating) is attempted with SIP signaling via IMS.

- IMS triggers network-initiated dedicated bearer establishment over 5GS for the voice bearer.

- During voice session establishment (dedicated bearer establishment for voice), gNB initiates EPS fallback via handover or redirection to EPS. If the UE has been in other non-voice sessions at this time, then those sessions will be moved to EPS as well.

- Voice session setup continues in EPS.

- Voice session is established in EPS.

- Migrating from EPS fallback to VoNR is simple. Once the network is able to support VoNR, gNB configuration to trigger EPS fallback can be disabled. This would allow IMS voice session to stay in 5GS from start to finish.

Table 4-6. *Impacted Nodes in 5G/4G Core due to EPS Fallback*

Requirement Type	E2E call Flow name	RAN	EPC	5GC
Support for Emergency and IMS service	EPS fallback for IMS voice	gNB , eNB	MME, PGW-C, PGW-U, HSS, DNN, PCRF	SMF, PCF, NRF , UDM, AMF, IMS
	NPLI for IMS calls	gNB , eNB	MME, PGW-C, PGW-U, HSS, DNN, PCRF	SMF, PCF, NRF , UDM, AMF, IMS
	Emergency service	gNB , eNB	MME, PGW-C, PGW-U, HSS, DNN, PCRF	SMF, PCF, NRF , UDM, AMF, IMS

Figure 4-21 illustrates a detailed call flow for an EPS fallback procedure.

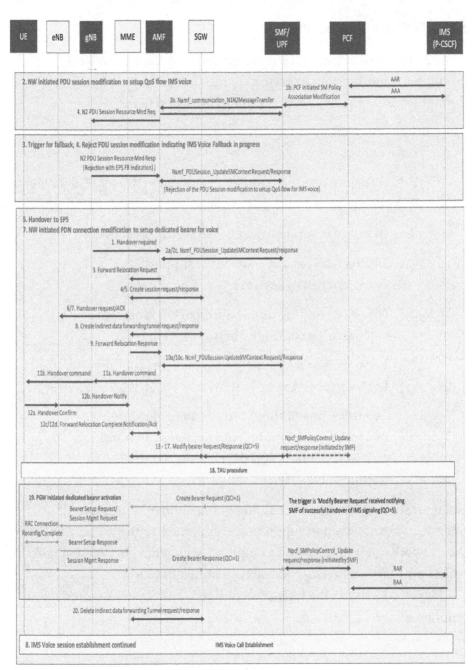

Figure 4-21. *Detailed call flow for an EPS fallback procedure*

Emergency Voice Service

Emergency services put more stringent demands on the network, compared to normal voice services. Some of the key requirements or demands for emergency service support are listed here.

- Must meet relevant regulatory requirements (e.g., accurate positioning)

- IMS emergency service can be offered natively over 5GS only if the following requirements can be met:

    1. Basic voice service must be supported over 5GS.

    2. UE, 5G RAN, and 5G core must support 5G emergency PDU session.

    3. N26 interworking must be supported for seamless voice service continuity between 5G and 4G.

    4. Location services must be upgraded to support SBI interfaces toward 5GC.

    5. "Accurate positioning" requirements must be met in NG-RAN; emergency services put more stringent demands on the network, compared to normal voice services.

If these requirements are not met or for some other reason the operator does not want to support emergency call natively over 5GS, then the network can be configured to support emergency services fallback, in which case the emergency call will be handled in EPS.

Figure 4-22 shows the high-level design architecture required for an emergency service fallback.

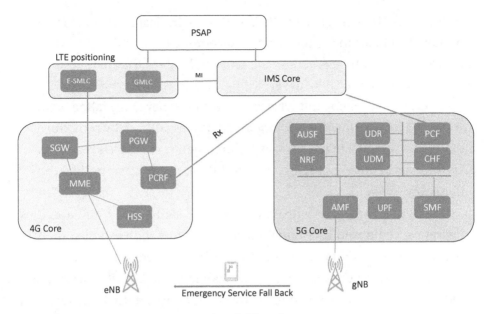

Figure 4-22. *Emergency service fallback*

Emergency Services Using EPS Fallback

The architecture for emergency services fallback is shown in Figure 4-22.

The emergency service allows a user registered/attached to 5GS to make emergency call over EPS when 5GS does not support emergency services.

The service can only be used by normally registered users and cannot be used by users in limited service state (e.g., by a SIM-less UE).

Users in limited service state can still use the emergency service in limited state in the 4G network. To support emergency call from users in limited service state, 4G RAN needs to advertise in a system information broadcast (SIB) message that IMS emergency bearer services for UEs in limited service mode is supported.

When the UE registers with 5GS, AMF shall indicate support for emergency fallback in the registration accept message to the UE. When it is time to make an emergency call, this would allow the UE to initiate a service request to the UE with service type set to emergency fallback.

AMF, upon receiving the service request for emergency fallback from the UE, triggers a request for emergency services fallback by providing an indication to gNB that a fallback for emergency services is required. gNB initiates handover or redirection to EPS so that UE can initiate the emergency call in EPS.

The UE then proceeds with emergency call setup in EPS and executes relevant procedures in EPS: emergency PDN connection establishment, emergency registration in IMS, and then IMS emergency call setup.

Once the emergency call has been established in EPS, it must not be handed back to 5GS, based on measurement reports, until the emergency call is finished.

Figure 4-23 shows the detailed call flow procedure for an emergency service fallback.

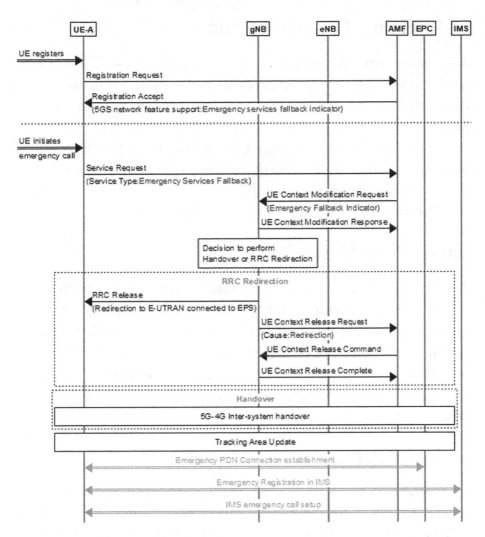

Figure 4-23. *Emergency service fallback call flow*

Redundancy Considerations

5GC NFs use stateless implementation as much as possible. The stateful part (i.e., the database) is typically planned for redundancy so that there is data replication across spanning across multiple PODs and data centers/ geographical locations.

This type of a deployment/desing for the 5G NFs enables the possibility to select an alternative NF service if the first selected service is not available or failed for some reason.

5G NFs shall have internal resiliency and not lose sessions.

Control Plane NF Resiliency

To ensure there is no single point of failure, NF applications must be resilient. The clause describes the resiliency of the NF implementation.

Control plane network functions (SMF, AMF, NRF, PCF, NSSF, etc.) are typically deployed as cloud-native solutions using container platforms like Kubernetes, which provides services like auto-healing and replica set creation; these ensure that any platform-related failures can be detected and resiliency can be provided accordingly.

Service Redundancy

In Kubernetes, services are exposed by using "external IP," which is assigned to Kubernetes worker node. The external IP address will be not available if the worker node fails. To avoid this single point of failure, CNFs can use different mechanisms (e.g., VIP) to ensure the external IP address attached to a CNF endpoint is always available.

In the following explanation, we will use KeepAliveD-based failure detection as the mode of failure detection for any service/PODs within the Kubernetes cluster as an assumption to detail the scenarios.

The overview is shown in Figure 4-24.

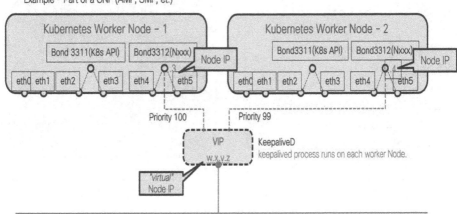

Figure 4-24. *Illustration of Service redundancy*

SBI-Based Interfaces Redundancy

HTTP2-based interfaces use Kubernetes normal networking mode (packets reach the endpoints with DNATing).

No Failure Scenario

Both worker nodes are active. In this case, packets toward CNF (Nxxx) come to Node Protocol-1, and those are then load-balanced to actual POD/containers (endpoint#1) by load balancer.

Figure 4-25 illustrates the no failure scenario.

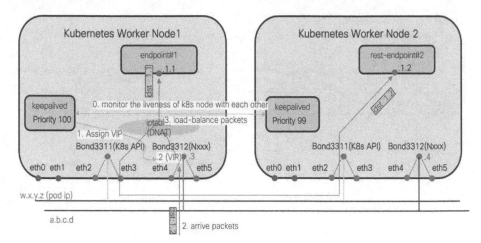

Figure 4-25.   *Normal working scenario*

Failure Scenario

In case Node Protocol-1 fails, KeepAlive detects it and changes association of VIP to another node. Packets toward CNF (Nxxx) then come to Node Protocol-2, and those are then load-balanced to actual containers (endpoint#2) by load balancer.

Figure 4-26 illustrates the failure scenario.

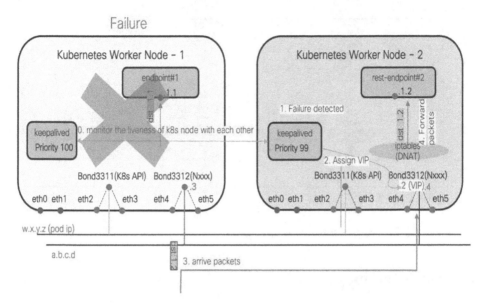

Figure 4-26. *Failure scenario*

Non-SBI Interface Redundancy (e.g., GTP/PFCP/SCTP)

These endpoints use "host-network" mode (packets reach to the endpoints without DNATing). These protocols cannot be NATed since 3GPP specifies that source IP and destination IP are the identity of the peer; therefore they should not be NATed.

No Failure Scenario

Both worker nodes are active. In host network mode, endpoint pods are act/sby (not load-balanced/DNATed by things such as iptables). In this case, packets toward CNF (Nxxx) come to Node Protocol-1, and those are then sent to actual containers (endpoint#1) by host network mode.

Figure 4-27 illustrates the no failure scenario.

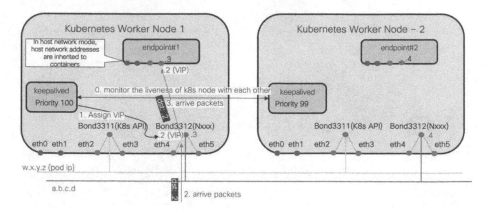

Figure 4-27. *Normal working scenario*

Failure Scenario

In case Node Protocol-1 fails, KeepAlive detects it and changes association of VIP to another node. Packets toward CNF (Nxxx) then come to Node Protocol-2, and those are sent to actual containers (endpoint#2) by host network mode.

Figure 4-28 illustrates the failure scenario.

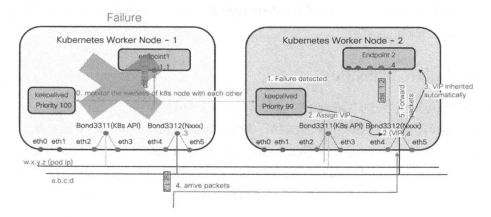

Figure 4-28. *Failure scenario*

Node Failure Detection and Handling

Figure 4-29 shows the generic node failure handling for a typical 5G deployment.

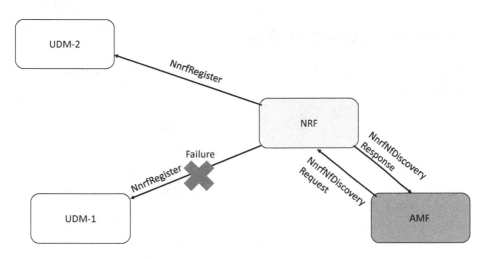

Figure 4-29. *Node failure handling*

In Figure 4-29, UDM-1 is primary and UDM-2 is secondary for the NF.

Both UDM-1 and UDM-2, upon coming up, register (NF registration) with NRF and start NF heartbeat with NRF. SMF uses the heartbeat response to track the operational status.

For any NFDiscovery request for UDM from the other network functions (e.g., AMF in the NFDiscovery response message), the NRF provides the details of UDM-1 toward the requested NFs.

In that case, the NRF detects UDM-1 failure by missing NF heartbeat response.

For any NFDiscovery request for UDM from the other network functions in the NFDiscovery response message, the NRF provides the details of UDM-2 toward the requested NFs.

If the NRF receives a register response from UDM-1, it detects that the UDM-1 is up again. The NRF marks UDM-1 as active once it recovers and sends back the details of UDM-1 in NFresponse messages to any NFs requesting UDM details.

NRF Failure Detection and Handling

Figure 4-30 shows the generic handling for NRF failure cases in a 5G deployment.

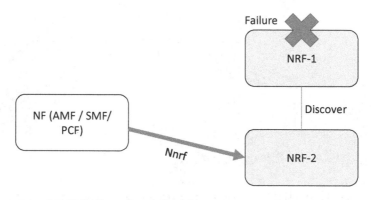

Figure 4-30. *NRF failure handling*

In Figure 4-30, NRF-1 is primary and NRF-2 is secondary for the NF.

The NF (AMF/SMF/PCF, etc.), upon coming up, registers (NF registration) with NRF 1 and starts NF heartbeat with NRF-1. SMF uses the heartbeat response to track the operational status.

In this case, the NF detects NRF-1 failure by missing NF heartbeat response, it registers to NRF-2 (secondary NRF), and starts sending NF heartbeat. The NF continues to send NF register message1 to NRF-1 to keep track of its status.

If the NF receives a register response from NRF-1, it detects that the NRF-1 is up again. The NF marks NRF-1 as active once it recovers and stops sending NF heartbeats to the NRF-2.

Geographical Redundancy

Figure 4-31 shows how geographical redundancy is deployed for control plane network functions.

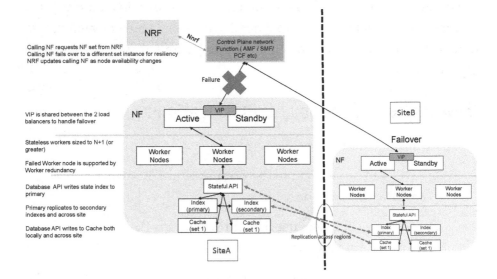

Figure 4-31. *Geographical redundancy for control plane network functions*

In Figure 4-31, there are two NFs that are geographically separated with primary in SiteA and the secondary in SiteB as shown.

In case of failure, where all the NFs within SiteA are not reachable and stop sending any heartbeat messages to the NRF within the site, then the NRF will remove the details of the the NF in that particular site and update the NF discovery response messages with the NF in SiteB as shown.

Geographical redundancy requires a periodic sync between the databases/stateful APIs between the two sites so that there is no impact to the sessions handled by the original site before the failure.

If the NRF receives register response from the NF from Site A, it detects that the NF is up again. The NRF marks the NF as active once it recovers and sends back the details of NF in Nfresponse messages to any other NFs requesting the failed NF's details.

Additionally it is also possible to introduce another layer on top of the NF that can internally detect the node failure within the site and redirect the requests toward the NF in redundant site (as shown in Figure 4-31). By doing so, additional messages that need to be exchanged between the NRF and other NFs and notifications to the other NF for failure of the failed NF can be avoided.

User Plane Redundancy Considerations

The UPF has two modes of resiliency:

1) UPF can be configured to mirror state and have one UPF active and one standby.

2) Group of UPFs can use one or two standby UPFs to recover the sessions.

Typically during design, 1:1 redundancy should be considered for UPFs that are serving delay-sensitive applications, like voice, uRLLC, and so on, but as the hardware requirement for 1:1 redundancy is high, network planning and design should have a good balance of 1:1 and N:M redundancy.

1:1 Redundancy

In 1:1 UPF resiliency configuration, there is one standby UPF for every active UPF. The active UPF synchronizes the session state with the standby UPF. As a result, when there is a switchover, the state is pre-programmed, and traffic processing can occur immediately.

The advantage of 1:1 redundancy is that recovery time due to failure is much lower than N:M, because the session state is pre-installed in the UPF. Further, the standby advertises the N3 and IP pool routes—albeit with a lower route prepend value—so, on switchover, BGP re-convergence time is reduced.

There should be procedures to ensure that the configuration of the standby UPF is updated frequnetly to reflect the changes on the active UPF. The active and standby UPF should have the same configuration so that when the switchover happens, there is no impact to the existing sessions.

Trigger and Switchover

The UPF monitors links and N4 interface using BFD and KeepAlive packets, respectively. Failure of an N3 or N6 link would occur when both physical interfaces have failed, or a KeepAlive timeout would trigger a switchover. The active UPF should be able to communicate with the standby UPF, and there should be notification to the standby UPF to take over.

The standby UPF should advertise the same N3 and pool routes to the BGP peers so the the BGP peer now sends traffic to the newly active UPF.

Figure 4-32 shows the user plane redundancy model where there is an standby user plane function for every active user plane function.

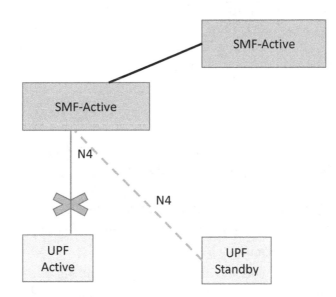

Figure 4-32. *1:1 user plane redundancy*

N:M Redundancy

In locations with big UPF deployments, the UPF redundancy scheme can be optimized by using the N:M feature. Rather than having one UPF back up another, and hence double the hardware needed, one or more UPFs can be standby for multiple active UPFs.

The state that each UPF holds is cached in a separate function (this is vendor-specific implementation) that has multiple functions.

Figure 4-33 shows the user plane N:M redundancy model and how the failure handling is executed in such a case.

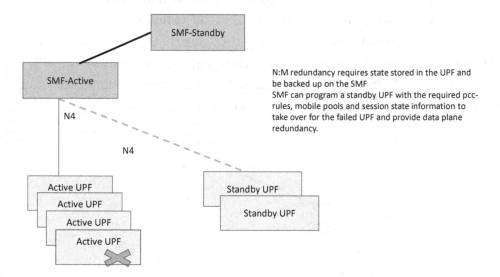

Figure 4-33. N:M user plane redundancy

The existing redundancy mechanism that is developed to support 1:1 is not suitable and scalable and is very expensive to implement in hardware and infrastructure cost.

Hence, there is a need for N:M where N > 1 and M is at least 1. So we need a solution where redundancy of UPF can be supported that meets the criteria of fast recovery of sessions.

To support N:M, we need to have a mechanism to store all the required information at a common location. This common information should be properly segregated.

On a switchover trigger, one of the M's available on standby should be selected to receive the appropriate data from the common location.

Fallback to Local Configuration

Even though there are redundancy considerations in place, there are chances that one of two NFs are not able to communicate with each other in a deployment scenario. For such cases, there is a need to have a fallback configuration that is local to the NFs.

Local policies on the NFs can take the least precedence and can be useful for node selection/communication when all other mechanisms fail.

Overload Protection

There are multiple cases where an NF can incur signaling storms—for example, during session establishment, where failures in other parts of the network require the NF to handle more requests than it was sized to support. In these scenarios, if not handled properly, the NF can become overloaded or even fail. During these incidents, it is important for the NF to apply back pressure to reduce the number of requests that it needs to process as well as prioritize the most critical requests to maintain optimal subscriber experience.

Overload protection requires the NF to drop or apply appropriate error codes to the requesting NF so that its resources are not overloaded and it can still function during a signaling storm. For example, a failure or reboot of an AMF may trigger subscribers to reattach, therefore causing a signaling storm toward the PCF. The signaling storm can impact multiple nodes in this scenario, including the NRF, SMF, PCF, NSSF, SCP, AF/IMS, UDM, AUSF, CHF, UPF, and AMF. Each of these NFs must provide overload protection to ensure they can handle the signaling storm. Typically, this requires a bound message queue to be implemented on the overloaded NF to drop or send the appropriate error codes to the NF initiating the storm.

While the receiving NF is overloaded, it should prioritize request/ response messages to maximize the subscriber experience and while maintaining resiliency. Typically, during failure scenarios, the NF is configured to prioritize session terminations, followed by session updates and eventual session creations. This will alleviate the congestion in the network to a certain extent while maintaining the service for existing sessions. If existing sessions are not prioritized, the typical behavior of the device is to completely disconnect from the network and reconnect, which creates an additional burden on an already overloaded network.

CHAPTER 5

5G Packet Core Testing Strategies

The shift from monolithic architecture to a service-based architecture (SBA) with applications realized by microservice has created many complex challenges for operators and service providers. On one hand, the shift toward microservice-based network functions (NFs) provides greater scalability and reliability advantages; however, on the other hand, it is expensive to realize and very complex to manage and test.

Testing for 5G core components is a complete game-changer, and the key challenge when it comes to testing is to be able to use existing successful frameworks from deploy-operate models and adapt them for cloud application testing.

To reduce the production risk, it becomes essential with the change in the architecture that the code can be deployed and tested in production at a fast pace, thereby providing the necessary feedback to the development teams. This process needs to be automated and be set as a continuous process of integration and development (CI/CD).

© Rajaneesh Sudhakar Shetty 2021
R. S. Shetty, *5G Mobile Core Network*, https://doi.org/10.1007/978-1-4842-6473-7_5

CI/CD is a must as far as testing and automation requirement goes to leverage the full benefit of 5G core innovations. Traditional telco operates a monolithic-type application provided by a vendor, integrated with different integration points clearly defined by 3GPP. With a change from monolithic to cloud-native and microservice-based architecture, there is an increase in these integration points, as there are no different protocols used between different network functions in 5G, and technically any of the NFs can communicate with any other NF in SBA.

With more and more service providers adapting to the open-source code and, in many cases, the service providers working on in-house software development teams wherein they start integrating vendor's third-party software to their existing infrastructure software platform. A Shift in focus towards automation and testing in a strategic manner is a clear trend.

Automation Level in Testing

Automating the testing process is a key to achieve all the benefits for microservices. A good target to achieve would be to automate at least 90% of test cases.

Automation testing has some benefits but also demands a level of ability that demands a high skill set. So it is eutopic to say that all test cases will benefit from automation, and test strategy definitions should be formed around the following possibilities.

Manual Testing

Sometimes testing an end-to-end flow or for problem reproduction is useful to execute manual testing. Some tests are also very hard to automate, and therefore they can be tested in and can be marked for future automation. Manual testing should be avoided in a microservice-type architecture because it creates several bottleneck in the deliver pipeline.

Semi-Automated Testing or Automated Assisted Testing

In semi-automated/automation assisted testing, there is a testing automation framework to prepare, execute, and collect information that can be online or offline validated by a human. This type of testing takes advantage of the human capacity to analyze patterns and unstructured data and takes advantage of automation capability to systematically execute tests step by step and collects data for manual verification. Drive tests are one example of a semi-automated testing.

Fully Automated Testing

As the name conveys, fully automated testing is a set of testing that is completely done by an automated system. This is a key to provide developers with early feedback and to improve the speed of releasing the code into production. Smoke testing can be an example of fully automated testing wherein when there are upgrades/change in version of the software, a regression test suite can be executed to check for the sanity of the new software.

Release Strategies for 5G SA Core Network

Microservices applications on SBA are often misconceived as the end solution. Some of microservice pitfalls and anti-patterns are described here. Considering the scope of this chapter, we will just reference briefly and let the reader do deeper digging on these topics.

- "Microservice as a goal": Organizations searching to adopt microservices but not to solve any organization requirement like velocity/releibility and scalability

- "Flying before walking": Adopting microservices without test automation, dev-ops, and automation pipelines

- "Redflag": Creating process that pitfall automation and creating organization barriers for software to flow into the different environments, increasing release cycles

- "Microservices as magic dust": They solve all problems in organization.

For operators transforming into 5G, it is required to have a fine balance between the complexity, operational speed, and visibility that needs to be taken under consideration when designing a release strategy.

There are several approaches and strategies to mitigate the drawbacks for software delivery, even if microservices are used in the build process. They should be selected according to business objectives, achievable targets, and risk–benefit analysis.

Following is a list of approaches toward release strategies that are often adapted by the 5G service providers.

Component Type Approach

This is the simple traditional approach. In this approach, several microservices are developed and wrapped together as a package to form a set of functionalities that can be termed as a NF; for example, an AMF or an SMF can be a bundle of microservices packaged together. The NF can be tested as a whole and can be lifecycle-managed during upgrades as one entity. This approach is very handy and can be easy to deploy, implement, and also manage from an operations perspective.

Each vendor in this approach will be provided with a cluster of their own to deploy and manage the microservices pertaining to the NF.

Figure 5-1 shows the microservices component structure for a NF wherein a set of microservices like management service, access token service, discovery service, endpoint service, and so on are bundled together to form the NF repository function (NRF).

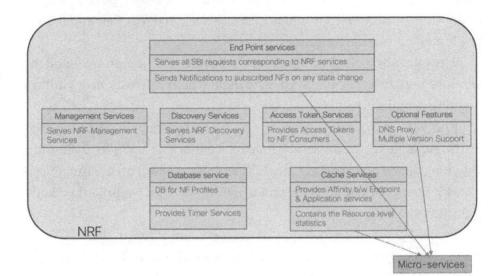

Figure 5-1. *Bundling of microservices within an NRF*

Advantages of component-type approach:

- Easy to implement

- Easy to debug/trace the source of problem

- Simple to deploy

- Simple to test if a manual process is used

Disadvantages of component-type approach:

- Longer release cycles for the NFs

- Intervendor/interteam dependency

Release-Centric Approach

In a release-centric approach, a vendor typically encapsulates his latest version of microservices into the code repository or in the form of binary artifact (e.g., rpm files). This is wrapper around a release type of testing cycle where several vendors' microservices are glued together and then implemented at same time.

The operator typically will manage a cluster that is common for all the vendors, and the vendors will go on to deploy their microservices within that one common cluster.

This is a very resource-efficient way to deploy a network wherein there are no separate clusters reserved for each vendor and scale-in/scale-out activities can be managed at a single cluster level based on the usage.

However, it can be an operational nightmare if not well-planned and rightly automated.

Figure 5-2 shows an example for a release-centric approach where there are multiple microservices services belonging to different NFs belonging to one repository.

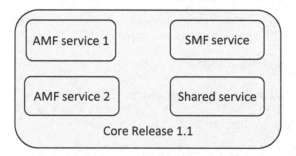

Figure 5-2. *Example for release-centric approach*

Advantages of release-centric approach:

- Reduces automation complexity, as the automation tool can be easily generalized for the cluster

- Can be used as an intermediate step toward a full CI/CD

Disadvantages of release-centric approach:

- Very complex to realize and deploy

- Can lead to very slow release cycles considering the complexity

CI/CD Centric Approach for 5G Delivery

Building a CI/CD pipeline with a conjunction of external software vendors is challenging because one of the main objectives is that the development teams of various vendors will contribute toward a common pipeline, where the source code repository will be maintained. This source code can be integrated into a common git repository and treated as an integral part of the entire repository.

In some cases, artifactory integration can also be used where multivendor repository integration is not possible/is complex. This artifactory integration will allow the binary produced by vendor to be integrated into the pipeline.

Figure 5-3 shows a very high-level view of how CI/CD integration can be planned and implemented in an operator environment.

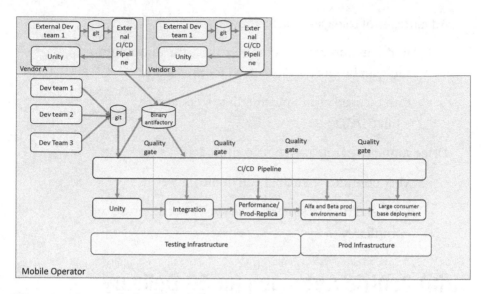

Figure 5-3. *High-level CI/CD architecture*

To help understand the CI/CD approach better, following is
an explanation of a few terms in Figure 5-3.

Pipeline

Pipeline is a set of tasks and processes to take the software from source
control and binary control to the several stages required for software
certification and into release in production.

A CI/CD pipeline should have close integrations with source code
control (git) and binary repository (artifactory) along with test automation,
security testing automation, and static code analyzers. There should be
means to ensure that code passess through the different stages of testing
and should enforce the validation of the criterium of quality gate.

Code Repository (git)

Code repository is the place where the source code is managed locally or
in the web. One popular code repository example is git.

Code repository also provides version control and branching mechanisms. Integration of code repository with the CI/CD pipeline is needed.

Artifactory

Once the binary repository for the code is created, there is a need to store these binary files for later reference. Artifactory is a place to store the binary files that can be used to install the source code into different environments.

One of the popularly known open-source versions of artifactory is Jfrog. In a Kubernetes environment, helm chart and metadata can be stored on Jfrog artifactory for the deployment.

Static Code Analysis

A static code analysis is a functionality often provided and integrated with the software that performs analysis metrics on source code or machine code. This functionality permits an inspection of the code and enforces code rules, measures the technical depth, and also identifies the unit test coverage. An example for static code analyzer is Sonarqube.

Quality Gate

Quality gate is a set of predefined software requirements/characteristics that must be met so that code can progress to the next stage of testing or to release into production.

The following can be incorporated on quality gate criteria:

- Test results report

- Technical depth increase: This is an estimation of software entropy increase (i.e., if a CI/CD pipepline is automated into production, code entropy should be limited by an increase of X amount; 3%-4% is usually a good rule of thumb).

– Code review or code approval process: This is a manual check from and approval by the team.

Figure 5-4 shows sample metrics extracted from the code analysis.

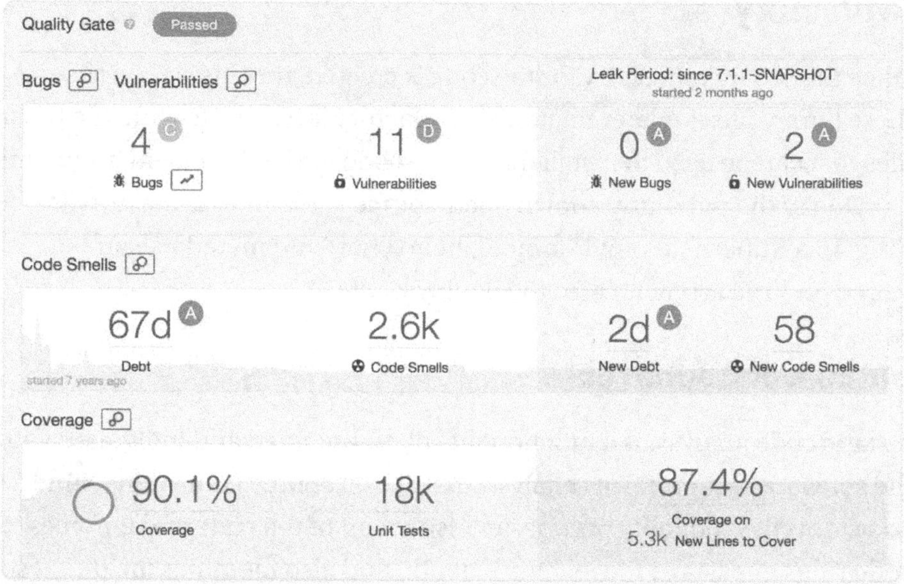

Figure 5-4. *Sample metrics*

Example quality gate for entering integration environment:

– All unit test pass

– 95% unit test coverage

– 4% technical depth increase

– Code was peer-reviewed

Example quality gate for entering prod-replica environment:

– 100% API testing coverage

– 100% API testing passed

- Maximum 2 minor/1 medium end-to-end failures

- Maximum 2 minor/redundancy and platform failures

- Maximum 2 minor security vulnerabilities

Example quality gate for production enviroment:

- 24 hours capacity testing with full call model with memory leak or central processing unit (CPU) spikes

- Maximum 5% memory increase on capacity testing

- Maximum 5% CPU increase on capacity testing

- Maximum 4% increase on number of database transactions

- Maximum 4% increase in I/O on network and transport

Advantages of CI/CD-centric approach:

- One of the biggest advantages of CI/CD-centric release approach is that this approach enables the operator to get early feedback.

- CI/CD-centric approach is the fastest and the most efficient approach to go to market.

Disadvantages of CI/CD-centric approach:

- Automation is a must, and the complexity of automation can be very high in the CI/CD-centric approach.

- Testing environment can be very complex.

Breaking the NFs software into microservices increases the delivery as well as the testing complexity. It becomes very important that the delivery process (software pipeline) as well as the testing process is completely automated for faster and more efficient delivery cycles and enables the operator to reap the flexibility provided by microservice architecture.

5G SA Testing Framework

For a successful testing infrastructure, it is important to formalize the testing procedure and have well-defined testing methodologies and priorities.

One useful concept is the testing pyramid explained in *Succeeding with Agile* by Mike Cohn (Addison-Wesley Professional, 2009). The testing pyramid provides guidelines for testing definitions and buckets, environments, and the number of test-cases to be executed. An example of a testing pyramid can be found in Figure 5-5.

As shown in Figure 5-5, the amount of testing to be done as end-to-end testing during the production phase should be the least, and more test cases should be identified and executed as a part of unit testing and integration testing. Similarly, in a testing pyramid, one should have more unit tests than integration tests, more integration than end-to-end, and so forth. An organization can nevertheless avoid some type of test (e.g., performance testing phase) or the organization can choose to change model testing pyramid, but the key is to define the testing strategy and stick to it.

It is important to avoid an ice-cream-cone mode of testing, where most tests are executed manually in production or a production-like enviroment with little or no automation and minimal unit testing.

Figure 5-5 represents the two testing models.

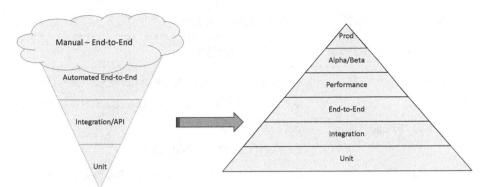

Figure 5-5. *Testing pyramid mode vs ice-cream-cone model*

5G SA Testing Type

Broadly, testing in 5G standalone (SA) can be classified into two categories:

- Functional testing
- Non--functional testing

Functional Testing

Under functional testing, the idea is to test the functionalities offered by each of the NFs as both standalone entities and also as an integrated unit.

From a 5G core network point of view, some of the key functionalities that need to be tested as a part of functional testing are listed in Table 5-1.

Table 5-1. *Test Categories in 5G Core Network*

Test objectives/functions	Funtion to be tested
Service discovery and selection	– Verify the correct discovery of services using NRF – Correct selection and balance across the SBA interfaces
Connection management	– Service request – Service parameter changes
Registration	– Registration/De-registration into the 5GC
Mobility management	– Session continuity in mobility scenarios
Session management	– PDU session establishment – PDU modification – PDU release
Policy framework	– Test policy framework between AMF and PCF; Access mobility and UE policy association – Test policy framework between AMF and SMF; session management
Charging	– Test charging scenarios – Online charging – Offline charging
Voice, IMS, and SMS services	– Voice service establisment – SMS over IP – SMS over NAS – Voice quality – EPS fallback
Redundancy and service restoration	– Node recovery – Node failure – Overload control (due to capacity needs maybe combined with capacity testing)

AMF, access and mobility management function; SMF, session management function; IMS, IP multimedia subsystem; SMS, short messaging service; NAS, non-access stratum; EPS, evolved packet system

There are various types of testing that can be clubbed within functional testing:

- Unit testing

- API testing

- Integration testing

Unit Testing

Unit testing is test type focusing on testing the minimum set of code/functionality that can be clubbed together to form a unit.

This test is typicaly done at the software development phase and at several levels of the software functions.

The software functions can be clubbed together with a debugger, as shown in Figure 5-6 and run on a framework.

Unit testing focuses on internal software functionality and targets to improve microservices integration quality. For example, a paging procedure can be divided in receiving downlink data notifiation, sending paging, and so on, and a unit test can be written to just test that specific functionality.

Unit testing doesn't provide a full view and can't guarantee that the system will work together to delivery a particular use-case.

Unit tests are often developed by the vendors internally, but in the case of a third-party software integration environment, there can be external providers who can perform these unit tests.

Figure 5-6 shows a high-level scope and architecture for the unit testing.

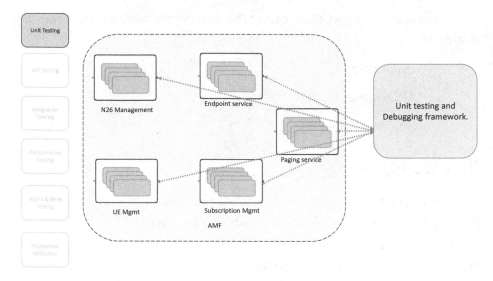

Figure 5-6. *Unit testing scope and architecture*

API Testing

API testing tests the possible interaction between a determined component (i.e., an NF) and matches that against an application programming interface (API) contract/definition.

This can provide an early clue that behavior is matching API contracts and that the component is ready for next level of testing.

The open API definitions for Release 16 can be found at `https://www.3gpp.org/FTP/Specs/archive/OpenAPI/Rel-16`. With the open API definitions, tests and interfaces can be automated and mock APIs can be generated using tools like swagger or specific API simulators and tested for the behavior of the NFs.

Mocking and simulation of APIs will provide capability to test the minimum external functionality if the system is "blackbox"-like.

API testing can also ease the integration testing complications, as in a multivendor environment. If each NF can individually validate the NF behavior with the API testing, then integration between the NFs can be simplied. Following is a scope/architecture for an API testing.

Figure 5-7 illustrates the API integration testing setup.

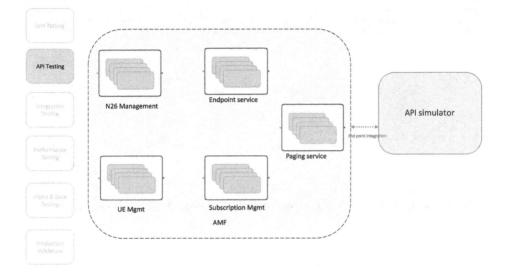

Figure 5-7. *API integration testing setup*

Integration Testing

Integration testing aims to verify the integration of the diferent components and data stores. Different NFs can be integrated with each other in this testing, therefore it is important to fine-tune the parameters, timers, and so forth between the NFs and test for the success as well as failure cases in this phase.

End-to-end testing can be an extention of integration testing wherein all NFs are integrated together and tested for the verification of the end-to-end call flow/use-case.

Figure 5-8 illustrates the integration testing for the 5G core NFs with simulated gNB and UE.

251

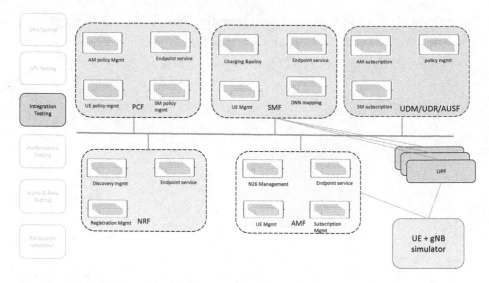

Figure 5-8. *Integration testing for the 5G core NFs with simulated gNB and UE*

Non-Functional Testing

Under non-functional testing, the following types of testing are typically performed:

- – Performance testing

- – Alpha & beta testing

- – Production validation

We will explain each of these types of testing and the focus against each in the coming sections.

Performance/Scale Testing

In performance testing, the aim is to be able to determine the capacity and sanity of the system/NF by subjecting it to load conditions with concurrent scenarios doing different actions.

Performance testing is important to determine any memory leakage, bottlenecks, or general degradation of any key performance indicators (KPIs) for a system.

Apart from the testing setup for the performance testing, one of the key requirements is to freeze on-call models that should be used for the various performance testing.

The main testing objective of performance testing is to determine the performance of the network elements in terms of CPU, RAM, I/O, and database utilization and identify any concurrency problems, memory leaks, disk and network utilization problems, inefficient database calls and utilization, and so forth.

There are different types of performance tests that can be applied to the 5G system such as to determine various KPIs such as:

- Signaling Performance Testing

- Data throughput performance testing

- Long Duration Tests

- Latency Tests

- Component-Based Performance Testing

- System Use-Case-Based Performance Testing

Signaling Performance Testing

In this type of testing, the system/NF is subjected to a high amount of signaling with various types of signaling over a period of time, and the performance of the network/NF is monitored for any call drops/NF failure or downtime in general.

There can be many variants of signaling performance testing, such as the following.

- Busy-hour testing with a call model running to monitor the system for KPI degradation

- NF capacity testing by bombarding the NF with a huge number of signaling transactions (attach/detach/ paging/handover, etc.)

Data Throughput Performance

In the throughput performance testing, the throughput capacity of a system/NF is determined by subjecting the system to a very high data rate and observing the system for any packet drops/KPI degradation.

Throughput testing can take different types:

- Single UE throughput cases

- Single UPF capacity/throughput cases

- System throughput cases

Long Duration Tests

Long duration testing is a very important part of the performance testing where the system/NF is subjected to a certain call model with either signaling-centric or user plane traffic-centric for a duration of around 24, 48, or 72 hours to observe for any degradation in KPI over time.

Latency Tests

Similarly to the long duration tests, it is important to observe the latency for procedures under different levels of load conditions to the system and to ensure that the latency under the different load conditions are not below the quality of service required for the sessions that are served by the system.

There are two main approaches toward performance testing: component-based performance testing and system use-case-based performance testing.

Component-Based Performance Testing

In this type of performance test, the network component can be isolated and built in a production-like infrastructure. With use of a load generator, different load conditions can be simulated to observe the component behavior.

This sometimes is smoke type testing, where the system is observed for some evaluation period (e.g., 24, 48, or 72 hours).

Figure 5-9 shows a simple setup for performance testing for AMF component.

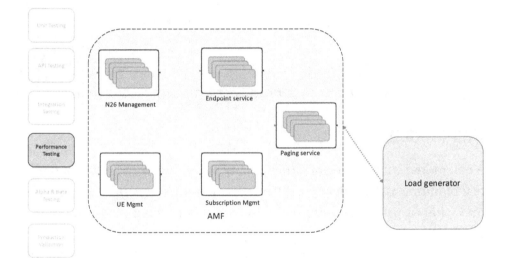

Figure 5-9. *Standalone performance testing for AMF using a load generator*

System Use-Case-Based Performance Testing

In this type of performance testing, there is a use-case-based approach toward testing (i.e., the users are simulated to test performamce of the system when working together). This will be very useful also to test failure and redundancy concepts in a non-production environment.

Figure 5-10 illustrates the architecture for an use-case-based performance testing setup.

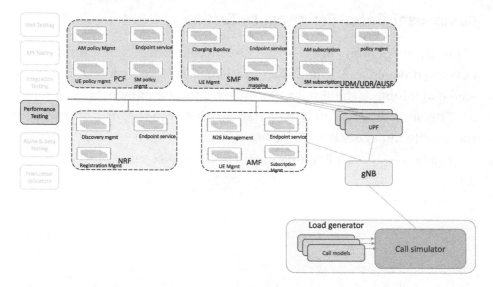

Figure 5-10. *System use-case-based performance testing setup*

Call Models

A call model is a key consideration for any network design/performance test planning. Call models will differ from operator to operator depending on various aspects like subscriber base, network coverage, usage pattern, and so on.

Call model is only indicative and acts as a reference for simulating the test environemnt closer to a production-like environment.

There can be multiple call models that can be used for the performance testing depending on the type of testing, and this will be discussed a little more in detail in the coming section.

Figure 5-11 shows a sample call model that can be termed as a generic call model applicable for the entire system. This can be further baselined to derive NF-specific call models, and the dimensioning of the entire network can be based on the call model.

Generic Call Model Parameters	
Event Rate per SAU per Busy Hour	
Registration	1
Deregistration	1
PDU Session Setup	1
PDU Session Modify (UE, PCF, UDM, CHF)	3
PDU Session Delete	1
Network Initiated release (UDM/PCF/CHF etc any notify)	1
Charging reporting	15
Release Request (Active to Idle)	100
Mobile Originated Service Request	60
Mobile Terminated Service Request	36
TAU	25
Paging	36
Xn Handover	60
N2 Handover	6
EPS Fallback for Voice	5
EPS Fallback for E911	0.001
NR to EUTRAN	15
EUTRAN to NR	6
Rx Dedicated Bearer Creation	6

Call Model Assumptions	
General Parameters	
PDU Per UE	2
Total UE	600000
5G Capable UE	100%
PCF Notify on Active / Idle transition	0
VM Core (HT Disable) -- Physical Cores	18
NRF Cache	50%
NF Cache copies	10
NF Instances	50
NF Services	4
NRF Spurt	5%
Number of gNB to page	5

Figure 5-11. *Generic call model for a 5G SA system*

There are multiple assumptions that go into creating a call model for testing. A few of these assumptions are listed here.

- Busy-hour call attempt assumptions: The rate of attach/detact/handover/PDU establishment/release/ modifications are all assumed based on either previous generation behavior or based on some traffic estimations.

- Hardware capacity assumption

- Capacity estimation provided for UE terminating over NR/EUTRAN

- Resource utilization assumptions: Most dimensions are made with a max resource utilization estimate of 75%-80%.

Figure 5-12 shows the access and mobility management function (AMF) call model that is derived from the generic call model shown in Figure 5-11.

Figure 5-13 shows the session management function (SMF) call model that again is derived from the call model shown in Figure 5-11.

AMF Call Model Parameters	
Event Rate per SAU per Busy Hour	
UE Registration	1
UE Deregistration	1
PDU session setup	1
PDU Session Modification	5
PDU Session Release	1
Service Release (Active to Idle)	100
Network Service Request (Idle to Active)	36
UE Service Request (Idle to Active)	60
Xn based handovers	60
N2 based handovers	6
IRAT 4G to 5G Handover	10
IRAT 5G to 4G Handover	20
TAU	26
Paging	200
Other Events	50

Call Model Assumptions	
General Parameters	
PDU Per UE	2
Total UE (M)	
5G Capable UE	100%

Figure 5-12. *Derived AMF call model from the generic call model*

SMF Call Model Parameters	
Event Rate per PDU Session per Busy Hour	
PDU session setup	1
PDU modify (UE/PCF/UDM/CHF)	5
UE Initiatted release	1
Network Initiated release (UDM/PCF/CHF etc any notify)	1
Usage report	15
Service Release (Active to Idle)	100
Network Service Request (Idle to Active)	36
UE Service Request (Idle to Active)	60
Xn based handovers	60
N2 based handovers	6
IRAT 4G to 5G Handover	10
IRAT 5G to 4G Handover	20
Other Service Requests	50

Call Model assumptions	
General Parameters	
PDU Per UE	2
Total UE (M)	
5G Capable UE	100%

Figure 5-13. *Derieved SMF call model from the generic call model*

Alpha and Beta Testing

In the Alpha and Beta test setup, a production-like environment is set up
with a very small set of users (test users) that are typically friendly to the
organization. This can be used to decrease risk of a large spread of a bug
into a production environment. The operator can take the use of slices to
completely isolate Alpha and Beta production environments, thus creating
an Alpha user slice and Beta user slice for the major market use-cases.

Implementing Alpha and Beta can reduce the need for costly
performance testing if the Alpha and Beta customers have significant
numbers to be statistically meaningful.

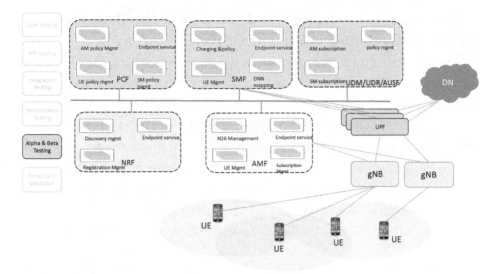

Figure 5-14. *Setup for Alpha and Beta testing*

Production Validation

This type of testing is executed in production environments in a continuous or on-demand way to test service availability and integrity. With traffic routing capabilities, this can be used to stimulate nodes after the upgrades in production.

Security Testing

Using cloud-native-based applications with microservices enhances the possiblity of security threats, because the 5G SA network uses open-source tools and open API for integration between the NFs and the tools, and use of MEC as a remote/edge data center also increases the threat because it exposes the NFs residing on these MECs to a less restricted access location.

Therefore, security testing should be considered for all steps of the process followed during the deployment of a 5G network. Also considering that in lab environments there are relaxed security restrictions, it becomes important that before the production rollout, there are production-like security considerations and testing performed.

One good practice would be to use transport layer security (TLS) on API that can be omitted in initial environments for the better understanding of call flows and messages and to ease the integration in general, but at least in the production-like environment, they should be enabled to overcome and flag any security threats.

Figure 5-15 shows the challenges with security introduced by 5G.

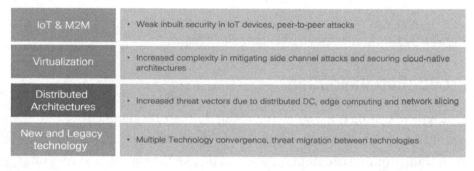

Figure 5-15.   *Challenges with security in 5G*

Figure 5-16 shows the different security threats that need to be addressed in 5G.

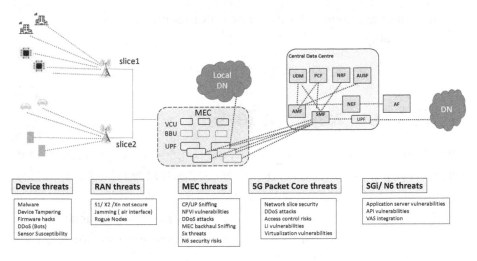

Figure 5-16. *Security threats in 5G*

As shown, there are different types of security threats in 5G, such as device threats, RAN threats, MEC threats, core network threats, N6/SGi threats, and so forth.

Vulnerability and distributed denial of service (DDoS)-related testing needs to be performed to address each of these threats as a part of the security testing for 5G.

Some of the key points to test for security vulnerability are:

- container secuirty testing

- virtualized network function (VNF)/cloud-native network function (CNF) security testing

- API security testing

- network security testing

- host security testing

- security considerations for roaming network

   – management/operation and automation security
     testing

   – security considerations for 4G integration

5G NSA Core Network Testing

With the introduction of NSA to the already deployed 4G network, there is
a significant amount of impact on the 4G nodes that need to be tested for
functional as well as performance stability.

Figures 5-17 and 5-18 show some of the key network elements that are
impacted due to introduction of NSA and the corresponding functional
impact on the network elements.

Device under test (DUT)	Functional impacts to be tested
MME	Support high bandwidth with extended QoS
	Support of secondary RAT procedures
	5G DCNR secondary RAT subscription control
	Support for flag on the NC-NR flag on DNS query for P-GW and S-GW
	Support the extended reporting of secondary RAN usage
SGW/PGW	Single user maximum throughput on DL and UL
	Support for extended QoS
	Generation of CDR with extended secondary RAT usage
	New QoS marking
	Potential TCP behavior and optimizations
HSS	Access restriction to 5G NR
	Extensions to AMBR for the extended bandwidth
DNS	Match the NC-NR tag
PCRF	Support for extended bandwidth support
Charging and OCS	Support for CDR with secondary RAT usage report
	Support for extended bandwidth support
	Capacity for charging at 5G speed and assignment of big quotas
Voice and IMS	Dedicated bearer creation with user falling back to 4G
	Correct transport of SMS and IMS signaling when in 5G

Figure 5-17. *Functional testing impact due to introduction of 5G NSA*

Test Area	Test Categories / Types
Device type testing	Test with 4G capable
	Tests with 5G NSA capable
	Tests with 4G APN
	Tests with 5G APN
Performance testing	Signaling testing because of introduction of new UE types
	User plane throughput testing
	Fair usage testing (between 4G and 5G NSA users using common resources)
	Long duration testing with 5GNSA specific call models
Redundancy testing	HSS / MME/ SAEGW-U / SAEGW-C redundancy and recovery testing
	DNS failure testing
	Secondary node failure testing
4G Regression testing	Handover testing
	IMS and emergency call testing
	Basic regression testing

Figure 5-18. *Other testing impact due to introduction of 5G NSA*

Testing Integration Points between 5G SA

The functional tests that need to be covered as a part of the 5G SA core network testing have already been discussed under the functional testing section.

In this section, we will discuss the testing required to validate the integration points between 5G SA and 4G/5G NSA. The design considerations for this were discussed in Chapter 4.

Following is a list of regression for a converged core approach needed for 4G and 5G NSA testing in the the SA core.

Scenarios for 4G-5G interworking that should be considered as a part of the test plan are listed here:

- mobility scenarios beween 5G SA and 4G/using N26 interface

- mobility scenarios without N26 interface

- EPS fallback for voice

- emergency services fallback

263

- interworking scenarios for UE with dual-registration capability

- node selection cases for UEs during mobility between 4G and 5G

- domestic roaming between 4G and 5G networks

Figures 5-19 and 5-20 show the various types of test scenarios that should be tested as a part of the interworking between 4G and 5G networks and also the impacted nodes in the 4G network and the 5G core network due to the interworking, which can help with the planning of test coverage.

Test Type	E2E Test Scenario	Impacted EPC Nodes	Impacted 5GC Nodes
Interworking with EPS	Interaction with PCC	PGW-C, HSS, DNN, PCRF, MME	SMF, PCF, NRF , UDM, AMF
	Mobility Restriction	PGW-C, HSS, DNN, PCRF, MME	SMF, PCF , NRF , UDM, AMF
	PGW Selection	PGW-C, HSS, DNN, PCRF, MME	SMF, PCF , NRF , UDM, AMF
	PDN connection establishment	PGW-C, HSS, DNN, PCRF, MME	SMF, PCF , NRF , UDM, AMF
	Network Configuration	MME	AMF
Handover Procedures	5GS to EPS handover using N26 interface	MME, SGW, HSS, PCRF DNS	AMF, PGW-c+SMF, PGW-u+UPF, UDM , CHF
	EPS to 5GS handover using N26 interface	MME, SGW, HSS, PCRF DNS	AMF, PGW-c+SMF, PGW-u+UPF, UDM , CHF
	Handover Cancel	MME, SGW, HSS, PCRF DNS	AMF, PGW-c+SMF, PGW-u+UPF, UDM , CHF
Idle Mode Mobility	5GS to EPS Idle mode mobility using N26 interface	MME, SGW, HSS, PCRF DNS	AMF, PGW-c+SMF, PGW-u+UPF, UDM , CHF
	EPS to 5GS Mobility Registration Procedure (Idle and Connected State) using N26 interface	MME, SGW, HSS, PCRF DNS	AMF, PGW-c+SMF, PGW-u+UPF, UDM , CHF
	EPS to 5GS Mobility Registration Procedure (Idle) using N26 interface with AMF reallocation	MME, SGW, HSS, PCRF DNS	AMF, PGW-c+SMF, PGW-u+UPF, UDM , CHF
Impact to EPS procedures	E-UTRAN Initial Attach	MME, HSS, DNS, SGW, PGW-C +SMF	-
	Tracking Area Update	MME, HSS, DNS,	-
	PDN Connection Request	MME, HSS, DNS, SGW, PGW-C +SMF	
	Registration procedure	MME	AMF
	UE Requested PDU Session Establishment procedure		AMF, PGW-c+SMF, PGW-u+UPF, UDM
	UE or Network Requested PDU Session Modification procedure		

Figure 5-19. *Test scenarios for 4G-5G interworking and its impact on EPC and 5G core nodes*

Requirement Name	E2E Call Flow Name	EPC	5GC
Support for Emergency and IMS service	EPS fallback for IMS voice	MME, PGW-C, PGW-U, HSS, DNN, PCRF	SMF, PCF , NRF , UDM, AMF, IMS
	NPLI for IMS calls	MME, PGW-C, PGW-U, HSS, DNN, PCRF	SMF, PCF , NRF , UDM, AMF, IMS
	Emergency service	MME, PGW-C, PGW-U, HSS, DNN, PCRF	SMF, PCF , NRF , UDM, AMF, IMS

Figure 5-20. *Test scenarios for EPS fallback/emergency service fallback*

Figure 5-21 highlights the summary of changes/functionalities that need to be tested or planned for testing during the integration on the 4G network side.

Considering that there can be scenarios in the operator network where there can be 4G, 5G NSA, as well as 5G SA all being served at the same time, corresponding integration should be planned as a part of the 4G-5G interworking so that there is no impact to the performance or functionality of the 4G or the 5G NSA network due to the introduction of the 5G SA network.

Device Under Test (DUT)	Function to be Tested
MME	N26 field and parameters
	Test the support of the of 5GC interworking on S5/S11
	AMF discovery using DNS based on TAC
	Selection of PGW-C based on SMF flag
SGW	Support for extended QoS
	New QoS marking
	Potential TCP behaviour and optimizations
	Aditional S5/s11
HSS	Access restriction to "CN type restriction"
DNS	Support of SMF tag to allow a selection of a PGW-C capable of acting as SMF.

Figure 5-21. *Impact on the 4G core network elements due to introduction of 5G SA*

Impact Changes to be Tested in 5G

Figure 5-22 shows the testing impacts on the 5G core network elements specifically due to the mobility of the UE from a 4G network to a 5G network.

Device under test (DUT)	Function to be tested
AMF	N1 mode support for UE
	CN restriction base on N8 subscription data :
	-EPC restriction
	-RAT restriction in EPS
	-Slice selection interworking for EPC based on DDN
	N11 - Interworking indication
	N26 - interworking and mapping of EPS parameters
SMF and PGW-C	Map the EPS service parameters into 5GC service parameters
UPF and PGW-U	

Figure 5-22. *5G core impact due to interworking with 4G*

Redundancy Testing in 5G

Redundancy testing can be classified into two types:

1) Node/NF failure testing

2) Platform failure testing

Node/NF Failure Testing

Node redundancy testing should consider the failure of each of the NFs one by one to ensure that the network is still able to sustain the failure without any loss in capacity or efficiency.

For each of the NF failure scenarios it is important to verify the following:

– The standby NF is able to assume the tasks of the active NF, and new calls are not impacted.

– There is no loss in KPIs because of any of the NF failure.

– Latency is not impacted because of the failure of one of the NFs.

– There is no impact on the performance of the system when an NF fails.

Figure 5-23 shows the redundancy layout for a simple Release 15 5G SA network.

Additionally, there can be other nodes like SCP, BSF, SEPP, EIR, SMSF, and so forth that again need to be tested and verified for failure and recovery.

Figure 5-23 is only indicative, and depending on the operator design for 5GSA, the node selection procedure can differ, which will have an impact to the redundancy model as well.

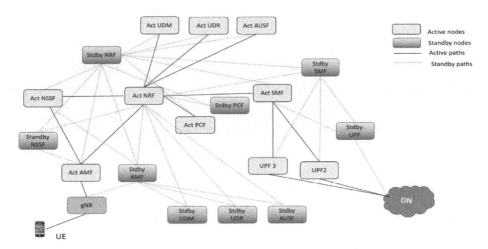

Figure 5-23. *Redundancy layout for a simple Release15 5G SA network*

Platform Failure Testing

Considering that the NFs in 5G SA are mainly microservices based and are hosted on container platforms like Kubernetes, it is important to plan, design, and also test the system for redundancy of the platform components.

Figure 5-24 shows a few example test-cases for the redundancy testing of the platform.

Kubernetes Failure	Expected Behavior
Failing multiple masters	The remaining master would become active No impact to any functionality Automatically recovered
Failing worker node	Automatically recovered → no impact The POD's on the worker node will be redeployed on other spare worker nodes
Nginx-ingress	These pods should move to other nodes Automatically recovered
Kube Proxy (iptables mode)	When a pod is added whenever the kube-proxy is down, then those iptables are not added and will be added when the kube-proxy comes up Automatically recovered → no impact
Helm failure	Automatically recovered → no impact
application POD failure (AMF pod / SMF POD / NRF pod etc)	Automatically recovered → no impact

Figure 5-24. *Sample Kubernetes failure redundancy testing*

Apart from the aforementioned redundancy planning, for an efficient functioning of the system, it is also important to plan for redundancy for the hardware and infrastructure components like NTP server, power supply to the hardware, and so on, and appropriate testing should be performed to verify the system performance by simulating the failure of these components.

Monitoring and Troubleshooting

An ideal Cloud native application as 5GC should be implemented on top of a robust framework for monitoring and troubleshooting. Due to the complexity increase this should be a day1 consideration.

Figure 5-25 illustrates a reference architecture for monitoring and troubleshooting.

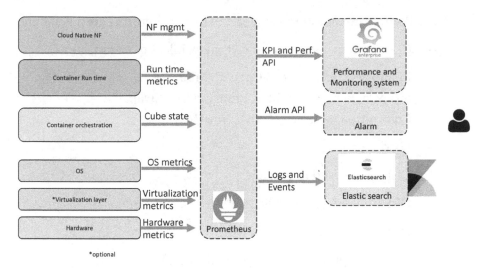

Figure 5-25. *Illustration of monitoring and troubleshooting*

Host-Level Monitoring

Host-level monitoring focuses on monitoring the hosts on which the NFs are deployed. This can cover the hardware, virutalization layer, and the operating system level performance monitoring to be able to correlate the alarms that are raised for a particular failure.

Figure 5-26 represents the reference architecture for host-level monitoring.

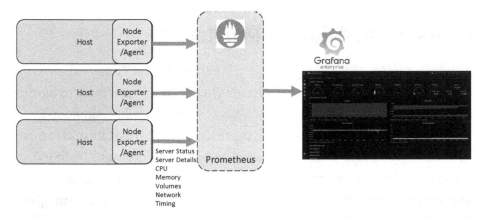

Figure 5-26. *Host-level monitoring*

The KPIs that are monitored as a part of host monitoring are listed here.

- CPU (system, user, nice, iowait, steal, idle, irq, softirq, guest)

- Memory (Apps, Buffers, Cached, Free, Sla, SwapCached, PageTables, VmallocUser, Swap, Committed, Mapped, Active, Inactive)

- Load

- Disk space used in percent

- Disk utilization per device

- Disk IOS per device (read, write)

- Disk throughput per device (read, write)

- Context switches

- Network traffic (in, out)

- Netstat (established)

- UDP stats (InDatagrams, InErrors, OutDatagrams, NoPorts)

A detailed view and possibility of correlation between NF failures and the running host is a must in any monitoring system allowing for an easy troubleshoot.

Container and Cluster Monitoring

Although we can think of an NF as a single entity, they run in several containers as part of a Kubernetes cluster. Therefore, it is vital that monitoring of the containers will provide more visibility during any failure situation.

Prometheus can be used to aggregate the metric and state and expose APIs as well as alerting base on those. Each container is monitor-based on KPI metrics, and the process run-time information can be collected. This can be taken into account to scale the microservices inside and give flexibility to the CNF.

Figure 5-27 represents the reference architecture for container and cluster monitoring.

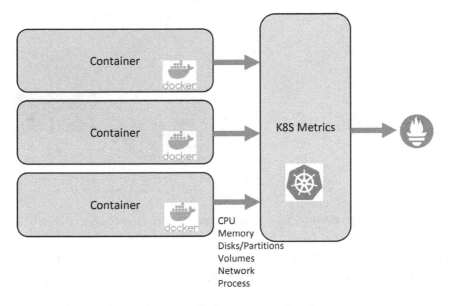

Figure 5-27. *Container and cluster monitoring*

Application/NF Monitoring

NF performance metrics are important for inferring the user experience and to start a top-down troubleshooting exercise. The NF will have an internal service that will be aggregating the metrics and send them to Prometheus for aggregation. Using those capabilities, a fullstack view can be useful when elaborated into graphana or any other reporting tool.

3GPP defines in TS 28.552 a set of metrics that can be use for different NF based on there procedure highlighting the following.

Figure 5-28 represents the reference architecture for application/NF monitoring.

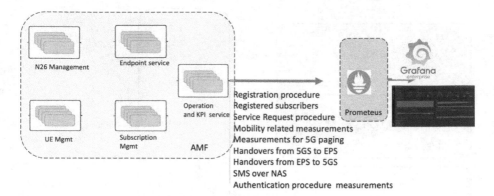

Figure 5-28. *Application/NF monitoring*

Figure 5-29, Figure 5-30, Figure 5-31, and Figure 5-32 show sample KPIs that can be used by the operator for the network functions UDM, NRF, PCF, and SMF, respectively.

NF Function	Procedure	KPI
UDM	Registered subscribers measurement	Mean number of registered subscribers through UDM
		Maximum number of registered subscribers through UDM
		Mean number of unregistered subscribers through UDM
		Maximum number of unregistered subscribers through UDM

Figure 5-29. *Sample KPIs for UDM NF monitoring*

NF Function	Procedure	KPI
NRF	NF service registration related measurements	Number of NF service registration requests
		Number of successful NF service registrations
		Number of failed NF service registrations due to encoding error of NF profile
		Number of failed NF service registrations due to NRF internal error
	NF service update related measurements	Number of NF service update requests
		Number of successful NF service updates
		Number of failed NF service updates due to encoding error of NF profile
		Number of failed NF service updates due to NRF internal error
	NF service discovery related measurements	Number of NF service discovery requests
		Number of successful NF service discoveries
		Number of failed NF service discoveries due to unauthorized NF Service consumer
		Number of failed NF service discoveries due to input errors
		Number of failed NF service discoveries due to NRF internal error

Figure 5-30. *Sample KPIs for NRF NF monitoring*

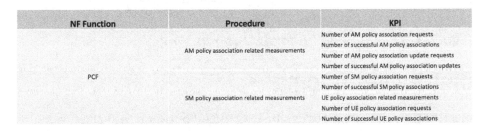

NF Function	Procedure	KPI
PCF	AM policy association related measurements	Number of AM policy association requests
		Number of successful AM policy associations
		Number of AM policy association update requests
		Number of successful AM policy association updates
	SM policy association related measurements	Number of SM policy association requests
		Number of successful SM policy associations
		UE policy association related measurements
		Number of UE policy association requests
		Number of successful UE policy associations

Figure 5-31. *Sample KPIs for PCF NF monitoring*

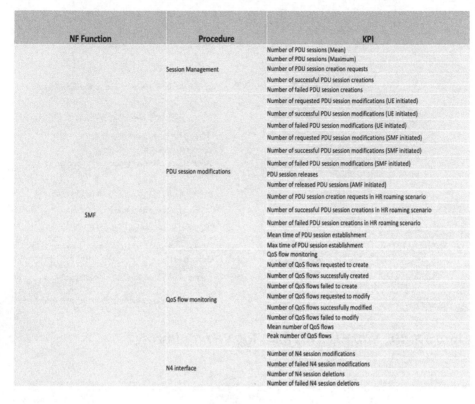

NF Function	Procedure	KPI
SMF	Session Management	Number of PDU sessions (Mean)
		Number of PDU sessions (Maximum)
		Number of PDU session creation requests
		Number of successful PDU session creations
		Number of failed PDU session creations
		Number of requested PDU session modifications (UE initiated)
		Number of successful PDU session modifications (UE initiated)
		Number of failed PDU session modifications (UE initiated)
		Number of requested PDU session modifications (SMF initiated)
		Number of successful PDU session modifications (SMF initiated)
	PDU session modifications	Number of failed PDU session modifications (SMF initiated)
		PDU session releases
		Number of released PDU sessions (AMF initiated)
		Number of PDU session creation requests in HR roaming scenario
		Number of successful PDU session creations in HR roaming scenario
		Number of failed PDU session creations in HR roaming scenario
		Mean time of PDU session establishment
		Max time of PDU session establishment
		QoS flow monitoring
		Number of QoS flows requested to create
		Number of QoS flows successfully created
		Number of QoS flows failed to create
	QoS flow monitoring	Number of QoS flows requested to modify
		Number of QoS flows successfully modified
		Number of QoS flows failed to modify
		Mean number of QoS flows
		Peak number of QoS flows
	N4 interface	Number of N4 session modifications
		Number of failed N4 session modifications
		Number of N4 session deletions
		Number of failed N4 session deletions

Figure 5-32. *Sample KPIs for SMF monitoring*

Distributed Tracing

In a CNF, several messages can be exchanged between the services and between several NFs. This makes PCAP-based troubleshooting very difficult, if not impossible. The normal approach is that APIs are instrumentalized with TAG ID on the message exchange. This provides the tracer with the capability to undertand the end-to-end flow of API messages, exporting this in a user-friendly way. The open tracing provides a framework that is compatible with several monitoring solutions, including Jaeger, Dynatrace, AppMon, and AppDynamics, making this implementation easier to achieve.

Figure 5-33 shows an example of distributed tracing.

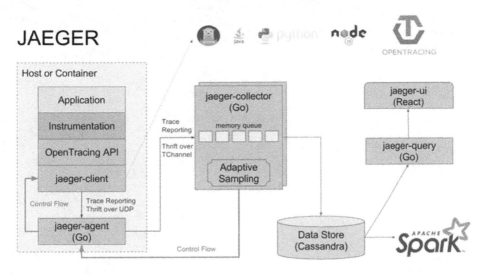

Figure 5-33. *Distributed tracing*

CHAPTER 6

Automation in 5G

Most of the mobile operators who are planning a transition from 4G to 5G will need to consider building a mobile network that is more standard-based and fully automated with a control on the complete network (software control). This will require the operators to plan their data center in a distributed manner, with a few data centers/sites marked as central data centers, where most of the network functions (NFs) and application functions will be deployed and several data centers marked as multi-access edge control (MEC) data centers. MEC data centers, where a few NFs like virtualized central units (vCUs), user plane functions (UPFs), local domain name systems (DNSs), and some local application functions will be deployed and many more smaller data centers where the virtualized distributed units (vDUs), and repeater interface units (RIUs) can reside are called far edge data centers.

Each of these locations can contain physical routers and (NF virtual infrastructure (NFVI) pods on which virtual network functions (VNFs)/NFs shall be deployed or provisioned. A mobile backhaul exists for all backhaul traffic between the edge sites and the central location.

Considering the complexity of the distributed architecture and the deployment, monitoring, and maintainence of all these NFs, it is inevitable for the operators to have a fully automated solution for network deployment, operation, and management with the following ask for the automation network.

© Rajaneesh Sudhakar Shetty 2021
R. S. Shetty, *5G Mobile Core Network*, https://doi.org/10.1007/978-1-4842-6473-7_6

- **Pervasive automation:** to enable a lean operations team

- **Resilient network:** resilient to human and natural faults

- **Ease of network rollout:** deploying a large number of sites in as seamless a manner as possible

- **Ease of service rollout:** deploying additional network services as seamlessly as possible

To be able to support these asks, the NF virtual orchestrator (NFVO) will need to have the technical capabilities to support the following:

- Provisioning and lifecycle management of all VNFs/NFs in the mobile network

- Configuration management of all VNFs/NFs in a phased manner as necessary

- Configuration of mobile backhaul elements as necessary for a successful end-to-end call flow

- Configuration of data center fabric to enable the provisioning and successful communication of all VNFs/NFs

- Managing and onboarding new virtual and physical network elements onto the network, as and when they are introduced

Network Slicing in 5G

Network slicing is fundamentally an end-to-end partitioning of the network resources and NFs so that selected applications/services/connections may run in isolation from each other for a specific business purpose. It enables a service provider to structure separate business relationships and processes toward customers with differentiated policies, charging, service level agreements (SLAs), isolated monitoring and identity, and so on.

The basic benefit of a network slice is that each separable business operation can be designed as a network slice and can be efficiently and reliably run.

Since it is possible to isolate network elements and group them together based on the business case that they are serving, it has a significant reduction on regression test cycles, and it ensures that the failure points are restricted to smaller groups of nodes and thus makes it very quick and easier to introduce new services to a system. Some of the key decision points while planning a slice are listed here.

- **UPF placement decision:** Depending on the business use-case and the slice SLA requirement, the placement of the UPF in MEC vs central DC must be planned.

- **Cloud-native 5G core requirements:** The decision between shared or dedicated mobility NFs is key while planning a network slice. The minimum requirement for a slice is a dedicated UPF; however, practically depending on the use-case and the billing requirement, the session management function (SMF), policy control function (PCF), charging function (CHF), and NF repository function (NRF) are also planned as exclusive NFs for a slice. The placement of these NFs is another aspect that needs to be considered while deciding on the slice design.

- **Transport network path behavior (SLA):** Some of the slices, like ultra-reliable low-latency communication (URLLC) slices, will require low latency; some other slices require high bandwidth and high reliability (fast reroute, shared risk link groups [SRLG], etc.). Some slices require encrypted paths, and so on. All these considerations should be a part of the transport network planning for a slice.

279

Fundamental Requirements for Slicing Automation

It should be possible for the service provider to dynamically create, modify, or delete a slice without impacting other slices.

- **Intent-based management:** Intent-based management as defined by [RFC7575] is "an abstract, high-level policy used to operate a network." Intent against SLA targets for each tenant instance is required for managing the volume and velocity of 5G services and resources.

- **Closed control loop (CCL):** For dynamic/real-time slice adjustment flexibility to be provided to any intent-based management, there is a need to support layered orchestration and CCLs (which does not imply multiple orchestrator implementations) to be able to warranty the SLAs.

- **Hybrid infrastructure management:** Cross-domain orchestration is a must to be able to impose segmentation in sub-slice/domain for scale and abstraction.

Figure 6-1 shows an 5G network slicing full stack with the provisioning orchestration and assurance platform working together to realize a business use-case across domains.

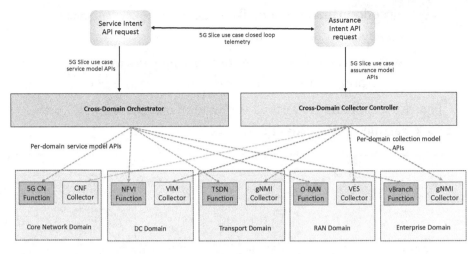

Figure 6-1. *Intent-based modeling concept*

Automation for a 5G Packet Core

Automation for a 5G packet core can be further classified into day0, day1, and day2 automation.

The day0 automation mainly focuses on the provisioning of the VNFs/cloud-native network function (CNFs), device onboarding onto the domain orchestrator. In some environments, where there is a continuous process of integration and development (CI/CD) integration required, the Day0 automation activity will include the CI/CD framework integration with the core network domain orchestrator.

The day1 automation focuses on the day1 configuration generation and applying the configuration to the VNF/CNFs.

In the day2 automation, there are various activities that need to be automated, such as:

– upgrades of the VNFs/CNFs

– differential configurations automation

– monitoring these VNFs/CNFs and analyzing the data

   – close-loop management like scale in/scale out, lifecycle management, and so on

   – service assurance for the entire core network by performing root cause analysis

Figure 6-2 explains the various automation use-cases for 5G core network classified as day0/day1 and day2.

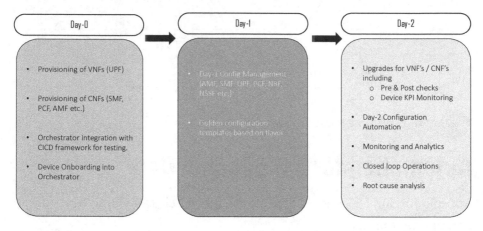

Figure 6-2. *5G core network automation use-cases*

The orchestration workflow for a 5G core network slice creation can be illustrated by the diagram in Figure 6-2, which consists of four main phases:

1. **Deploy phase:** In the deploy phase, the images, flavors, network design, and model definition for the VNFs per slice are deployed on an NFVI

2. **Install:** In the install phase, the Kubernetes cluster is deployed with the assignment of roles of master and worker nodes within the cluster.

3. **Configure:** In this phase, the day1 configuration for the NFs is applied and the NSI and NSSIs are created and NFs are assigned to the slice.

4. **Execute:** In the execute phase, the slice is activated and ready to handle traffic and provide service to the subscribers.

Figure 6-3 shows the flow that is used for a network function deployment and configuration to achieve different slices within the domain.

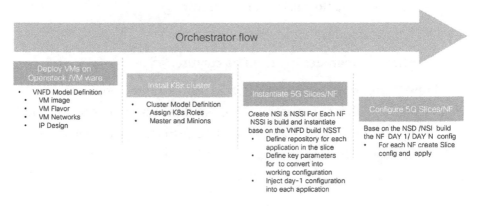

Figure 6-3. *5G core NF and slice creation*

While deploying the 5G core network, there are different layers of the 5G core that require automation other than the 5G core network slice creation/orchestration workflow.

The following are the different layers of 5G core network that needs to be automated.

- – Infrastructure
- – Deployment
- – Function
- – Configuration
- – 5G Abstraction

Infrastructure

From the infrastructure automation perspective, there can be many alternatives depending on the customer requirements, such as Openstack, VMWARE, baremetal deployment, and so on. There also can be a hybrid

283

setup where there are different VNFs/CNFs hosted on different types of infrastructure. The infrastructure automation should be able to:

- onboard platforms into orchestrator,

- understand the network topology, and

- handle upgrades in the infrastructure.

Figure 6-4 represents one such hybrid infrastructure environment.

In Figure 6-4, the deployer is an element that should be able to install new cluster, modify/upgrade cluster, add node to cluster, as well as remove node from cluster, thereby managing the critical node detection problem (CNDP) nodes for any NF deployment.

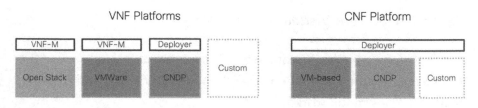

Figure 6-4. *Hybrid infrastructure with different platforms*

Deployment

In the deployment layer, the automation framework needs to support the onboarding of the different infrastructure options as listed in the infrastructure section. There is also a need for the infrastucture to be kept isolated from the aforementioned layers.

Some of the key automation tasks in this phase include:

- deployment of the cluster nodes that can perform the cluster management tasks for the cluster

- configuration of the CNF clusters

- image management

- lifecycle management of the cluster manager

— network configurations and node replacements,
  if required, for the cluster nodes

Deployment layer automation is illustrated in Figure 6-5.

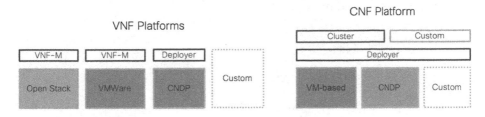

Figure 6-5. *Deployment layer automation*

Function

In the function layer, the main automation ask is to support the onboarding of the different network functions on top of different infrastructures.

For a hybrid scenario (as shown in Figure 6-6), there should be different automation flows to onboard the NFs on the cloud-native platform vs the VNFs on the VMWARE/openstack infrastructure.

Apart from deploying the VNFs and NFs, in this layer there is a need to automatically allocate the addresses and also perform the lifecycle management, such as upgrade, failure detection and recovery, status handling, and so on for these VNFs/CNFs.

Figure 6-6 illustrates the automation for the network function layer.

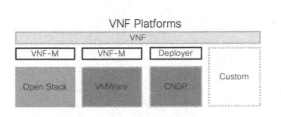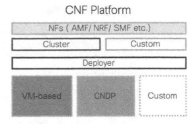

Figure 6-6. *Function layer automation*

Configuration

In the configuration layer, there is a need to automate the day1 configurations for the VNF and the CNF nodes that are deployed on the 5G core system, as shown in Figure 6-7.

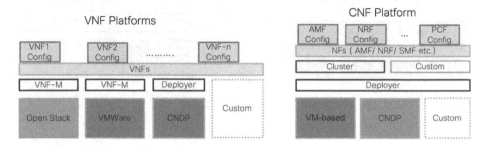

Figure 6-7. *Configuration layer automation*

5G Abstraction

In the abstraction layer, there is a need to aggregate the slices and sub-slices and bundle the NFs according to the slices. The slice-specific bundling, configuration, and provisioning can be automated as a part of this layer.

Figure 6-8 illustrates the 5G abstration layer automation.

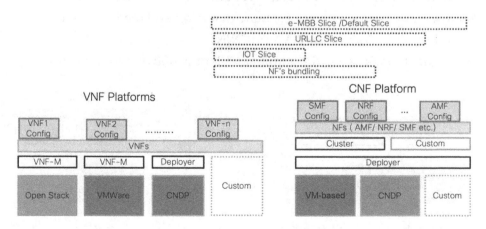

Figure 6-8. *5G abstraction*

Figure 6-9 shows an example of one of the 5G packet core VNF (UPF) with an automated slice lifecycle management for the VNF.

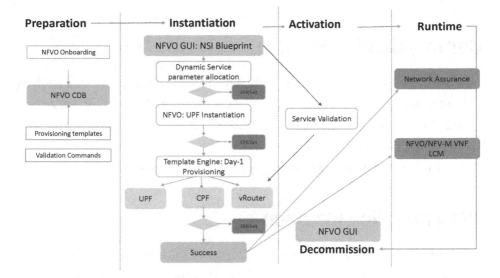

Figure 6-9. *UPF slice lifecycle with core network domain slice orchestrator*

End-to-End Slice Automation and Management

5G networks will consist of three main domains:

- − access network domain

- − core network domain

- − transport network domain

While planning network slicing as a feature to offer various use-cases, it is important to consider the impact of slicing on all three domains and the switching of these three domains together to realize an end-to-end slice.

Before we can discuss the end-to-end orchestration and its automation requirements, it is important to understand a few terminologies and some concepts behind the same.

Communication Service

A communication service can include a bundle of specific services, such as voice service, data service, uRLLC service, and so on. Each of the services should be realized/served by different PDU sessions.

Also, a specific PDU session makes use of a single network slice, and different PDU sessions may belong to different network slices.

Network Slice Instance

Network slice instance (NSI) is a set of NFs and network slice subnet instance (NSSIs) that comibned together can support a certain set of communication services which serves a certain business use case.

Network Slice Subnet Instance

Network slice subnet instance (NSSI) is introduced for the purpose of NSI management. NSSI is a subset of NSI and can be a combination of one or more NFs within a particular domain. NSI can consist of multiple NSSIs across different domains, like RAN and core network domains.

The RAN domain can have multiple NSSIs in standalone (i.e., NSSI-a or NSSI-b). Similarly, core network domain can also have multiple NSSIs (i.e., NSSI-c, NSSI-d, etc.). NSI can be achieved by logically combining the NSSI's from different domains together (as shown in Figure 6-10), NSI-1 is achieved by combining the NSSI-a and NSSI-c. Similarly, NSI-3 is achieved by combining the NSSI's NSSI-E and NSSI-B together.

Figure 6-10 shows the relationship between NSI and NSSI.

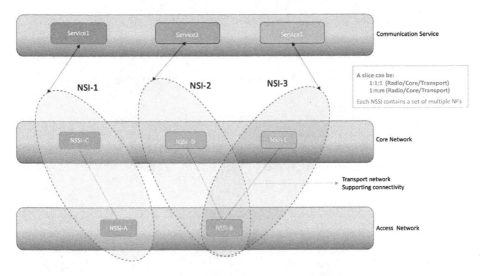

Figure 6-10. *Relationship between communication services NSI and NSSI*

Some key points include:

- Two NSIs can be physically/logically isolated from each other either fully or partially.

- Two or more NSIs can share a common NSSF. This is also called a shared constituent of NSI.

- Two or more NSSIs can share a common NF. This is also called a shared constituent of NSSF.

- An NSSI may contain only a core network function or only an access network function or multiple network functions within the same domain.

Network Slice Instance Lifecycle

In an operator's networks, the NSI is a managed entity that has a lifecycle of its own and is independent of the lifecycle of the service instances that are associated with it.

A network slice lifecycle consists of the following phases:

- preparation phase

- instantiation, configuration, and activation phase

- runtime phase

- decommissioning phase

Figure 6-11 shows the 3GPP representation for the lifecycle phases of an NSI.

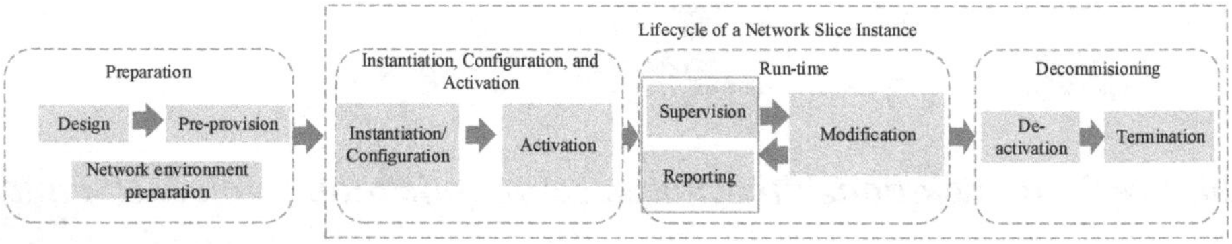

Figure 6-11. *Lifecycle phases of a NSI ➤ 3GPP spec 23.801*

Preparation Phase

The NSI does not exist during the preparation phase. It includes the creation of the network slice templates, slice design, creation of the network environments, onboarding of the templates to support the lifecycle of the NSIs, and other preperation activities. During the preparation phase, these templates that are created can also be verified.

Instantiation, Configuration, and Activation Phase

During this phase, all the NSI-related resources are created and are configured to ensure that the NSI is ready for operation. In the activation step, the NSI is made active by steps like diversion of traffic, activation of database, and so on. Network slice instantiation, configuration, and activation can include instantiation, configuration, and activation of other shared and/or non-shared NFs.

During this phase, the "Create a NSI" operation is supported, which may trigger the creation of NSSIs or setting up the associations for an existing NSSIs.

Run-Time Phase

In the run-time phase, the NSI is capable of traffic handling to support the corresponding communication services. The run-time phase includes monitoring and reporting and corresponding modification activities like upgrades, reconfiguration, NF association and disassociation with an NSI, and so on.

The following three operations are supported in the run-time phase:

- **Activate an NSI:** As the name suggests, the activation of NSI includes actions that enable the NSI to provide the services marked for the NSI. This may trigger activation of the corresponding NSSIs as well.

- **Modify an NSI:** During the NSI modification, the NSI is reconfigured and several workflows such as change in NSI capacity and topology can be triggered. NSI modification can be triggered by change in the network slice requirement or change in the communication service requirements or can be a result of assurance action from the NSI monitoring automatically. NSI modification may trigger corresponding NSSI modification.

- **Deactivate an NSI:** As the name suggests, the deactivation of the NSI would stop the NSI from providing the corresponding communication service. Before modifying an NSI, there might be a need to deactivate the NSI to perform the necessary changes followed by activation of the NSI. NSI deactivation trigger NSSI deactivation to deactivate corresponding NSSIs that are not used by other NSI(s).

291

Decommissioning Phase

The decommissioning phase includes deactivation of the NSI and repurposing the dedicated resources of the NSI for other activities. The NSI will not exist anymore after the decommissioning phase.

The operation performed in the decommissioning phase is the "Terminate an NSI" action.

Service Orchestration Solution

Service orchestrator abstracts all the underlying network domains and provides a single interface to upstream OSS/BSS systems and portals, thereby reducing integration tax with upstream OSS/BSS solutions. Service orchestrator will then interface with multiple resource orchestrators using, for example, Network Configuration Protocol (NETCONF) downstream.

Resource/Domain orchestrator's role is to manage the specific network domain interfacing with the network and its controller. This helps in performing cross-domain orchestration using different resource orchestrators (e.g., IP transport, data center, etc).

Service orchestrator and resource orchestrator can both use the same orchestration engine, allowing services to be modeled as stacked services, whereas a complex service can use multiple other service models.

The service orchestrator is a mandatory automation requirement as far as 5G is concerned.

The key requirements around a service orchestration solution from an operator's point of view are:

- The service orchestration solution should be able to perform an end-to-end service lifecycle management in centralized and distributed data center scenarios by fulfilling requests for network functions, applications, and network connectivity needed for the service.

- It should be possible to configure the service orchestration solution through service templates and other metadata.

- It should support open modeling languages (e.g., YANG, TOSCA, YAML) and follow open modeling standards.

- The service orchestator should be able to provide onboarding tools/adaptors to allow different vendors' specific descriptors to map to common models and vice versa for network service and NFs.

- The service orchestator should support API management and monitoring.

- The service orchestator should manage an inventory of service instances, including the components that make up each service instance.

- The service orchestrator should be able to handle triggers from service assurance models for scale-in/scale-out.

- It is very important for the service orchestrator to support/realize zero-touch provisioning, especially considering the complexity of the 5G network provisioning.

- The service orchestration solution should be able to support the following capabilities to secure and protect data:

  - database fail-over mechanisms

  - data backup

- secured data storage

- data consistency

- The service orchestation solution should support
  the "Network-as-a-Service" concept that enables
  WAN transport services to be created, managed, and
  monitored by a tenant.

- The service orchestration solution must support
  orchestration of multiple domains (e.g., transport, RAN,
  core network domains) and also be able to manage
  these network domains in a multi-vendor environment.

In cases where the service provider plans to provide enterprise solutions in the 5G network, the service orchestration solution should be designed to be able to fulfill enterpise service requests (e.g., network connectivity, NFs, and applications orchestration).

One of the most popular cloud orchestration softwares that is used widely in the telecom industry is network service orchestrator (NSO) by Cisco.

Figure 6-12 shows an end-to-end orchestration overview where a particular communication service is translated into network slice management function inputs that, together with inputs from the OSS/BSS of the operator, is able to orchestrate an end-to-end slice across the various domains like RAN domain, core network domain, and transport domain by providing the required configuration changes as inputs to these various domain slice managers.

The domain slice managers, in turn, provision the slice parameters/ configurations to the respective NFs in the domains, thereby realizing an end-to-end slice in a completely automated manner.

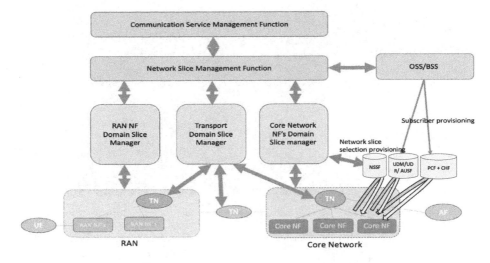

Figure 6-12. *End-to-end slice orchestration overview*

End-to-end orchestration in an ideal network should be able to support integration with the following components:

- inventory (resource pool)

- bare metal services (BMaaS)

- OSS, service manager (which interact w/K8s orchestrator for LCM)

- configuration manager for all network functions (CMaaS, VNF/PNF/CNFs)

- element management system (EMS)

- security (platform, application, password manager)

- slice manager/policy manager

Figure 6-13 shows the end-to-end orchestration flow with different automation touch points for a typical 5G network.

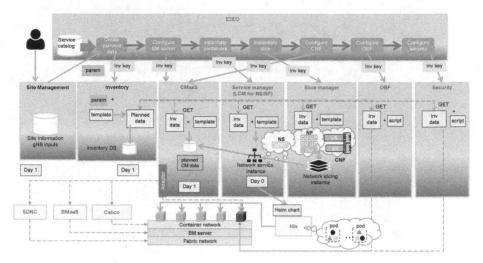

Figure 6-13. *End-to-end orchestration functionalities*

Service Assurance in 5G

The 5G network features network slicing capability to support diverse services, such as IoT, cloud-based services, industrial control, autonomous driving, mission-critical communications, and so on. Each kind of service has its specific performance requirements—for example, massive connectivity, super-high bandwidth, ultra-low latency and ultra-high reliability.

The performance of 5G networks, including network slicing, needs to be ensured in order to meet the performance requirements of the services. The performance of the NFs, NSSIs, and NSIs needs to be monitored and analyzed based on a set of management services with the relevant management data—for example, performance measurements, KPIs, and management analytical data.

Service assurance is used to monitor, model, and analyze network data to make sure service quality levels are achieved and maintained. Its purpose is to deliver an optimal customer experience according to network policy resource availability and commercial terms.

The service assurance solution should be able to provide the following features and functionalities with the objective to any operator's operations team toward service-centric operations.

1) Fault supervision/monitoring: The service assurance solution should have the fault supervision/active monitoring/detection with alert capability on different network layers and interdomains from the same or different vendors.

2) End-to-end network performance monitoring, measurement, and assurance based on SLA/QoS/QoE

3) Close-loop assurance approach with the automated and preventive healing/scaling before the hardware or software of the network and services fail based on the anomaly detection of the trending and forecasting analysis from the automated alarm correlation, root cause analysis and service impact analysis driven by the machine learning (ML) and artificial intelligence (AI).

4) Almost zero-touch orchestration on automated fault detection, correlation and root cause analysis. One-stop process or workflow to isolate a network or customer alarm instead of troubleshooting current multiple steps from one NOC to another on a cross-domain service. Enhancing operational efficiency and productivity on network operations to internal and external customers.

5) Self-Reliance: Able to maintain and establish new rules/used cases pertaining to an operator's environment easily

6) The service aassurance solution should be able to perform automatic scale-out/scale-in based on collected alarms, KPIs, or correlation of both by triggering service orchestrator.

7) The service assurance solution should be able to support the capability to notify about virtualized resource capacity shortage per compute, per tenant, per VM, and so on.

Figure 6-14 shows how the service assurance can improve the network KPIs by providing inputs to the service orchestrator.

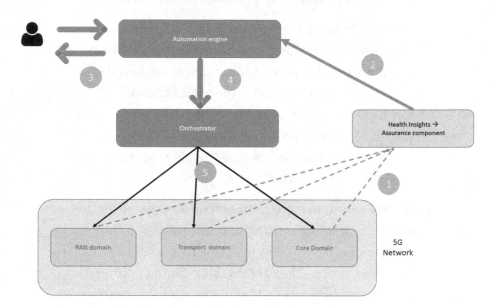

Figure 6-14. *Closed-loop automation with the help of service assurance*

In the aforementioned scenario shown in Figure 6-14, all the 5G network elements are set with KPI thresholds by the service assurance health insight component.

Step 1: When there is an exception taking place on any of the domains, it will be reported and detected by the service assurance component.

Step 2: The health insights will apply the required filters and determine with internal logic a proper response that will help resolve the exception that was detected in step 1 and provide this response to the associated automation engine (playbook)

Step 3: The automation engine can either be fully automated or, as in this case, can have a manual intervention to verify the action guided by the service assurance model before delegating the action toward the service orchestrator.

Step 4: The correction changes are pushed toward the service orchestrator.

Step 5: The service orchestrator pushes changes back to network.

Figure 6-15 shows how the service orchestrator, along with the service assurance automation, can help the network close the loop from device level to intent level, where device level means being reactive to the anomalies flagged by the devices and proactively fixing them and intent level means adding logic to the network by streamlining events from multiple sources into a holistic view across the layers.

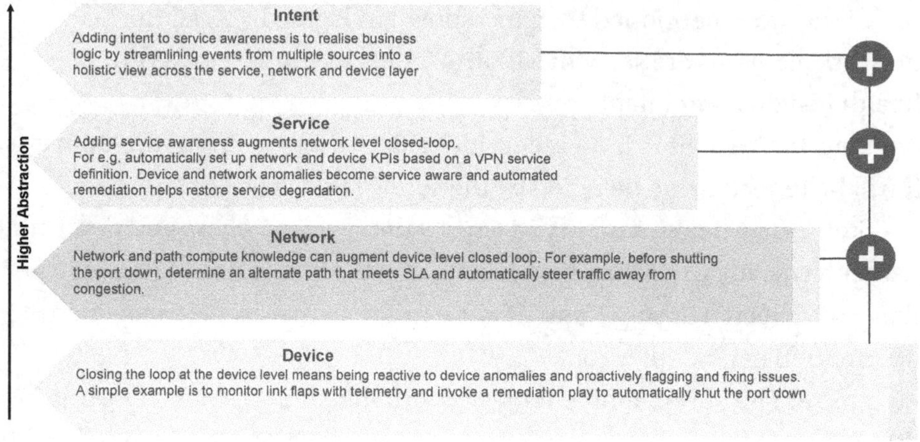

Intent

Adding intent to service awareness is to realise business logic by streamlining events from multiple sources into a holistic view across the service, network and device layer

Service

Adding service awareness augments network level closed-loop. For e.g. automatically set up network and device KPIs based on a VPN service definition. Device and network anomalies become service aware and automated remediation helps restore service degradation.

Network

Network and path compute knowledge can augment device level closed loop. For example, before shutting the port down, determine an alternate path that meets SLA and automatically steer traffic away from congestion.

Device

Closing the loop at the device level means being reactive to device anomalies and proactively flagging and fixing issues. A simple example is to monitor link flaps with telemetry and invoke a remediation play to automatically shut the port down

Higher Abstraction

Figure 6-15. *Closing the loop – from device to intent*

CHAPTER 7

Architectural Considerations by Service Providers

In this chapter, we will discuss some of the Release 16 features, like enhanced service-based architecture (e-SBA), where we will discuss NFset and NF service set followed by indirect communication and different types of indirect communication.

Further the reader will be introduced to the 5G policies and the different types of policies in 5G, how we can optimize some signaling, and how an application can be mapped to a network slice with the help of UE policies (URSP).

Toward the conclusion of the chapter, the reader will be introduced to some advanced 5G topics like local area data network (LADN), non-public 5G, and their types.

© Rajaneesh Sudhakar Shetty 2021
R. S. Shetty, *5G Mobile Core Network*, https://doi.org/10.1007/978-1-4842-6473-7_7

Enhanced Service-Based Architecture

Some of the key functionalities that are addressed by 3GPP Release 16 that are based on the architecture-SBA include:

- the concept of network function (NF) set and NF service set

- indirect communication (via SCP) with delegated discovery

NF Set and NF Service Set

Let's start by defining these terms.

NF Set

A set of control plane NFs that are similar/equivalent in nature, perform similar tasks serving as producers for a similar type of consumers, and are interchangeable can belong to one NF set.

One NF cannot belong to more than one NF set (per public land mobile network [PLMN]).

NF Service Set

Each of the NFs (only control plane NFs) can be composed of one or more NF services.

The NF services can be of similar type or can be very different from each other. The similar NFs can share context data among themselves and can be interchangable. Such NF services that share the context and are similar in nature and are interchangeable clubbed together form an NF service set.

These NF service sets can be spread across multiple NFs within the same NF set as well or can all reside within the same NF.

One NF service cannot belong to more than one NF service set.

Service Binding

Binding between the consumer node and the producer node in 5G with e-SBA can occur at multiple levels.

- – NF set binding

- – NF service binding

- – NF service set binding

- – NF instance binding

We will discuss in detail the NF set binding and the NF service set binding, as they are the most commonly used ones.

NF Set Binding

Figure 7-1 shows an example of NF set binding.

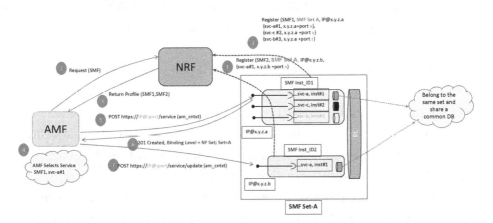

Figure 7-1. *NF set binding example with communication model B (without service communication proxy [SCP])*

As shown, there are two session management functions [SMFs], SMF1 and SMF2, that are a part of SMF set A.

SMF1 has three NF services within the NF (i.e., svc-a, svc-b, and svc-c), whereas SMF2 has only one NF service (i.e., svc-a).

For this example, 3GPP Release 15 communication model B is considered, which does not include SCP for indirect communication between the producer and consumer NFs but involves the NRF for discovery of the producer NFs.

In **step 1,** the two SMFs register themselves with the NF repository function (NRF). Apart from the NF itself, the NF services and the NF set are also communicated to the NRF in the registration procedure along with the IP addresses and the port details for the NF services.

In **step 2,** the access and mobility management function (AMF) desires to use service svc-a from an SMF and initiates a discovery procedure with the NRF for the requirement.

In **step 3,** the NRF in return provides the details of SMF1 and SMF2 with the NF services and port details of the services within the two SMFs to the AMF in response.

In **steps 4 and 5,** with internal logic, AMF selects SMF1, svc-a for the communication and sends the request to SMF1 svc-a on the IP address and the port notified by the NRF.

In **step 6,** the SMF responds back to the AMF with 201 ack (indicating success response) along with the binding details indicating the binding at NF set level (e.g., binding level= NF set;SetA).

In **step 7,** the AMF is able to understand the redundancy structure in the producer NF and can send the subsequent messages (e.g., update message to the SMF2 svc-a).

NF Service Set Binding

Figure 7-2 shows an example cae of NF service set binding.

As shown in the example, there are two SMFs, SMF1 and SMF2, that are a part of SMF set A.

SMF1 has three NF services within the NF (i.e., svc-a instance #1, svc-a, instance #2, and svc-b), whereas SMF2 has only one NF service (i.e., svc-a instance #1).

Out of these NF services, svc-a instance #1 and svc-a instance #2 from SMF1 and svc-a instance #1 from SMF2 all are a part of one NF service set.

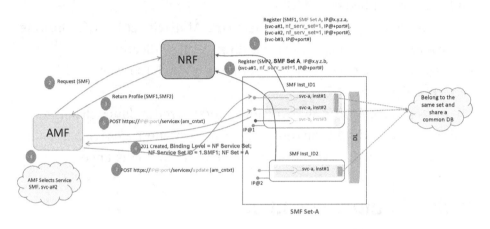

Figure 7-2. *Binding to NF service set example with communication model B (without SCP)*

As shown in Figure 7-2, 3GPP Release 15 communication model B is considered, which does not include SCP for indirect communication between the producer and consumer NFs but involves the NRF for discovery of the producer NFs.

In **step 1,** the two SMFs register themselves with the NRF, apart from the NF itself. The NF services and the NF set along with the NF service set are communicated to the NRF in the registration procedure along with the IP addresses and the port details for the NF services, as shown.

In **step 2,** the AMF desires to use service svc-a from an SMF and initiates a discovery procedure with the NRF for the requirement.

In **step 3,** the NRF, in return, provides the details of SMF1 and SMF2 with the NF services and port details of the services within the two SMFs to the AMF in response.

In **steps 4 and 5,** with internal logic, AMF selects SMF1, svc-a for the communication and sends the request to SMF1 svc-a on the IP address and the port notified by the NRF.

In **step 6,** the SMF responds back to the AMF with 201 ack (indicating success response) along with the binding details indicating the binding is at NF service level (e.g., "binding level= NFserviceset;NF servicesetID=1SMF1 NFset=A").

In **step 7,** the AMF is able to understand the redundancy structure in the producer NF and can send the subsequent messages (e.g., update message) to the SMF1 svc-a instance #2 or SMF2 svc-a instance #1.

Indirect Communication

The indirect communication functionality provides the flexibility for the operators to retain the NRF only for any NF-related discovery procedure and NF selection procedure and introduces SCP to provide any service-related communication between the NFs, thereby keeping the discovery and selection logic separate from the business logic for service selection.

Indirect communication can be of two types:

1) indirect communication without delegated discovery

2) indirect communication with delegated discovery

Indirect Communication Without Delegated Discovery

In indirect communication without delegated discovery procedure, for the discovery of the producer node, the consumer NF always contacts the NRF with a set of criteria that can be used for filtering the right producer NF.

The NRF then uses these filtering criteria and provides back the consumer NF with a list of candidate producer NFs.

The consumer NF should then use some internal logic to narrow down on one of the producer NF for the service communication and send the service communication request to the target NF via the SCP.

Figures 7-3 and 7-4 show an example for an indirect mode of communication without delegated discovery wherein the AMF wants to forward a PDU session establishment message to a candidate SMF for a particular slice and DNN within a particular region.

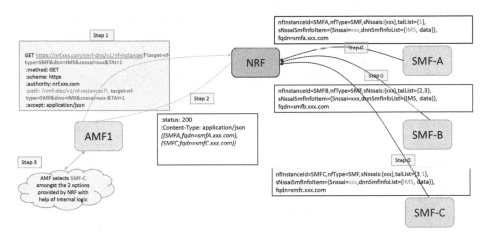

Figure 7-3. *Indirect communication without delegated discovery (1/2)*

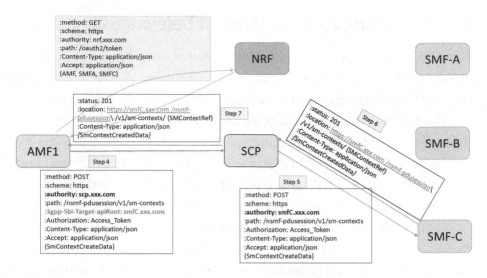

Figure 7-4. *Indirect communication without delegated discovery (2/2)*

Figures 7-3 and 7-4 show a procedure for indirect communication without delegated discovery.

For this example:

In **step 0,** the SMFs SMF-A, SMF-B, and SMF-C all register themselves with the NRF.

All of these SMFs serve the slice with sNSSAI{xxx}, with all of them serving the data network names (DNNs) {data, IMS}.

SMF-A serves to the tracking area identity (TAI){1}, whereas SMF-B serves to TAI{2,3} and SMF-C serves to the TAI{1,3}.

In **step 1,** the AMF desires to communicate with SMF serving the slice with slice ID sNSSAI-xxx, DNN=IMS and serving the TAI 3 and requests a discovery procedure with NRF accordingly providing the aforementioned parameters.

In **step 2,** the NRF returns back the SMFs that match the criteria mentioned in step 1 by the AMF. In this case, the SMF-B and SMF-C match the criteria, and the fully qualified domain names (FQDNs) of these two SMFs are returned back to the AMF by the NRF as shown. Additionally the access token is also optionally provided by the NRF to the AMF, which can be used for communication authorization with the SMFs.

In **step 3,** the AMF with its internal logic decides on one of the provided SMFs—in this case, SMF-C for further service communications.

The logic within the AMF for the selection can be round-robin or based on some load contol/overload protection algorithm that is vendor-specific.

In **step 4,** once the AMF has selected the SMF, it sends the request toward the SCP. In the request toward the SCP, the target node (in this case SMF-C) is selected and the access token is also sent that was received by the AMF in the discovery procedure with NRF.

In **step 5,** the SCP reads the header of the message and decides to route the received message to the target SMF (SMF-C) with the content that was sent to the SCP by the AMF.

In **step 6,** the SMF responds back to the SCP with a 201 message along with the relevant binding details—in this case, context creation for the session—and sends across the SM context details to the AMF.

In **step 7,** the SCP forwards the received message from SMF-c back to the AMF. The AMF stores the SMF and the context details for further communication.

Indirect Communication with Delegated Discovery

In indirect communication with delegated discovery procedure, for the discovery of the producer node, the consumer NF will not contact the NRF for selecting the candidate producer node. Instead it will send across a list of criteria that needs to be used as filtering criteria to the SCP for selection of the candidate producer NF.

The SCP uses the filtering criteria communicated to it and initiates a discovery procedure with the NRF, asking for a list of candidate producer NFs.

If the response from NRF has multiple NFs, then the SCP uses an internal logic to narrow down one of the candidate NFs and sends across the request message from the consumer to the selected producer.

Figures 7-5 and 7-6 show an example for an indirect mode of communication with delegated discovery wherein the AMF wants to forward a PDU session establishment message to a candidate SMF for a particular slice and DNN within a particular region.

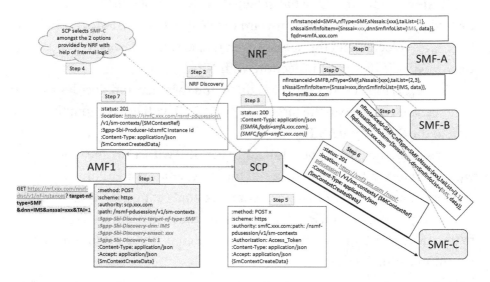

Figure 7-5. *Indirect communication with delegated discovery (1/2)*

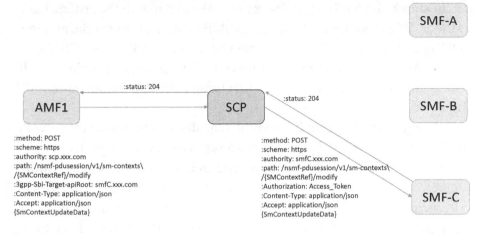

Figure 7-6. *Indirect communication with delegated discovery (2/2)*

Figures 7-5 and 7-6 show a procedure for indirect communication with delegated discovery.

For this example:

In **step 0,** the SMFs SMF-A, SMF-B, and SMF-C all register themselves with the NRF.

All of these SMFs serve the slice with sNSSAI{xxx}, with all of them serving the DNNs {data, IMS}.

SMF-A serves to TAI{1}, whereas SMF-B serves to TAI{2,3} and SMF-C serves to TAI{1,3}.

In **step 1,** the AMF desires to communicate with SMF serving to the slice with slice ID sNSSAI-xxx, DNN=IMS and serving TAI 1 and sends across a request message directly to the SCP with the above parameters along with the POST message, which needs to be redirected toward the right candidate SMF.

In **step 2,** the SCP initiates a discovery procedure with the NRF asking for a candidate SMF matching the criteria that were sent to the SCP by the AMF in step 1.

In **step 3,** the NRF returns back the SMFs that match the criteria back to the SCP. In this case the SMF-A and SMF-C match the criteria, and the FQDNs of these two SMFs are returned back to the SCP by the NRF as shown. Along with this, the access token is also optionally provided by the NRF to the SCP, which can be used for communication authorization with the SMFs.

In **step 4,** the SCP with its internal logic decides on one of the provided SMFs—in this case, SMF-C—for further service communications.

If the SCP is also performing the load-balancing functionality within the network, then the SMF selection will be based on the load-balancing criteria in SCP. If SCP is also performing overload control functionality, then the overload control inputs can also be considered in the logic for candidate producer selection by the SCP.

In **step 5,** the SCP decides to route the received message from the AMF in step 1 to the target SMF (SMF-C) with the content that was sent to the SCP by the AMF.

In **step 6,** the SMF responds back to the SCP with a 201 message (i.e., context creation) for the session and sending across the SM context details to the AMF.

In **step 7,** the SCP forwards the received message from SMF-c back to the AMF. The AMF stores the SMF and the context details for further communication as shown.

Failure Handling with NF Service Set and Indirect Communication Without Delegated Discovery

In advanced 5G deployments where NFset, NF service sets, and indirect communication are all enabled, it becomes important to carefully plan and design the mode of communication that should be enabled/used between the NFs to ensure optimized signaling.

Figure 7-7 is an example of such a deployment where indirect communication without delegated discovery is planned between the AMF and SMF wherein the AMF requests to establish communication with one of the services that is offered by the SMF service within the NF set.

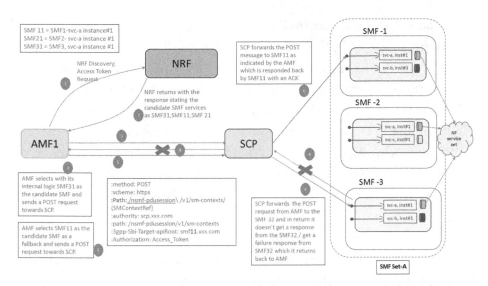

Figure 7-7. *Service failure handling with indirect communication and without delegated discovery*

Figure 7-7 shows a procedure for redundancy handling with indirect communication and without delegated discovery.

For this example:

In **step 0,** the SMFs SMF-1, SMF-2, and SMF-3 all register themselves with the NRF. Also there are individual services within these SMFs (i.e., svc-a, svc-b, and svc-c) that are also registered with individual port numbers during the discovery procedure.

The svc-a in SMF-1, SMF-2, and SMF-3 are all within an NF service set as shown. All of these SMFs are part of the NF set—that is, they all serve to the same slice, DNNs, and the same set of TAIs.

In **step 1,** the AMF desires to communicate with an SMF that can provide a service (i.e., svc-a) to the AMF and in turn initiates a discovery procedure with the NRF with the service requirements.

In **step 2,** the NRF returns back the SMFs that match the criteria mentioned in step 1 by the AMF. In this case, the SMF-1 svc-a (SMF11), SMF-2 svc-a (SMF21), and SMF-3 svc-a (SMF31) and the FQDNs of these three SMFs are returned back to the AMF by the NRF, as shown. Additionally the access token is also optionally provided by the NRF to the AMF, which can be used for communication authorization with the SMFs.

In **step 3,** the AMF, with its internal logic, decides on one of the provided SMFs (in this case, SMF-31) for further service communications and sends the request to the SCP, which is then forwarded to SMF31, as shown.

In **step 4,** the SMF3 svc-a instance #1 is down and there is a failure response / no response provided back to the SCP by the SMF which is sent back to the consumer AMF by the SCP as shown.

In **step5:** The AMF reselects a new SMF i.e in this case SMF1 svc-a (SMF11)and sends the request to the SCP.

In **step6:** The SCP reads the header of the message and then forwards the same to SMF11 which is acknowledged back by the SMF to the SCP and in turn is sent back to the AMF by the SCP as shown.

Failure Handling with NF Service Set and Indirect Communication with Delegated Discovery

Figure 7-8 is an example for such a deployment where indirect communication with delegated discovery is planned between the AMF and SMF, wherein the AMF requests to establish communication with one of the services that is offered by the SMF service within the NF set.

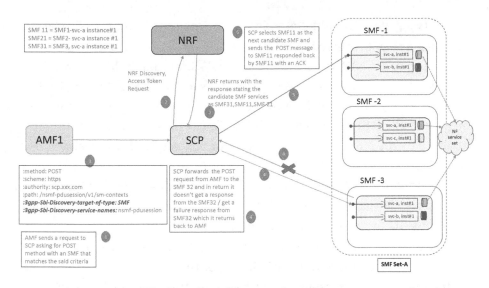

Figure 7-8. *Service failure handling with indirect communication and with delegated discovery*

Figure 7-8 shows a procedure for redundancy handling with indirect communication and with delegated discovery.

For this example:

In **step 0,** the SMFs SMF-1, SMF-2, and SMF-3 all register themselves with the NRF. Also there are individual services within these SMFs (i.e., svc-a, svc-b, and svc-c) that are also registered with individual port numbers during the discovery procedure.

The svc-a in SMF-1, SMF-2, and SMF-3 are all within an NF service set, as shown. All of these SMFs are part of the NF set (i.e., they all serve the same slice, DNN, and the same set of TAIs).

In **step 1,** the AMF desires to communicate with an SMF that can provide a service (i.e., svc-a) to the AMF and in turn sends a POST message to the SCP with the parameters that it can use to select the right SMF for discovery procedure.

In **step 2,** the SCP initiates a discovery procedure with the NRF with the criteria that it received in the message from the AMF.

In **step 3,** the NRF returns back the SMFs that match the criteria. In this case, the SMF-1 svc-a (SMF11), SMF-2 svc-a (SMF21), and SMF-3 svc-a (SMF31) and the FQDNs of these three SMFs are returned back to the SCP by the NRF, as shown. Additionally the access token is optionally provided by the NRF to the SCP, which can be used for communication authorization with the SMFs.

In **step 4,** the SCP, with its internal logic, decides on one of the provided SMFs (in this case, SMF31) for further service communications and sends the request to SMF31 as shown.

The SMF3 svc-a instance #1 is down and there is a failure response/no response provided back to the SCP by the SMF.

In **step 5,** the SCP reselects a new SMF (in this case, SMF1 svc-a [SMF11]) and sends the request to the SCP.

As it is evident from these two examples of indirect communications with and without delegated discovery, for failure handling cases, it might be beneficial to use the indirect communication with delegated discovery, which optimizes the signaling as the SCP will be able to retry the redundant NFs or NF services and can also use the stored logic for any further communications with the provider node.

Benefits of Indirect Communication

Apart from the obvious use-case of keeping the service communication logic separate from the discovery and registration logic, the indirect communication also provides the following benefits to the operators for any advanced 5G deployment.

- **Load balancing and overload control for the NFs:** As seen in the previous examples, when there are multiple candidate producer NFs returned by the NRF for a particular discovery procedure, the SCP can apply the load balancing/overload control logic to select one candidate producer NF out of the candidate list.

– **Failover handling of NFs:** In case of failure of one of the candidate NFs—especially in the indirect mode communication with delegated discovery—the SCP can retry another redundant producer NF from the candidate list provided to it by the NRF.

– **Centralized monitoring and tracing:** If the indirect mode of communication is centralized and all service traffic is flowing through the SCP, it becomes easy for the operators to monitor and trace the calls/flows and becomes simpler with the help of SCP and will require fewer integration points.

– **Application programming interface (API) interoperability:** In multi-vendor deployment models where the NFs are from different vendors using different versions of APIs, SCP can be a very useful addition to such a network that can bridge the gap between these two types of NFs.

– **Topology hiding:** In some networks, SCP can act as a entity that can hide the topology to the external NFs that are trying to acccess the NFs within the operator private network.

There are other benefits, because of which the operators will prefer using an SCP in the network for indirect communication over direct communication. These include:

– SCPs can offload alternate routing.

– SCPs can support 5G mediation.

– SCPs can be used for supporting canary testing.

– SCPs can handle hybrid deployments.

- SCPs can be made aware of 5G subscriber location function (SLF).

- SCPs can provide synergies with NRF beyond standards.

- SCPs reduce network complexity and maintenance cost.

5G Policies

In 5G, unlike 4G, there are three types of policies that can be applied to a UE. The three types of policies are:

- access and mobility-related policies

- UE-specific policies

- session management-related policies

The access and the mobility-related policies (referred to as AM policies) are the policies that are provided to the AMF during the registration of a UE. The policy control function (PCF) that communicates these policies to the AMF is referred to as AM-PCF.

The UE-specific policies are a set of policies that are sent to the UE via the N1/N2 interface from the AMF to the UE fetched during the registration of the UE by AMF via a PCF referred to as UE-PCF.

Session management-related policies (referred to as SM policies) are the policies that are provided to the SMF during the PDU establishment procedure of a particular session/UE by a PCF referred to as SM-PCF.

We will discuss the details and contents of each of these policies and how an operator can use these policies to optimize signaling and strategize the traffic steering within this network in the relavent sections.

Figure 7-9 shows how the three policies are clearly separated in the unified data repository (UDR) and how different PCFs can be used to fetch AM + UE policies and SM policies for a particular user.

Often the AM-PCF and the UE-PCF for a deployment are the same; however, depending on the slicing strategy and traffic seperation strategy the SM-PCF can be the same or different for a particular UE session.

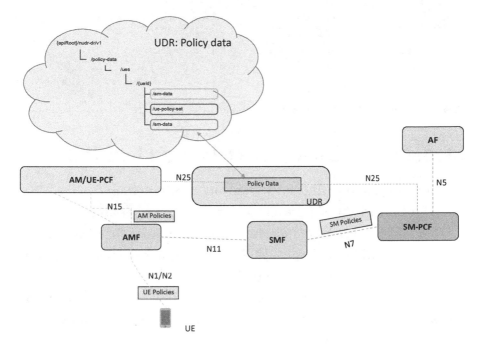

Figure 7-9. *Separation of AM, SM, and UE policies*

As shown in Figure 7-9, the SM policies are fetched from the UDR by the SM-PCF and stored in the SMF for a particular session of the UE.

Similarly the AM and UE policies are fetched from the UDR by the AM-PCF and the AM policies are stored in the AMF, whereas the UE policies are sent to the UE for usage during the PDU establishment procedure via N1/N2 interface by the AMF.

Figure 7-10 shows the structure in which UE, AM, and SM policy data is stored in the UDR and how these policies are fetched by the AM/UE and SM PCF's.

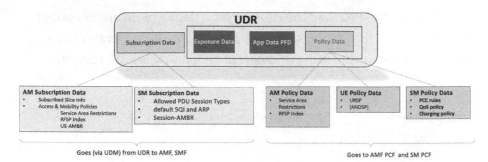

Figure 7-10. *UE, AM, and SM policy data in UDR*

Choosing the SM-PCF, AM-PCF, and UE-PCFs

For optimal signaling within an 5G network, it is important that the AM-PCF, UE-PCF, and SM-PCF are all the same wherever possible.

This can significantly reduce the signaling, as the policies will need to be retrieved and stored by the PCFs seperately if there are two different PCFs for UE+AM policies and SM policies.

Additionally, separate PCFs for AM, UE, and SM policies would mean extra signaling procedures required with the NRF from AMF and SMF for the discovery of the PCFs.

3GPP Release 15 allows the use of the same PCF for UE policies, AM policies, and SM policies.

In the **Nsmf_PDUSession_CreateSMContext** request message that is sent by the AMF during the PDU establishment procedure, there is a possibility for the AMF to include a parameter (i.e., **PCF ID**), along with the other parameters like subscription permanent identifier (SUPI), selected DNN, single-network slice selection assistance information (s-NSSAI), PDU session IDs, and so on.

Once this parameter is included in the message, the SMF need not perform a PCF discovery procedure with NRF and can bypass the step and use the PCF ID that was indicated by the AMF to retrieve the SM policies for the UE session.

However, the operator will need to have a clear strategy on PCF sharing between the slices, as the SMFs can belong to different set of slices and the AMF can be common for many slices.

For interworking cases wherein the UE is handed over from the 4G network to the 5G network, it might not be possible to retain the same PCF for AM+UE policies and SM policies.

As discussed in Chapter 4, the packet data network gateway (PGW)-c+SMF combo node selection in the 4G network needs to be designed in a manner such that when the UE moves from a 4G coverage area to a 5G coverage area, the selected PGW-c+SMF node remains the same to ensure session and IP address continutiy.

In such cases, the PCF selection for the SM policies is done already in the 4G network during the session establishment procedure; however, the AM and UE policies for the UE need to be applied when the UE moves into the 5G coverage area.

Therefore, AM-PCF and UE-PCF selection will be done independently by the AMF when the UE moves from the 4G network to the 5G network.

Access and Mobility-Related Policy Control

The access and mobility policy control is instrumental for the following functionalities:

- service area restriction management

- RAT frequency selection priority (RFSP) functionality management

- UE aggregated maximum bit rate (AMBR) management

- SMF selection

Service Area Restriction Management

Figure 7-11 represents some of the highlights of service area restriction management.

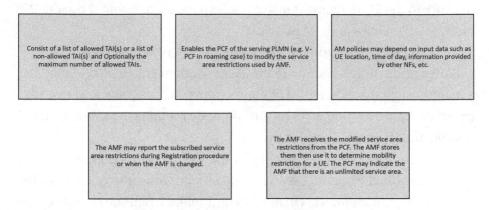

Figure 7-11. *Service area restriction management highlights*

The service area restriction management allows subscribers to only transmit in certain areas (allowed areas, TAI-list).

The AMF receives the service area restriction list from the UDM for the UE as a part of the subscription data during the UE registration procedure.

The AMF notifies the PCF about the service area restriction list from the subscription data, and if the PCF receives the AM policies from the UDR with a delta service area restriction list, it communicates the same to the AMF via the N15 interface, which is now updated in the AMF.

When the UE tries to access the TAIs that are marked as restricted/ forbidden TAIs for the UE in the AM policies, then the AMF can initiate a "CN-initiated PDU session inactivation procedure" by communicating with the relevant SMFs and can stop the data transmission for these UEs.

For UEs in idle state, the AMF ensures that the UEs are not allowed to intitiate any session management procedures for TAIs that are marked as forbidden or not allowed for the subscriber.

Not allowed subscribers (e.g., except MPS users), to transmit in certain regions (not- allowed areas TAI-list).

Figure 7-12 represents a geographical area where different service area restrictions are applied for a particular subscriber.

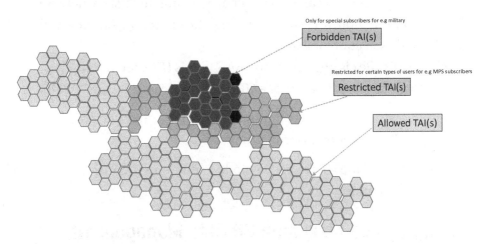

Figure 7-12. *Sample service area restriction applied for a geography*

RAT Frequency Selection PriorityFunctionality Management

RAT frequency selection priority (RFSP) index is used to control idle-mode camping behavior of UEs wherein the operators can plan the network such that the voice-centric mobiles can be made to camp on the 4G cells and the data-centric UEs can be made to choose 5G cells in their idle mode.

This is possible by designing and creating a specific RFSP index for each different type of UEs. The RFSP index in RAN specifications is called subscriber profile ID for RAT/frequency priority (SPID).

Similarly to the service area restriction management, the AMF shall have the RFSP subscription details for the UE, which it would derive from the UDR during the registration procedure, and the PCF can modify the RFSP index used by the AMF. These dynamic policies can be pushed from the PCF at any time and can be a result of accumulated usage, network slice load information, and so on, allowing the operator to strategize the UE idle mode selection policies.

The RFSP index is applied by the RAN and is UE-specific, and it is applied to all the radio bearers of a UE and can be used by the RAN to:

- control idle mode camping for the UE by modifying the cell reselection priorities for it, and

- redirect the UEs in active mode to different RATs or frequencies.

UE Aggregated Maximum Bit Rate Management

The UE AMBR value enforcement is done by the RAN, but the AMBR value for a particular UE is provided by the AMF to the RAN.

The AMF gets the AMBR subscription value for the UE from the UDM during the registration procedure. This AMBR value can be updated by the PCF at any time if there is a change in the policy for a particular UE.

Based on the received UE-AMBR value, the AMF sends across the same to the RAN and the RAN enforces the UE-AMBR value to the UE.

Figure 7-13 explains the UE-AMBR management key points.

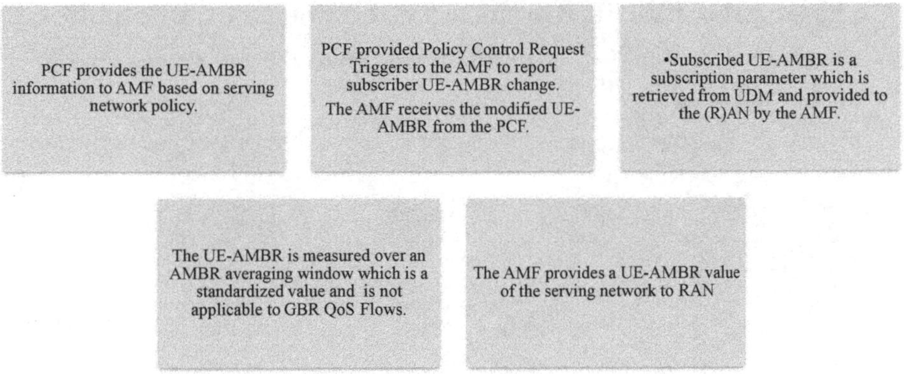

PCF provides the UE-AMBR information to AMF based on serving network policy.	PCF provided Policy Control Request Triggers to the AMF to report subscriber UE-AMBR change. The AMF receives the modified UE-AMBR from the PCF.	•Subscribed UE-AMBR is a subscription parameter which is retrieved from UDM and provided to the (R)AN by the AMF.
	The UE-AMBR is measured over an AMBR averaging window which is a standardized value and is not applicable to GBR QoS Flows.	The AMF provides a UE-AMBR value of the serving network to RAN

Figure 7-13. *UE-AMBR management*

AM and UE Policy Triggers

Figure 7-14 provides some, but not all, of the policy control request triggers for the AM policies.

Policy Control Request Trigger	Description	Condition for reporting
Location change (tracking area)	The tracking area of the UE has changed.	PCF (AM Policy, UE Policy)
Change of UE presence in Presence Reporting Area	The UE is entering/leaving a Presence Reporting Area	PCF (AM Policy, UE Policy)
Service Area restriction change	The subscribed service area restriction information has changed.	PCF (AM Policy)
RFSP index change	The subscribed RFSP index has changed	PCF (AM Policy)
Change of the Allowed NSSAI	The Allowed NSSAI has changed	PCF (AM Policy)
UE-AMBR change	The subscribed UE-AMBR has changed	PCF (AM Policy)
SMF selection management	UE request for an unsupported DNN or UE request for a DNN within the list of DNN candidates for replacement per S-NSSAI	PCF (AM Policy)

Figure 7-14. *Access and mobility-related policy control triggers (not complete list)*

These can be subscribed by the PCFs, and when the AMF reports the trigger back to the PCF, a modified AM policy can be applied to the subscriber accordingly.

Figure 7-15 shows the procedure for AM and UE policy management.

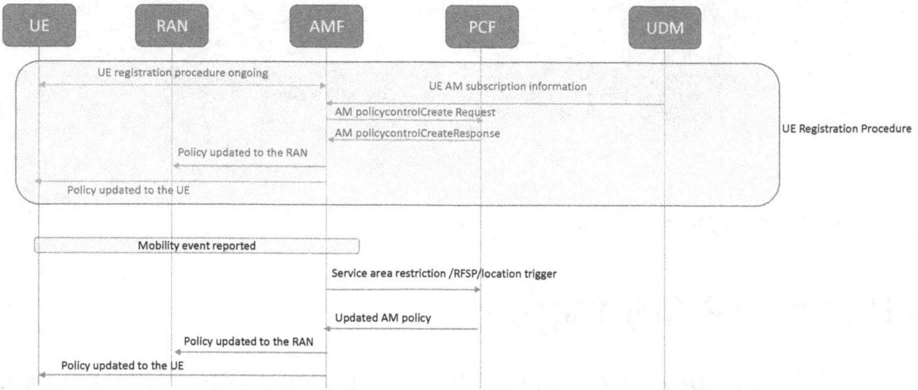

Figure 7-15. *AM and UE policy management procedure*

Figure 7-15 shows the procedure for AM and UE policies management in a typical 5G network.

The AM policy assocation establishment can happen in three instances.

1. during the UE initial registration with the network

2. during handover when the AMF relocation is required with PCF change

3. during handover from 4G to 5G when the UE doesn't have any existing AM policy association between AMF and the PCF

For the AM policy modification, there are three cases.

1. There is a scenario where the policy control trigger condition is met and the AMF sends the notification to the PCF about the same.

2. When the local decision changes or triggers for the policy enforcement changes in UDR and the PCF decides to initate the policy modification with the AMF.

3. AMF relocation is initiated and the AM policy association needs to be changed from the old AMF to a new AMF. In this case, the AMF initiates the modification procedure.

For the AM policy termination procedure, the following can be the triggers.

1. UE deregistration from the network

2. an AMF relocation due to mobility where the new AMF is not in the same PLMN as the old AMF

Figures 7-16 and 7-17 describe the AM policy association establishment, modification, and termination procedures.

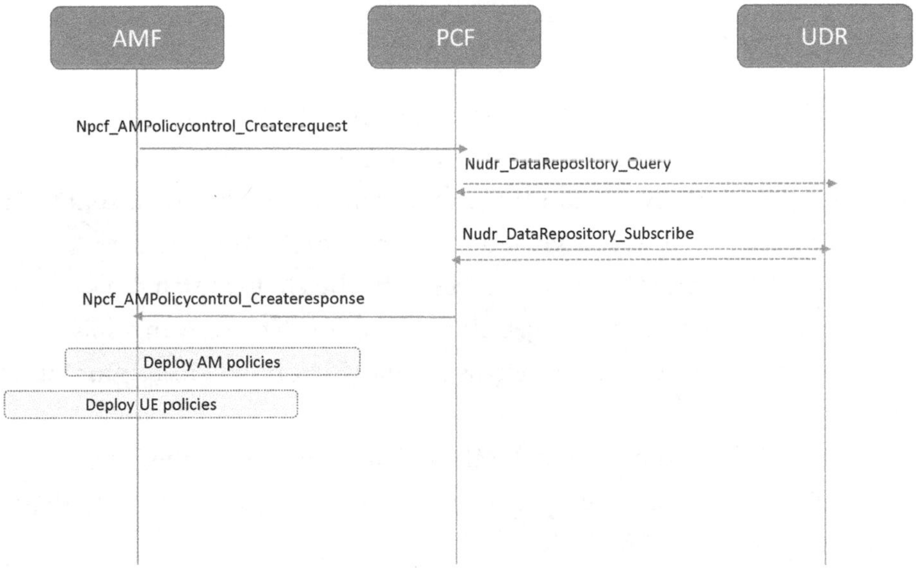

Figure 7-16. *AM policy association establishment*

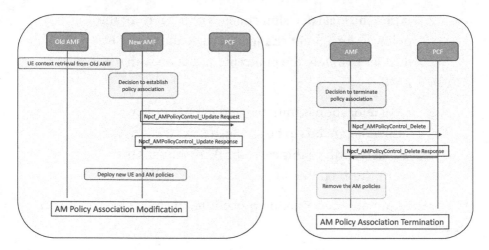

Figure 7-17. *AM policy association modification and termination*

The SMF selection has been discussed in the node selection section of Chapter 4.

UE Policy Control

On the UE, there are UE route selection policies (URSPs) and access network discovery and selection policy (ANDSP), which it follows.

The URSP and ANDSP are either preconfigured in the UE or sent to the UE by the network during registration as a part of the UE policies.

Both ANDSP and URSP rules are used by the UE to match the application traffic to a matching traffic desciption. The UE can apply default traffic rules whenever there is no matching traffic descriptor for any application.

The UE follows the serving PLMN policies provided in the form of URSP within the home network, and during roaming it follows the VPLMN policies in the form of ANDSP.

During roaming, the home PCF (h-PCF) can send the policies to the visited PCF (v-PCF) via the roaming interface.

Like AM policies, the UE policies are also provided by the PCF and can be based on the operator local policies and configurations.

For accurate policy delivery, the PCF may subscribe to the UE location/ state to ensure delivery of the updated policies to the UE upon right trigger.

Access Network Discovery and Selection Policy

The ANDSP is a policy that is used by the UE for selecting non-3GPP accesses and deciding how to route the traffic among the selected non-3GPP accesses and 5G core network. It is an optional policy and applicable only to UEs that support non-3GPP access to the 5G core.

The ANDSP can be already preconfigured in the UE or provided to the UE by the PCF via the N1/N2 interface, as explained in the AM policy control section.

ANDSP contains the rules that the UE can use to select a WLAN access network. The WLAN access network then can be used for registering against a 5G core network with the use of a non-3GPP access network (selection rules for which are provided by the network) and traffic offloading by the UE (i.e., sending the traffic to wireless local area network [WLAN] and not to the PDU session).

Table 7-1 provides the information and description of an ANDSP rule.

Table 7-1. *Access Network Discovery and Selection Policy*

Information name	Description	Category	PCF permitted to modify in a UE context	Scope
WLANSP rules	1 or more WLANSP rules	Mandatory	Yes	UE context
E-PDG identifier configuration	The UE uses this information to select e-PDG	Optional	Yes	UE context
N3IWF identifier configuration	The UE uses this information to select N3IWF	Optional	Yes	UE context
Non-3GPP access node (N3AN) selection information	The UE uses this information to select ePDG or N3IWF	Optional	Yes	UE context

As shown in Table 7-1, the UE can be provided with one or more WLAN Selection Policy (WLANSP) rules. Each of these rules can be applied to the UE based on the trigger criteria for these WLANSP rules.

The UE constructs a prioritized list of the available WLANs by discovering the available WLANs and comparing their attributes/capabilities against the groups of selection criteria in the valid WLANSP rule(s). When there are multiple valid WLANSP rules, the UE evaluates the valid WLANSP rules in priority order. The UE evaluates first if an available WLAN access meets the criteria of the highest priority valid WLANSP rule. The UE then evaluates if an available WLAN access meets the selection criteria of the next priority valid WLANSP rule.

UE Route Selection Policy

UE route selection policy is used by the UE to determine how to route the outgoing traffic or new traffic when initiated by the UE.

URSP is used by the UE for application binding to a particualar rule. In other words, with the help of URSP, the UE is able to determine if an application can be associated to an established PDU session, can be offloaded to non-3GPP access outside a PDU session, or can trigger the establishment of a new PDU session.

The URSP additionally also provides the following to the UE:

- SSC mode selection policy (SSCMSP)

- Network slice selection policy (NSSP)

- DNN selection policy

- Non-seamless offload policy

- Access type preference

Figure 7-18 shows the URSP assistance to the UE.

| SSC MODE SELECTION POLICY (SSCMSP) FOR THE UE TO ASSOCIATE THE MATCHING APPLICATION WITH SSC MODES. | NETWORK SLICE SELECTION POLICY (NSSP) FOR THE UE TO ASSOCIATE THE MATCHING APPLICATION WITH S-NSSAI. | DNN SELECTION POLICY FOR THE UE TO ASSOCIATE THE MATCHING APPLICATION WITH DNN. | PDU SESSION TYPE POLICY FOR THE UE TO ASSOCIATE THE MATCHING APPLICATION WITH A PDU SESSION TYPE. | NON-SEAMLESS OFFLOAD POLICY FOR THE UE TO DETERMINE THAT THE MATCHING APPLICATION SHOULD BE NON-SEAMLESSLY OFFLOADED TO NON-3GPP ACCESS OUTSIDE OF A PDU SESSION. | ACCESS TYPE PREFERENCE INDICATING THE PREFERRED ACCESS (3GPP OR NON-3GPP) WHEN THE UE NEEDS TO ESTABLISH A PDU SESSION FOR THE MATCHING APPLICATION. |

Figure 7-18. *URSP assistance to the UE*

For any new application detected by the UE, it evaluates the URSP rules in the order of precedence and matches it with the traffic descriptors in the URSP rule.

Upon matching with the traffic descriptor, the UE detemines if any of the existing PDU sessions for the UE can satisfy the traffic description and either initiates a new PDU establishment or sends the traffic for the application through an existing PDU session.

The network can send updated URSP rules to the UE depending on some of the trigger conditions being met. A few example triggers include:

- the UE performs mobility from 4G to 5G core network

- there is a change in allowed/configured s-NSSAIs for the UE

- change in the availability of LADN DNN.

- PCF updates the URSP for the UE

- UE registers in a non-3GPP access

Figure 7-19 shows the flow for the delivery of URSP from the network to the UE when any of the trigger conditions are met.

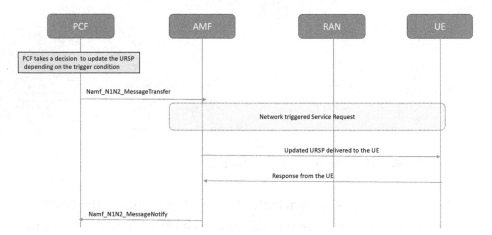

Figure 7-19. *Delivery of URSP to the UE from the network*

Figure 7-20 shows the content within an URSP rule and the content for a route selection description within the URSP rule.

UE Route Selection Policy Rule

Information Name	Description
Rule Precedence	Determines the order the URSP rule is enforced in the UE.
Traffic descriptor	This part defines the traffic descriptors for the policy
Application identifiers	Application identifier(s)
IP descriptors	IP 3 tuple(s) (destination IP address or IPv6 network prefix, destination port number, protocol ID of the protocol above IP)
Non-IP descriptors	Descriptor(s) for non-IP traffic
List of Route Selection Descriptors	A list of Route Selection Descriptors

Information Name	Description
Route Selection Descriptor Precedence	Determines the order in which the Route Selection Descriptors are to be applied.
Route selection components	This part defines the route selection components
SSC Mode Selection	One single value of SSC mode.
Network Slice Selection	Either a single value or a list of values of S- NSSAI(s).
DNN Selection	Either a single value or a list of values of DNN(s).
Non-seamless Offload Indication	Indicates if the traffic of the matching application is to be offloaded to non-3GPP access outside of a PDU Session.

Route Selection Descriptors

Figure 7-20. *Sample URSP rule and the content within the URSP descriptor*

Session Management Policy Control

The session management policy control provides the policy and charging control functionality along with event reporting for service data flows.

The SM-PCF determines and applies the SM policies for a particular PDU session after considering the subscription policies for the UE in the UDR and the other operator-defined policies received from the SMF, AMF, AF, and CHF.

N7 interface between the PCF and SMF is used to exchange the session management policy information corresponding to a particular UE's PDU session. The SMF selects the PCF during the PDU establishment procedure with the help of either NRF, AMF, or local configuration within the SMF.

The following services are provided by PCF for session management policy toward the SMF:

- – Policy create

- – Policy update

- Policy delete

- Policy update notification

QoS Negotiation

The SMF negotiates the QoS with the PCF by initiating a policy association establishment procedure.

The sessionAMBR and 5G Qos profile parameters received from subscription are included in the Npcf_SMPolicyControl_Create request to PCF.

The response from PCF may contain the following:

1) Session rules

   A session rule consists of policy information elements associated with the PDU session. The QoS-related information is authorized session AMBR and authorized default QoS.

2) PCC rule

   The PCC rule includes the FlowDescription, FlowDirection, and RefQosData parameters, among other information. There could be one or more PCC rules in the response from PCF.

3) QoS characteristics

   The QoS characteristics include parameters such as:

   - Resource type (GBR, delay critical GBR, or non-GBR)

   - Priority level

   - Packet delay budget or packet error rate

   - Averaging window

   - Maximum data burst volume

4) QoS description

The QoS description parameter consists of the following:

- 5QI: standard or non-standard from the QoS characteristics attribute

- Uplink and downlink GBR

- Uplink and downlink MBR

- Maximum packet loss rateoQosId referenced in PCC rules

- Default QoS indication

There could be more than one QoS description attribute in the response from PCF.

Figure 7-21 shows a the procedure for SM policy association establishment.

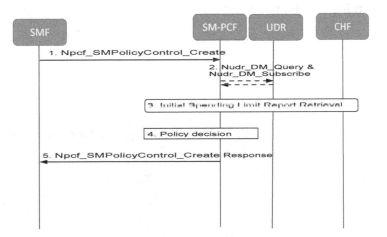

Figure 7-21. *SM policy association establishment*

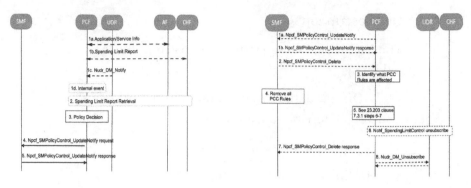

PCF initiated SM Policy Association Modification

SM Policy association termination

Figure 7-22. *SM policy association modification and termination procedure*

Figures 7-21 and 7-22 show the procedure for SM policy association addition, modification, and termination procedures. The different scenarios and triggers are mentioned in detail for these procedures in 3GPP 23.502 Section 4.16.4 through Section 4.16.6.

Figure 7-23 shows a high-level representation for the N7 QoS and charging rules applied to SMF from SM-PCF.

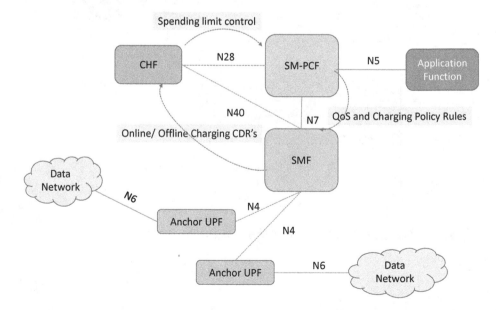

Figure 7-23. *N7 QoS and charging rules applied to SMF from SM-PCF*

Local Area Data Network

LADN is a Release 16 feature in 5G that enables the user to access a particular data network in a very specific region with the help of a separate DNN.

The subscriber will be able to access this particular DNN only in the specific regions (TAIs), and outside of this region, the UE will not be able to access access the DNN at all.

Operators planning a specific QoE for users in, for example, a local stadium, shopping center, or college campus can plan and implement the LADN service.

Typically a list of tracking areas are classified and configured as a serving area for the LADN, where the LADN DNN can be accessed and used by the UE.

The list of tracking areas can be configured on the AMF against a particular DNN called the LADN DNN.

The LADN service area can be provided to the UE during the initial registration, thereby making the UE aware of the specific region where the LADN DNN is available and can be used.

The UE selects the LADN DNN and sends a PDU establishment request to the AMF, which forwards it toward the SMF, indicating the location of the UE that is used by the SMF to either accept or reject the request, as shown in the Figure 7-24.

In Figure 7-24, the UE is equipped with the LADN subscription and is within the LADN region and tries to access the LADN APN.

The AMF detects that the UE sends a PDU establishment request message with LADN DNN and indicates to the SMF that the UE is within the LADN service area. The SMF then allocates a UPF that is reserved for the LADN service in that region, and the data path for the UE is as shown in the figure.

When the UE moves outside the LADN service area, the AMF will indicate the same to the SMF, and the SMF will initiate a UPF relocation procedure for the UE or terminate the call for the UE, depending on the operator policy for the same.

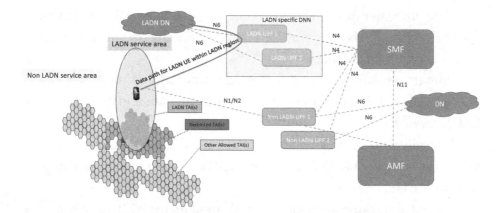

Figure 7-24. *LADN representation in an operator network*

Non-Public 5G (Private Network)

Non-public 5G (or private 5G) is often used to describe the use of 5G technology restricted to a private network that is focused on serving very specific users (e.g., factory use-case, campus use-case).

The 5G system, according to the specifications, should be able to support private/non-public networks (NPNs) that provide coverage restricted to a specific area.

A private network provided by 5G operators has the following edge over 4G offerings for private network.

> 1) **Network slicing:** Unlike 4G, one of the biggest advantages that a 5G network provides is the possibility of network slicing.

It is possible that the service provider dedicates a slice for the private 5G usage only.

The infrastructure for a private 5G network can be completely separated end-to-end with the help of slicing, and the slicing can be planned in a manner so that the nodes handling the signaling as well as data traffic for the private 5G network can be isolated from the public usage with the concept of slicing.

2) **Support of MEC:** MEC, as descibed in Chapter 2, is a cloud evolution to move certain types of application for a user to be hosted and served at the edge data center closer to the UE.

Some of the low-latency applications, such as URLLC applications hosted by the private networks, can benefit from the MEC approach wherein the stringent latency and throughput targets can be met, thereby allowing the private network to be able to provide faster and futuristic services to the end-users.

3) **Higher bandwidth and better spectral efficiency:** Apart from the higher bandwidth and speed that the 5G offers to provide to the private 5G network, antenna techniques like massive MIMO, and adaptive trasmission modes, it is possible to efficiently focus the transmitting energy onto specific users, thereby improving the spectral efficiency and increasing the average revenue per user.

4) **API exposure:** Interaction with third-party service providers through an API-based core network makes it easier for the private 5G networks. The network exposure function (NEF) acts as a bridge by providing APIs to the third-party applications with the 5G core network entities. This makes it easy for third-party applications to perform functions like monitoring, provisioning, and so on.

Figure 7-25 summarizes the advantages of a non-public 5G network over a private LTE network.

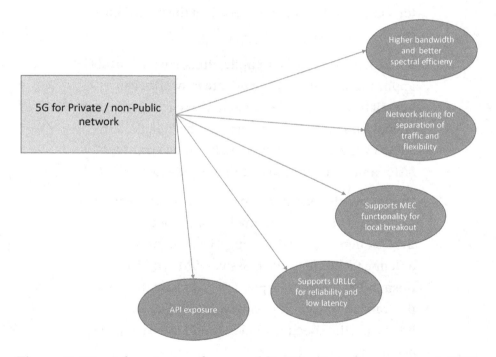

Figure 7-25. *Advantages of non-public 5G network over private LTE*

Deployment of Non-Public 5G Network

An NPN may be deployed as:

- standalone NPN (SNPN) (deployment isolated from the PLMN of the service provider)

- public network-integrated NPN (deployment with PLMN support)

Standalone Non-Public Network

In the standalone deployment model, the **non-public** 5G network is completely isolated from the public 5G network, as shown in Figure 7-26.

The combination of a PLMN ID and network identifier (NID) identifies an SNPN.

NIDs are either globally managed (unique in this universe) or locally managed.

NID value ranges are separate for globally managed and locally managed spaces.

Standalone mode has all the characteristics of PLMN selection, including unified access control.

As shown in Figure 7-26, the cell can operate in standalone mode by broadcasting cellReservedForOtherUse. This will ensure that all UEs that are not subscribed for non-public 5G are kept away.

PLMN-ID can be the operator PLMN ID and does not have much significance from access grant/restriction to the operator's network.

Standards support the possibility for a cell to be operating as both standalone as well as PLMN mode, and in such cases, the PLMN ID for standalone non-public 5G network and for MNOs needs to be completely different. SIBs will need to include the PLMN ID for NPN in such cases.

This model of deployment can be followed where there is no need for interactions between the private and the public 5G networks.

The cost for implementing a standalone private network can be very high, as all the NFs need to be deployed on premise for such a deployment, and the complete network needs to be managed end to end as well.

However, the upside to this type of a deployment model is that security in such a deployment can be completely controlled, and the private network operator can have complete control over the network.

Optionally there can be a connectivity between the private and the public network for select application fallbacks such as voice service fallback.

Interworking with EPC is not supported for standalone networks. The issue is that authentication can be very different for standalone network, and mapping of context may not be simple.

If a UE performs the registration or service request procedure in an SNPN identified by a PLMN ID and a locally managed NID, and there is no subscription for the UE, then the AMF shall reject the UE with an appropriate cause code to temporarily prevent the UE from automatically selecting and registering with the same SNPN.

If a UE performs the registration or service request procedure in an SNPN identified by a PLMN ID and a universally managed NID, and there is no subscription for the UE, then the AMF shall reject the UE with an appropriate cause code to permanently prevent the UE from automatically selecting and registering with the same SNPN.

Figure 7-26 shows a typical deployment for a standalone non-public 5G deployment (private 5G).

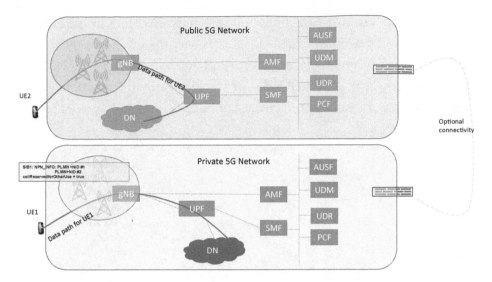

Figure 7-26. *Standalone private network deployment*

Public Network Integrated NPN

Public network integrated NPNs are NPNs made available via PLMNs either by using a dedicated DNN or by allocating a unique s-NSSAI value to the slice instance reserved for the NPN.

The network slicing functionalities as explained in Chapter 4 apply for the NPN.

Since the network slicing concept cannot block the UE from accessing the network itself in areas outside the NPN areas, the access restriction in the form of closed access groups (CAGs) is combined along with network slicing to achieve the desired behavior.

A CAG identifies a group of subscribers who are permitted to access one or more CAG cells associated to the CAG.

CAG is used for the public network-integrated NPNs to prevent UE(s), which are not allowed to access the NPN via the associated cell(s), from automatically selecting and accessing the associated cell(s).

In integrated **non-public** and public 5G networks, the **non-public** 5G network will share some of the resources with the public 5G network. Figure 7-27 shows an integrated private and public 5G network where the RAN resources for the two networks are common and the core network resources are separated for private and public 5G networks.

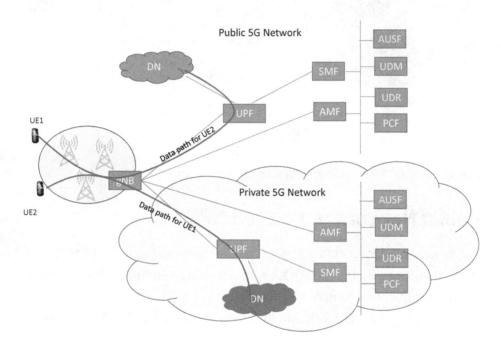

Figure 7-27. *RAN sharing with public and non-public 5G network*

Figure 7-28 shows an integrated private and public 5G network where the core network resources for the two networks are common and the RAN resources are separated for private and public 5G networks.

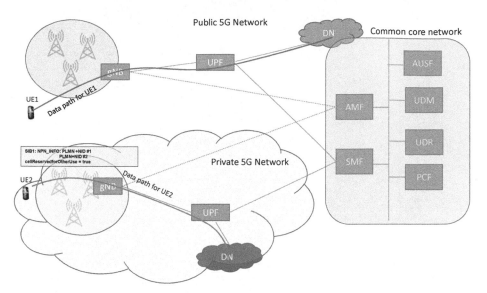

Figure 7-28. *Core network sharing between public and non-public 5G network*

Key Notes

Finally, some key notes to remember:

- **NPN Cell:** a cell that is only available for normal service for NPN subscribers.

- An NPN-capable UE determines that a cell is NPN-only cell by detecting that the "cellReservedForOtherUse" IE is set to true while the NPN-IdentityInfoList IE is present in CellAccessRelatedInfo."

- Emergency services are not supported in standalone networks.

Index

A

Access and mobility function
  (AMF), 22–26
Access and mobility management
  function (AMF)
  access node (gNB), 185
  AMFs serving different
    slices, 178
  deployment scenario, 178
  forward request, 187, 188
Access node (gNB), 185–187
Access Point Name (APN)
  planning, 137, 138
Alpha and beta testing, 259, 260
API integration testing, 251
Application function, 52
Authentication server function
  (AUSF), 38, 39
Automation
  abstraction layer, 286, 287
  activities, 281
  classification, 282
  deployment layer, 285
  function layer, 285
  infrastructure, 283
  layers, 283
  packet core, 281
  phases information, 282

service assurance, 296–300
service orchestrator, 292–296
Automation network
  operators, 277
  physical routers, 277
  slicing (*see* Slicing automation)
  technical capabilities, 278
Automation testing
  fully automated testing, 237
  manual testing, 236
  semi-automated/automation
    assisted testing, 237

B

Buffering Action
  Rule (BAR), 17

C

Charging data records (CDRs), 34
Charging function (CHF)
  ChargingDesc, 38
  charging trigger function, 36
  data block, 37
  details, 34
  online and offline charging, 35
  Qos mapping, 36, 37
  service provider, 35

S